Multiculturalism and the Canadian Constitution

Law and Society Series
W. Wesley Pue, General Editor

The Law and Society Series explores law as a socially embedded phenomenon. It is premised on the understanding that the conventional division
of law from society creates false dichotomies in thinking, scholarship,
educational practice, and social life. Books in the series treat law and
society as mutually constitutive and seek to bridge scholarship emerging
from interdisciplinary engagement of law with disciplines such as politics,
social theory, history, political economy, and gender studies.

A list of the titles in this series appears at the end of this book.

Edited by Stephen Tierney

Multiculturalism and the Canadian Constitution

UBCPress · Vancouver · Toronto

16 15 14 13 12 11 10 09 08 07   5 4 3 2 1

Printed in Canada on ancient-forest-free paper (100% post-consumer recycled) that is processed chlorine- and acid-free, with vegetable-based inks.

Library and Archives Canada Cataloguing in Publication

Multiculturalism and the Canadian constitution / edited by Stephen Tierney.

(Law and society, ISSN 1496-4953)
Includes bibliographical references and index.
ISBN 978-0-7748-1445-4

1. Multiculturalism – Canada. 2. Multiculturalism – Law and legislation – Canada. 3. Civil rights – Canada. 4. Constitutional history – Canada. I. Tierney, Stephen J. A., 1967- II. Series: Law and society series (Vancouver, B.C.)

KE4381.M84 2007   342.7108'73   C2007-905384-X

Canadä

UBC Press gratefully acknowledges the financial support for our publishing program of the Government of Canada through the Book Publishing Industry Development Program (BPIDP), and of the Canada Council for the Arts, and the British Columbia Arts Council.

This book has been published with the help of a grant from the Canadian Federation for the Humanities and Social Sciences, through the Aid to Scholarly Publications Programme, using funds provided by the Social Sciences and Humanities Research Council of Canada.

Printed and bound in Canada by Friesens
Set in Stone by Artegraphica Design Co. Ltd.
Copy editor: Joanne Richardson
Proofreader and indexer: Dianne Tiefensee

UBC Press
The University of British Columbia
2029 West Mall
Vancouver, BC V6T 1Z2
604-822-5959 / Fax: 604-822-6083
www.ubcpress.ca

Contents

Acknowledgments

I am extremely grateful for all the work done by the UBC Press team to make the production of this book such a smooth process. In particular, Randy Schmidt has offered unstinting support and helpful insights from the moment the project was conceived through to its completion. The production team led by Holly Keller, and assisted by Megan Brand, has also shown great professionalism. The comments of three anonymous referees are also much appreciated.

I am also very grateful for two grants that have aided in the publication of the book: an Aid to Scholarly Publications Programme grant from the Canadian Federation for the Humanities and Social Sciences, and an award from Princeton University. We are particularly indebted to Jameson Doig for his considerable efforts in helping to secure the latter award and for his encouragement and helpful advice throughout.

Multiculturalism and
the Canadian Constitution

Introduction:
Constitution Building in a
Multicultural State

Stephen Tierney

Canada has long been the focus of international attention for its success as a multicultural society and, in particular, for its ability to manage its cultural diversity through a federal constitution. Constitutional provisions across a range of areas, including the relationship between English and French Canada; federalism more generally, including the status of Quebec; language rights; the status of Aboriginal peoples; Canada's immigration and integration strategies; constitutional guarantees for religious schools; affirmative action; and a general guarantee of equal protection to men and women all tell a complex story of diversity, embracing First Nations, settler communities, and new immigrants, and consolidated through a long and incremental period of constitution building.

This book brings together eleven essays by leading scholars of cultural diversity from backgrounds in law, political science, and sociology, and in doing so addresses several key components of the evolving Canadian story: the evolution over time of multicultural law and policy in Canada; the territorial dimension of Canadian federalism, which also embraces Canada's language policy; and the role of constitutional interpretation by the courts in the development and enhancement of Canada as a self-consciously multicultural state.

Multiculturalism and the Canadian Constitution is divided into two parts. The first addresses the historical evolution of multiculturalism and federalism in the development of the Canadian constitution. It comprises five retrospective accounts that identify key factors in the development of Canada's unique approach to managing cultural diversity. Together these chapters help build a picture of why Canada has adopted such a constitutional commitment to the accommodation of diversity, what its successes have been, and what challenges remain in reconciling different visions of the Canadian state. Several themes emerge from these chapters, which raise key questions for the further exploration of the Canadian experience. First, how might we attempt to explain in ideological terms the Canadian commitment to both cultural and territorial diversity? From contributions by Forbes, Temelini, and Chevrier, we can see that different approaches to, or understandings of, liberalism have been at work throughout the evolution of Canadian multiculturalism and that ideological tensions remain today regarding how the state should move forward. Second, what explanations can we find for the successes of Canadian constitutional law and policy in this area? Has Canada found a particularly successful approach or has it, as Will Kymlicka argues, simply been lucky in a variety of ways? Third, a related question is whether the experience of Canada can correctly be termed a distinctive "Canadian model" that differs from approaches taken elsewhere or whether it has adopted a similar approach to that taken in other countries but is unique simply because Canadian constitutional policy has played out in different circumstances. And last, the book examines the tensions that emerge between the accommodation of territorially based identities through federalism and a multicultural policy that accentuates the identities of non-territorial groups and thereby undermines, in the eyes of certain provinces (particularly Quebec), provincial prerogatives. Part 2 of *Multiculturalism and the Canadian Constitution* is concerned with the accommodation of diversity in constitutional law and practice. Taking the form of a series of case studies, these chapters illustrate the extent to which multiculturalism has become embedded in the Canadian Constitution and, indeed, within Canadian constitutional identity. Studies of language policy, federalism, the role of the courts, and the problematic issues raised by the concept of equality all serve to highlight the ongoing challenges Canada faces not only in responding to such a range of often competing political agendas but also in finding a model of liberalism that can allow it to meet these challenges consistently.

Part 1 opens with three reflective chapters by Hugh Donald Forbes, Michael Temelini, and Will Kymlicka respectively, each of whom, in different ways, addresses the patterns of Canada's constitutional evolution over the past four decades. Forbes discusses the influence of Pierre Trudeau on this process; Temelini focuses upon the pathways of political mobilization from which Canada has developed its multicultural policy; and Kymlicka analyzes the structural conditions within which this policy emerged. Forbes' chapter is a short intellectual biography of the person who, perhaps more than any other, influenced contemporary Canadian attitudes to federalism and cultural diversity: Pierre Trudeau (prime minister from 1968 to 1979 and from 1980 to 1984). His role in developing Canada's multicultural policy is of course well-recognized, but Forbes' argument is that Trudeau's commitment to this policy was not simply a transient flirtation reflecting the strategic opportunism of a skilful political actor; rather, it was based upon a deep, philosophically developed and enduring set of political principles. As such, contemporary multiculturalism in Canada today is in many respects the progeny of Trudeau's self-conscious, long-term planning.

Forbes contends that, before the management of cultural pluralism in Canada can be properly understood, attention must be given to its underlying principles. Although the task of theorizing political principles is normally left in the hands of academics, Forbes argues that Trudeau, himself an intellectual as well as a practising politician, developed a sophisticated vision of Canada as a multicultural state. His role, therefore, became even more pivotal in that, by bridging the gap between theory and political practice, he was able to give constitutional effect to the normative theory he developed. Such was his role that Forbes describes him as "the first and ... most authoritative theorist of Canadian multiculturalism"; hence, any attempt to understand the phenomenon of Canadian multiculturalism requires an appreciation of Trudeau's thought and actions.

In ideological terms, Trudeau's model of liberalism exerted a strong influence over constitutional development. Forbes explains that Trudeau's ambitions extended beyond accommodating diversity in Canada to a wider vision of a cosmopolitan world in which culture should belong to the private realm, with state and society playing a neutral role. Ideally, culture would become a matter of individual choice, which a policy of multiculturalism would be designed to facilitate. One highly controversial aspect of Trudeau's approach was his firm opposition to Quebec nationalism and his consequent eschewal of any sense of Canada as bicultural or binational. Canada should develop a strong bilingual policy, encapsulated in the *Official Languages Act*, 1969, and reinforced with further constitutional protection for the French and English languages within the *Charter of Rights and Freedoms*, 1982, but it would remain a uninational federation of one demos, within which cultural diversity would be encouraged mainly as an aspect of private life rather than as a constitutionally fostered identity. As such, Canada could also become an example, and perhaps a template, for the wider transition across the world towards global governance and the weakening of national attachments that should attend such a process. It was essential that, as a possible model for postnationalism, Canada should not present itself as a binational or multinational state; such a concession would be a serious impediment to its destiny as a haven beyond the divisiveness of national particularities. Fatally, according to Trudeau, a recognition by Canada of its own national pluralism would simply see the old antagonisms of the age of the nation-state fought out in different ways, not only between states but now also within them; and instead of Canada's offering a remedy for the plague of nationalism, it would instead provide a conducive environment for a new mutation of the virus.

Trudeau's cosmopolitan aspiration has, of course, come under challenge from Quebec nationalists for decades, but it has also recently been attacked by liberal theorists of cultural pluralism (most prominently Will Kymlicka), who present an alternative model of liberalism suitable for a deeply diverse state. They argue that the cosmopolitan model misses the fact that liberalism can – and, indeed, in the interests of liberal justice, must – recognize deep cultural diversity and the importance of the political institutionalization of this diversity for individual members of cultural groups and substate national societies. Kymlicka has also criticized the idea that the state can be neutral with regard to culture: "I think this common view is not only mistaken, but actually incoherent. The idea of responding to cultural differences with 'benign neglect' makes no sense. Government decisions on languages, internal boundaries, public holidays, and state symbols unavoidably involve recognizing, accommodating, and supporting the needs and identities of particular ethnic and national groups."[1] This critique rests on the fact that national societies, or "societal cultures," are universal phenomena within which people live out their cultural lives, rather than sites of collective identity that can or should be wished away.

Forbes recognizes the deep paradox in Trudeau's endeavours. In his efforts to turn Canada into the first postnational state, Trudeau employed a strategy that was itself a nation-building one: "an experiment in creating a nation designed to show the world how to overcome nationalism," in Forbes' words. But of course fostering nationalism, even an open, civic, tolerant, and multicultural nationalism, in the very endeavour to overcome nationalism, is by definition self-defeating. Indeed, Quebec nationalists, and many Aboriginal people, would argue that Trudeau's vision simply led to a new model of nation building in English Canada, from which they were excluded and through which they felt further marginalized. Therefore, for Forbes, Trudeau's appeal to national feeling is ultimately a valuable reminder that, when trying to decide how applicable the Canadian model may be for other states, in which the conditions for a cosmopolitan displacement of nationalism are even less favourable, such a grand vision should be embraced only with caution.

Like Forbes, Michael Temelini considers the ideological underpinnings that have served to shape the Canadian approach to diversity, and, in doing so, he suggests that, in its early manifestations, the dominant ideological position promoted a much more participatory model of citizen engagement than did the heavily legalistic and remedy-driven model that we find in the post-Trudeau era. In other words, he identifies within postwar Canadian history a largely forgotten approach to multiculturalism (what we might call liberal republicanism), which did then, and might yet, offer a rival vision to the liberal individualist model that remains dominant today. His historical overview focuses particularly upon the Canadian parliamentary debates establishing the Royal Commission on Bilingualism and Biculturalism (the B and B Commission) in 1963 and the political movement for multiculturalism that emerged from this process. His principal thesis is that Canadian multiculturalism as it has developed in recent years tends to be addressed as a heavily juridified concept; in other words, it is conceived in rights-based terms as a principle of procedural justice and is expressed in juridical terms as a liberal theory of minority rights. In fact, he argues, multi-culturalism in Canada has far deeper roots than the *Charter of Rights and Freedoms* through which the juridified model has now been crystallized, and, therefore, we should reinvestigate the alternative political model that was so influential in the early 1960s.

Temelini's task is not to deny either the existence or the normative value of multicultural rights (in fact, he argues that these rights have made a considerable contribution to the development of Canadian civilization); rather, it is to retrieve from its state of neglect the political and deliberative tradition of multiculturalism from which the principle initially developed through the language of civic humanism and political virtue. The value in recalling this alternative tradition is not only historical accuracy with re-gard to the rediscovery of an important political process that has been largely written out of contemporary historiography, but also the possibility of re-suscitating the values that this process inspired. The idea of multicultural-ism as expressed at the time of the B and B Commission was driven not only by political or judicial elites but also by citizens, who did so in an organic way, through public deliberation. Thus the principle was expressed through the mode of civic virtue and was entrenched within the political mind-set of citizens as an essential component of the Canadian democratic state dec-ades before its official adoption by the state through the *Charter*.

For Temelini, a crucial lesson that emerged from Canada's 25th and 26th Parliaments (1962-65) was that a multicultural state cannot be built only by elite-driven institutions or by constitutional engineering; rather, the citizenry must be fully engaged with an issue that pervades all aspects of daily life and that requires the day-to-day support and practice of citizens. These par-liaments recognized that citizen engagement was essential, in Temelini's words, to "strengthen the bonds of civic solidarity, build allegiance to Can-ada, and bolster citizenship." For Temelini, there is considerable value in ar-ticulating multiculturalism as a good rather than merely as a right since the former construction gives all citizens, not only those making rights claims, a sense of ownership over the policy and a sense of responsibility for its success. In this context, he cites Charles Taylor's view that this sense of civic ownership also formed the essential groundwork upon which multicultural rights could be entrenched through the *Charter* because people now under-stood the values that these juridical rights were designed to embody.[2] In short, Temelini's chapter argues that the success of multiculturalism depends upon its organic development and acceptance within the body politic. It is argu-ably a more republican model than that presented by Trudeau, and it asks the fundamental question of whether an individualistic, juridical model can ultimately be sustained without popular commitment and participation. Without such a developed level of civic acceptance, efforts to establish multiculturalism through elite-led institutions and juridical social-engineering become much more difficult, if not impossible, to achieve, a point that seems to resonate in Peach's chapter (discussed below).

These first two chapters highlight a tension between different liberal ideologies in the development of postwar Canadian multiculturalism. They also demonstrate that the Canadian model of multiculturalism was, in many ways, the result of self-conscious policy decisions by elites rather than a mere accident of history. At this point, the book turns to two related questions: whether the Canadian model is unique and whether its success is the result of wise decision making rather than the felicitous circumstances within which it has developed. Will Kymlicka's chapter responds to these questions in an iconoclastic way. He begins by observing that Canada has been perceived abroad, and presented by the Canadian government and others at home, as a global model for the accommodation of ethnocultural diversity. Although agreeing that the Canadian model has been an undoubted success, Kymlicka sets out to dispel certain myths about Canada's approach to multiculturalism, arguing that the Canadian experience is not unique but is, in fact, broadly similar to the models adopted by many other Western democracies over the past thirty years. Focusing upon immigrant multiculturalism and also, to some extent, upon bilingual federalism, he argues that, although these policies have been most successful in Canada, this success can be explained more by fortunate circumstances than by the more generally assumed explanation: namely, the combined political will of elites and citizens to make it happen.

Kymlicka explains how the conventional story of Canada's success in this area tells of the country's tradition for openness and tolerance and of a multicultural vision promoted by enlightened political leaders and received by citizens sufficiently mature and tolerant to assimilate it. Kymlicka, however, in a more incremental account of how and when Canada's immigration policy developed, paints a more complex picture, suggesting that various less dramatic factors, such as timing, geography, and luck, made multiculturalism a less risky business for Canada than it otherwise might have been (and than it has been elsewhere). Kymlicka's conclusion – that, in light of these fortunate circumstances, Canada's record in accommodating diversity is in fact fairly modest – acts as a thought-provoking riposte to those more self-satisfied accounts that often eulogize the unmitigated success of Canadian multiculturalism.

The next two chapters focus upon the issue of federalism and highlight some of the tensions that exist both between (1) a federal conception of the state and a cosmopolitan approach to individual rights (which were strengthened in the Trudeau era) and (2) varying conceptions of federalism itself, which are to be found in the different cultural traditions of anglophone and francophone Canada and in the contrasting approaches to the scholarship of federalism that emerge within these respective traditions.

Ian Peach's chapter addresses the failed processes of constitutional change in the post-patriation period of the 1980s and 1990s[3] – in particular, the unsuccessful attempts to amend the federal Constitution at Meech Lake and Charlottetown, processes that culminated in 1987 and 1992, respectively. By this time, the influence of Trudeau was fully cemented in the minds of many elite actors and ordinary citizens and, as such, Peach argues in a strongly polemical way that the patriation process, completed in 1982, marked a fundamental shift in the attitudes of ordinary Canadians towards the Constitution. Peach explores the events that led to the adoption of the *Charter* in particular and argues that the influence of equity groups participating in the Parliamentary Committee on the Constitution in the winter of 1980-81 was crucial in shaping its substance; this fact gave these groups, and Canada's citizens more widely, a sense of ownership over the 1982 *Constitution Act* in general and the *Charter* more specifically. Therefore, Peach contends, the elite-controlled negotiations leading to the draft Meech Lake Accord set up a process from which ordinary citizens felt excluded; this top-down approach defied the expectations citizens had built up during patriation of a direct involvement in processes of constitutional change; and, in consequence, by the late 1980s deference to government was close to death in Canada.

Peach identifies two separate critiques of the Meech Lake style of intergovernmental decision making – one concerning method and the other membership – that finally combined, he argues, to kill any lingering deference among Canadians towards their political elites. The former critique concerns the lack of openness in the Meech Lake process and the absence of full republican deliberation. The latter addresses exclusion and, in particular, the lack of involvement in the negotiations of territorial governments and Aboriginal peoples as well as other interest group representatives. His account reflects Forbes' discussion of Trudeau's role in building a new Canadian nationalism. Peach identifies Trudeau's vision as a liberal democratic one that invited the participation of citizens, whereas Prime Minister Mulroney was wedded to an older Tory vision of elite accommodation; as such, Mulroney misread the popular mood, and the extent to which Canadians had adopted a new participatory model of Canadian democracy with its eschewal of deference to political elites.

Peach identifies the aftermath of the failed Meech Lake Accord as an opportunity for possible renewal of public faith in constitutional process; but, ultimately, the pre-Charlottetown efforts at finding a breakthrough in the impasse between Quebec and the rest of Canada – given the deep unhappiness within Quebec concerning the patriation process from which many felt Quebec had been excluded – was to prove to be an opportunity lost. This was a period of radical experimentation in public engagement. The "Renewal of Canada" conferences were for him "truly remarkable events" in terms of the extent to which people both engaged in discussion and had their views taken seriously. But Peach argues that, despite the seeming realization by elites that full public engagement was now essential to any process of constitutional renewal, in the intergovernmental negotiations leading to the draft Charlottetown Accord, the people once again found themselves as passive observers watching from the outside as elites determined the direction of constitutional change.

Peach draws two main lessons from this troubled period in modern Canadian history. The first is that the methodology of Meech Lake and Charlottetown has left a sour taste and a deep distrust of political elites. Second, Peach offers an optimistic message concerning the management of cultural difference in Canada. Greater public scepticism with elite-led constitutional deliberations does not equal scepticism with attempts to accommodate it through constitutional processes; instead, the discussions wherein the public has been involved have shown that Canadians are well able to reach decisions about the accommodation of difference if they are only given the chance to participate and to debate these issues. In focusing upon the role of ordinary citizens in these processes, Peach's account recalls Temelini's discussion of democratic deliberation and the way in which Canadian citizens at different times have developed an expectation of high levels of participation. Referring to Temelini's chapter, it may be that much of the discomfort felt by many Canadians over the elite-driven machinations of both Meech Lake and, to a lesser extent, Charlottetown finds its provenance not only in citizen debates over the constitutional changes of 1980-82 but also through earlier engagement with processes such as the B and B Commission. Temelini's account may also help explain why disaffection with elites has not resulted in popular distaste for the policies of multiculturalism that these elites pursued at Meech Lake and Charlottetown. Temelini describes Canada's receptiveness to its multicultural reality as a grassroots phenomenon, arising among the people through public deliberation and through an ensuing sense of popular ownership of the Constitution and of the multicultural pattern it represented. Therefore, it should perhaps not be surprising that, even if disaffection with intergovernmental negotiation methods has been a consequence of Meech Lake and Charlottetown, there has not been a concomitant backlash against the ongoing substantive efforts by Canadians, elite and ordinary, to manage diversity more successfully within the state.

It might be noted that Peach's account of citizen dissatisfaction is largely the story of English Canada's reaction to the events of the 1980s and 1990s, and that the reaction in francophone Canada, and especially in Quebec, was very different, with disaffection expressed not so much with the elite-driven process of constitutional negotiations as with the failure of these negotiations, in substantive terms, to alleviate Quebec's dissatisfaction with the Constitution as patriated from the UK in 1982. In this context, Marc Chevrier addresses the nature of Canadian federalism from a very different perspective than that adopted by Peach. As a starting point, it is important to note that the federal nature of Canada predates contemporary debates about multiculturalism by a century, and, indeed, the federal system itself embodies a constitutional commitment to diversity – diversity based upon territorial identities. Indeed, it is the territorial control offered by federalism that has facilitated the development of Quebec's distinct national identity around a set of governmental and other institutions within a discrete territorial space. And, in addition, distinctive identities of a regional rather than a national type have also developed in other provinces.

Whereas Peach's account seems to presuppose a unicultural, or certainly uninational, conception of the Canadian demos, Chevrier addresses the differences in understandings over the nature of the Canadian Constitution that arise between anglophone and francophone Canada. He argues that this is pronounced not only among ordinary citizens but also among political scientists and legal scholars, with each of these groups tending to adopt very different views about the nature of the Canadian federation and of federalism more generally, depending upon the linguistic community from which they come. Chevrier notes that Canadian federalism developed in a fairly ad hoc fashion, without a grand vision or the accompaniment of a rich theoretical tradition similar to the American Federalist Papers to explain, and thus normatively underpin, the union of three colonies in 1867. Also, he observes that, despite the vast literature that exists on the topic of Canadian federalism, there is no common set of criteria used by Canada's two linguistic communities to define the federal system or to locate it within wider and more general theories of federalism. According to Chevrier, the story tends to vary between anglophone and francophone commentators. By his account, French-speaking authors are more likely to focus upon the history of the federal system, arguing that unitary or imperial aspects enshrined in its early development remain intact. Furthermore, francophones are less interested than are anglophone political scientists in the workings of the federal system in terms of economic efficiency; rather, they concentrate more on the distribution of powers between the two levels of government, with frequent reference to what is seen as the centralizing tendencies of the Canadian system and federal control over intergovernmental relations. This contrasts sharply with many anglophone political scientists, who tend to present Canada as heavily decentralized, certainly in comparative perspective. Chevrier's work, therefore, highlights that one of the ongoing challenges facing constitutional responses to deep diversity is that these responses must be able to accommodate very different understandings of the purpose of the Canadian state and of its federal model.

Chevrier observes that, since 1982, it has become common for the nationalist movement in Quebec to be seen as the main force of resistance to federalism. This again highlights the prevalence of a story of the post-1982 Canadian experience in anglophone Canada, which contrasts with that advanced by francophone scholars. For example, although, as Donald Forbes has pointed out, the *Charter* is in many ways popular in Quebec, it has also been seen there as a device that endangers territorial diversity by uniting minorities around the idea of one national Canadian community. The strategic alliance in the 1960s between cultural minorities and the federal government in the building of a multicultural vision of the Canadian state (as also discussed by Forbes and Temelini) is often identified in Quebec as a strategy to weaken Quebec nationalism. Indeed, Chevrier argues that the demands for recognition advanced by non-territorial cultural groups since 1982 have created a process that promises to undermine even federalism itself. This became apparent in the constitutional reforms attempted at Meech Lake and Charlottetown, with Chevrier offering a very different picture of these processes from that given by Peach. According to Chevrier, there was a major clash between those seeking to strengthen the federal powers of the provinces and those who increasingly challenged federalism itself in the name of their diverse and deterritorialized cultural and other interests. Charlottetown, he suggests, tried to square the circle by meeting both sets of demands. Although the failure of this process can, in part, be explained by the complexity of the amending formula contained in the *Constitution Act*, 1982, and in general by political differences in a diverse state, he offers a further hypothesis that, since 1982, the relationship between federalism and federation has changed in Canada. In particular, the tension between those seeking a further territorial division of powers and those seeking to undermine federalism in the name of deterritorialized interests was too great to accommodate. As he puts it: "In this sense, the societies in Canada can be viewed as torn by a double process of federalization and defederalization."

Chevrier's chapter therefore highlights the deep tension that can exist between accommodating territorial diversity through federalism and the aspirations of non-territorial groups for recognition. This has become tied to the related divide between Quebec and the rest of the country over the former's status. Exacerbating this, a unitary nationalism has developed around the *Charter* and a vision of rights, as alluded to by Temelini and Peach, that has reshaped perceptions of the nature of the Canadian political community in an increasingly monistic way and that, in many ways, sees federalism as an unwelcome constraint upon this nation-building exercise.

Chevrier also notes that, although the *Charter* seeks closer Canadian integration with respect to identity and citizenship, it is important not to ignore that the Aboriginal challenge to the Canadian state, when advanced by way of claims for self-government, is federalist in texture since it seeks to establish autonomous governments on a clearly territorial basis. In a sense, this has added a further dynamic to claims that Canada is a multinational state, a claim traditionally advanced by Quebec but now also finding a new impetus in the discourse of Aboriginal peoples. In light of these tensions, Chevrier does not envisage a finalized agreement on the nature of Canadian federalism in the near future.

Part 2 of *Multiculturalism and the Canadian Constitution* addresses the ways in which multiculturalism has become embedded in the constitutional practice of the Canadian state. Here a series of case studies demonstrates the all-pervasive reach of multiculturalism in terms of language policy, the role of the courts, and the ongoing struggle to define adequately and to implement the deeply contested concept of equality. This part of the book begins with a topic that is tied closely to federalism; namely, the management of Canada's linguistic diversity. This issue is also linked to the search for stronger national unity, as Daniel Bourgeois and Andrew F. Johnson explore in their account of the 2003 *Action Plan for Official Languages*. They view this plan as one of several major policy initiatives designed to strengthen the authority of the Canadian state, which is under challenge not only from within in terms of Quebec nationalism but also from without as a consequence of globalization. They assess the plan in this light and also with reference to the accountability issues, relating to federalism and moral choice, which it raises. The plan seems to offer strength to arguments that the constitutional accommodation of Canada's diversity is the result of self-conscious policy making and also that the Canadian approach to language rights is in many ways unique in terms of creating a level of officially protected and promoted bilingualism that is unrivalled in almost any other state (Belgium being one of the few feasible comparators).

Bourgeois and Johnson begin by discussing the *Action Plan* in terms of its strategic role as a bulwark against forces of globalization and nationalism. As part of a coordinated response by the federal government to Quebec nationalism, it was the "carrot" of an official "carrot and stick" policy, balanced against measures such as the *Clarity Act*, 2000, which followed the Quebec referendum on sovereignty in 1995 and the Supreme Court of Canada's opinion in the *Secession Reference* of 1998. Next, the authors discuss the implications of the plan in terms of the accountability of federal political institutions. They observe that the plan presents twenty-five goals and sixty-four specific means to attain them, with the goals themselves being divided into eleven priority sectors. Of these, Bourgeois and Johnson focus on education and health since these have traditionally been policy areas that the provinces have sought to protect from the interference of the federal government's spending power. They note widespread criticism, particularly in the area of education, that much of the money allocated for French-language (mother tongue) education has not been spent by the federal government and, more especially, by provincial governments.

In the view of Bourgeois and Johnson, the Canadian state is not less interventionist than it was prior to 1995; rather, it is repositioning itself in the context of globalization. Although the process is a quiet one, it has a "discrete centralizing tendency" that also requires "complacent federalism" and provincial acceptance of this type of investment. Furthermore, a related problem is moral accountability. Although the policy of national integration via the *Action Plan* appears to be effective in dealing with the challenges posed by globalization, this could all collapse if a crisis of legitimization occurs, whereby the federal government neglects its obligations to transfer funds to the provinces to promote social equality. If such a scenario occurs, the authors offer the stark warning that "the Canadian state may well wither in the face of the moral accountability challenges posed by globalization."

Hugh Kindred addresses another complex issue within the Canadian federal system: the legal implementation of international instruments. This issue is always difficult, but it has, in recent years, been the focus of attention before the courts following a landmark case. Kindred notes that, in the area of foreign affairs, the federal government has the prerogative power to bind Canada to international agreements but that it does not have the unilateral authority to implement these treaties by legislation. Depending upon the subject matter of the agreement, the power to implement may lie with the federal parliament or, alternatively, with provincial legislatures. This, of course, allows the provinces the option of refusing to implement treaties negotiated by the federal government, leaving the latter with no constitutional authority to force the issue and, thereby, potentially in breach of international undertakings it has given to implement the agreements to which it has adhered. This is now a particularly prominent issue since, in light of mass immigration, international relations with states that many Canadians view as their "home countries" are important in the maintenance of cultural links.

The fact that transnational relations now increasingly embrace cultural links between Canada and other countries to which Canadian citizens have ties, leads Kindred to observe that the issue of respective federal/provincial competences in this area is an ever more complex one; the reason being that treaty commitments undertaken by the Canadian government regarding culture and related matters increasingly cover subject areas that are within provincial competence. Furthermore, matters are made more complex yet by the recent development of a more activist approach on the part of the courts to the status of unimplemented international obligations. Kindred identifies this as part of the fall-out of a broader culture of judicial activism that arrived with the *Charter of Rights and Freedoms*, following which the Supreme Court of Canada determined that, in interpreting the *Charter*, it should have regard to international laws and conventions on human rights; a position taken even though the *Charter* makes no reference to such international instruments. In other words, there is now a general requirement on courts to interpret the meaning of statutory language in the broadest possible context. As Jameson Doig also notes (discussed below), this new activism marked a move away from a traditional deference to Parliament. One aspect of this deference involved the principle that an unimplemented treaty would have no domestic consequences; indeed, the courts would not even take cognizance of such a treaty until it had been implemented through the relevant legislature.

Although with the *Charter* came the new principle that Canada's international human rights obligations should assist in the interpretation of this document, Kindred observes that the courts have not drawn a distinction between incorporated and unincorporated treaties. Instead, the Supreme Court has, in his view, generally been "quite circumspect" in the way it has been prepared to invoke international legal sources. This is not to go so far as to say that judges are in effect "applying" unimplemented treaties as though they were sources of law, but they are using them as part of the legislative context of the statute under interpretation. Here his focus moves to the important case of *Baker*,[4] which he suggests clarifies the approach of the Court somewhat. In this case, Justice L'Heureux-Dubé expressed the view that "the values reflected in international human rights law may help inform the contextual approach to statutory interpretation and judicial review."[5] In Kindred's view, this case shows the preparedness of the Court to refer, and perhaps even to defer, to binding but unimplemented international agreements as a positive aid to statutory interpretation. It seems to require, rather than merely permit, courts to make use of international law in interpreting domestic legislation.

But there must surely be a concern here that this endangers provincial prerogatives. It is traditionally understood that provinces have the power to choose whether, and if so how, to implement international agreements in the area of provincial jurisdiction. It now appears that courts are being mandated to give some degree of weight, if not quite legal effect, to such measures even if the province had expressly chosen not to implement. It would seem that only when legislation to the contrary exists, and where that is, in Kindred's words, "insurmountably in conflict" with the international obligation in question, that the international agreement will not be used to inform the application of Canadian law. But Kindred's point that many international agreements that cover cultural and other matters, the implementation of which are very important to cultural minorities in Canada, in fact fall within the area of provincial jurisdiction, adds further complexity to this whole issue. And so once again we see the potential for a clash between the interests of territorial diversity embodied in provincial constitutional jurisdiction, on the one hand, and the non-territorial interests of other cultural minorities, on the other. The story from *Baker* is, therefore, certainly far from complete, creating as it does another difficult area for the courts in the management of Canadian cultural and territorial diversity.

The role of the courts in the development of the multicultural tenor of the Canadian Constitution has, of course, grown in recent times, as Temelini also observed, and the issue of judicial activism, seen in the context of the *Baker* case, is a point of more general importance in the post-*Charter* era. In the next two chapters, Jameson Doig considers the growing assertiveness of the Supreme Court of Canada under the chief justiceship of Brian Dickson, while Robert Currie analyzes how the issue of culture raises the difficult question of whether traditional assumptions about the objectivity of adjudication must be opened to further scrutiny and critique in light of new research highlighting the extent to which culturally informed attitudes and presuppositions affect judges in their decision-making processes.

As has been discussed, perhaps the most significant institutional legacy left by Pierre Trudeau in the area of cultural pluralism is the *Charter of Rights and Freedoms*. Jameson Doig explores how Canada's multicultural identity developed in the post-*Charter* era and, in particular, the role played in this process by Brian Dickson, chief justice of Canada from 1984 to 1990, who, by authoring many of the leading judgments in this era, served to advance the rights of Aboriginal peoples, members of particular religious and ethnic groups, and other vulnerable groups. In addition to exploring these substantive developments, Doig also assesses deeper cultural developments undergone by the Court itself in the very methodology of adjudication. He observes how, on the one hand, Canadian judges brought into being a new culture of judicial activism in application of the *Charter*, which was alien to Canada's constitutional tradition of parliamentary sovereignty, and, on the other, resisted the adoption of a strongly individualist approach to civil liberties as practised in the United States of America. That position, if adopted, would have offered a set of precedents, in particular in the area of free speech, that might have stifled a more collectivist approach to the cultural rights of groups that, as Kymlicka has shown, are so central to the Canadian multicultural experience. Certainly, the *Charter* itself contains a body of group rights that is not to be found in the American Bill of Rights; nonetheless, the way in which the judiciary would apply these remained, in 1982, a largely unknown quantity, and the convenient reference point of American precedents may have proved tempting to Canadian judges. It is in this dual context, Doig argues, that the leadership of Chief Justice Dickson became crucial.

Doig observes that Dickson's commitment to a bilingual and multicultural Canada was evident from his time as a trial judge in Manitoba in the 1960s and later on the Manitoba Court of Appeal. When appointed to the Supreme Court of Canada, and in time to the post of chief justice, his leadership was evident when, in the early case of *Hunter*,[6] he applied a broad, purposive approach to the interpretation of the *Charter*. This was an acknowledgment that, as a constitutional document, the *Charter* could not be approached with the same interpretative tools as an ordinary statute but, rather, would need a more expansive reading – one that would take full account of the normative commitments within the *Charter*. And this approach was reinforced in subsequent cases, establishing itself as a leitmotif of *Charter* adjudication to the present day.

Chief Justice Dickson also took the lead in developing discrete areas of case law that enhanced the management of cultural diversity in Canada. One such area involved Aboriginal rights, where, most notably in the *Sparrow* case,[7] the Supreme Court set out basic principles for the weighing of Aboriginal rights against the legislative prerogatives of the federal Parliament and the provincial legislatures. Here, Dickson's judgment was central in holding that existing Aboriginal rights must be "interpreted flexibly so as to permit their evolution over time."[8] A liberal interpretation was to be given to section 35 of the *Constitution Act*, 1982, and in general government interference with existing Aboriginal rights was to be closely scrutinized, with such interference required to clear a high hurdle.

Doig also discusses how Dickson showed sensitivity to the issue of language rights, bringing a creative interpretation to the constitutional guarantees for linguistic minorities in Canada. This involved a recognition that the purpose of language rights is not simply to facilitate communication but also to allow the culture and identity of linguistic communities to thrive. In this sense, Chief Justice Dickson and the Supreme Court as a whole showed themselves alive to the advancement of group as well as individual rights, even in the face of criticism that the Court was being excessively activist.

A third area of importance during Dickson's chief justiceship was hate speech. In *Regina v. Keegstra*,[9] the Supreme Court, led by Dickson, found that, although section 319 of the *Criminal Code* (which outlawed the promotion of hatred) was prima facie contrary to the *Charter*, the Court should be guided by the values and principles essential to a free and democratic society, which include respect for cultural and group identity. Unlike in the United States, where hate speech is most often protected, in Canada, regard has to be given to the special character of equality and multiculturalism in the Constitution. As such, section 319 was a reasonable limit on free speech.

Therefore, Doig, in conclusion, argues that, through both his expansive approach to *Charter* interpretation and his application of this approach in several important areas of substantive law, Dickson helped establish a methodology and a judicial ideology that continue to be used to advance the cause of vulnerable individuals and groups and, hence, to boost their sense of inclusion within Canadian civil society. In this we see a more nuanced approach to liberalism – one that moves away from a rigid, individualist approach towards greater recognition of the importance of group identities and group membership for the diverse communities that constitute Canadian society.

It has been observed that Temelini's chapter highlights the extent to which the agenda of multiculturalism has crystallized into a narrative of rights and how, in many ways, the focus of attention has shifted from broader political participation by citizens towards a juridical understanding of cultural rights, remediable before the courts. While it would certainly be very unfortunate were the former tradition of civic virtue to be forgotten, when we reflect on Doig's chapter, there is nonetheless something of the inevitable about the growth of litigation in the development of any multicultural policy, in particular with the creation of legally enforceable *Charter* rights and the passage of specific legislation designed to protect minorities. Nor is this necessarily inconsistent with republican democracy; the opportunity to litigate was itself intended by the deliberative commitment of Canadians as a whole when such laws were adopted, either as constitutional principles or through legislation enacted by their representatives in Parliament. It is an inescapable fact that, in a democracy, legislation turns political claims into legal rights. Besides the *Charter*, it is also notable that Trudeau advanced a strong anti-discrimination strategy, an affirmative action policy, and a law outlawing hate speech; and that each of these measures either invited individual applicants to bring cases or threatened with court action those citizens or institutions that breached the relevant provisions.

Robert Currie focuses on the issue of equality and, in particular, upon the way in which equality of citizenship is encapsulated in the notion of the rule of law as embodied in the *Charter*. But the issue of equality, although almost universally accepted as a key principle underpinning so many other human rights, is, when explored a little more thoroughly, in fact deeply contested. There are profound disagreements about whether equality can be conceptualized simply in formalistic terms without reference to a wider context, or whether it is necessary to look behind equality, in the narrow sense, at structural factors that favour certain groups and prejudice others. In this context, Currie asks whether Canadian courts and judges are indeed prepared to move beyond conceptions of formal equality, and, if so, whether they have the tools they need to take into account complex social and cultural realities, which, as commentators such as Kymlicka have shown in appeals for a more sophisticated understanding of liberalism, highlight deeper inequalities.

Currie concentrates upon the law of evidence to explain how legal principles do not always adapt to the need for contextualization. He suggests that an analysis of what evidence is admitted and the way it is treated will help explain the impact that culture has upon adjudication and jury deliberation, offering pointers as to which aspects of the judicial process might be reformed and how. In light of this, he devotes much of his chapter to the important 1997 case of *R. v. S. (R.D.)*,[10] where the Supreme Court of Canada articulated the view that the proper accommodation of diversity and multiculturalism required judges to take account of social and cultural contexts in embracing the principle of equality. As well as the principle of equality, the *Charter* of course also contains a commitment to multiculturalism in section 27, and it is against the backdrop of the interaction of these two principles that this case should be considered.

The case of *RDS* arose from the arrest of a black teenager by a white police officer in Nova Scotia. Currie discusses how the broader cultural context was considered in this case by the trial judge who, unusually, took into account interracial conflict within the relevant community, particularly the poor relations between white police officers and black community members. The trial judge therefore adopted a contextual approach and, on appeal, this was supported by the Supreme Court. Currie commends the approach taken, and in a wider sense he argues for a differentiation to be made between what he calls "adjudicative neutrality," which is necessary for non-biased decision making, and "fact neutrality," which is an excessively formalistic approach that doesn't properly take context into account. He contends that it is wrong to begin from the assumption that everyone is "equal" and "neutral" until the facts prove otherwise because such a formal equality analysis may fail to take into account social forces that may have had a strong bearing upon the factual circumstances that, in the end, come before the court. In this sense, the *Charter* is very significant since the constitutionalization of multiculturalism forces courts to address this debate when developing the law of evidence, and also encourages a new "cultural discourse" within the judicial system concerning the very meaning of terms such as "neutrality," "fairness," and "equity."

The final two chapters of *Multiculturalism and the Canadian Constitution*, written by Joan Small and Katherine Eddy, respectively, also address the issue of equality. Small's chapter, like Currie's, identifies a possible strain between equality and the principle of multiculturalism. She argues that the effect of Canada's policy of multiculturalism upon the law of the *Charter*, and in particular upon the principle of equality, remains in many respects to be worked through. However, what is clear is that there are considerable tensions between these principles since multiculturalism as a legal principle challenges substantive equality law both for individuals and for the collective protection of groups.

Within the principle of multiculturalism itself, Small argues, there is a possible paradox between, on the one hand, fostering social cohesion, integrating immigrants into Canadian society, combating discrimination, and the like (all of which have the principle of equality as their basis) and, on the other hand, policies to promote diversity for the distinctive cultures within Canada, including the provision of public assistance to maintain this diversity, which of itself is a move away from formal equality. She suggests that, since the *Charter* came into force, the former dynamic has been the real driving force, aimed at ethnic participation in employment and combating racism, all in the name of promoting equality. Small's contention is that this vision of equality should not come to dominate the Canadian approach to multiculturalism. According to her, this drive towards equality must be set in the context of section 27, which expresses multiculturalism as a Canadian constitutional value that is relevant to subsequent constitutional decision making. As was seen in Jameson Doig's account of the Dickson court, interpretative obligations arising from the *Charter* are of a different kind from ordinary principles of statutory interpretation, and, in particular, they lead the courts to scrutinize measures closely when they conflict with *Charter* provisions. On this basis, Small argues, the constitutional commitment to multiculturalism in section 27 must be taken very seriously, despite other and possibly rival commitments to formal equality. Small's approach highlights again the different approaches to liberalism that attend the accommodation of cultural diversity: the formal equality of a traditional liberal model on the one hand, and the more contextualized account that promotes the value of diversity (perhaps at the expense of formal equality), on the other. However, despite so much jurisprudence on the issue of equality in the context of Canada's multicultural framework, Small finds that, in general, the courts' consideration of these issues lacks theoretical depth.

One way in which the Canadian Constitution compromises formal equality is in accrediting special protections to certain groups and territories: Aboriginal peoples, Quebec, denominational communities, and English and French linguistic minorities. They each have separate institutional and legal rights, and, Small argues, despite the Supreme Court's assertion to the contrary,[11] the special status accorded to these groups creates a hierarchy within the Canadian constitutional settlement that privileges them. All of this raises for Small a series of questions vis-à-vis section 15 of the *Charter*. How does, or should, Canada's constitutional commitment to a multicultural society affect judicial understanding of equality law? And what sorts of claims for cultural protection or promotion can persons or groups who are not given special constitutional status make, if any? In fact, there has been little jurisprudence on the relationship between sections 15 and 27, despite the wide use of section 27. One difficult area involves the concept of "dignity." Here she argues that a whole range of questions have not yet been answered by the Supreme Court, such as how a group, rather than an individual, can be said to feel self-respect or self-worth; whether the Court is concerned with the feelings of the totality of the members, on the one hand, or of the group as a group, on the other; and how to determine who speaks for the group, or how group sentiment is to be measured. She concludes that section 15 is capable of promoting a positive interpretation of section 27 by embracing a contextualized approach that recognizes cultural diversity as an important aspect of human dignity. The Supreme Court has not yet developed this as it might, but, in Small's view, it is obliged by the *Charter* to give full effect to section 27, taking seriously the concept of dignity as well as that of equality.

Katherine Eddy also addresses the interface between the important values of equality and dignity in any multicultural society, with a focus upon welfare rights as equality rights. Although her chapter is not about culture directly, clearly the concept of equality in general has important implications for all minorities. Her principal questions concern whether individuals are morally entitled to social assistance to help them meet their basic subsistence needs and, in particular, whether they have a constitutional "welfare right" to such provision. She begins by observing that the Canadian Constitution does not contain any commitment to the alleviation of severe poverty or the meeting of basic subsistence needs; and it certainly does not create rights to these things. Although according to section 36(1) of the *Constitution Act*, 1982, Canada is committed to providing "essential public services of reasonable quality to all Canadians" and the promotion of "equal opportunities for the well-being of Canadians," there are no specific provisions in this regard to be found in the *Charter of Rights and Freedoms*. However, the issue is open to some debate because the *Charter* does contain an equality guarantee and does entrench the rights to life, liberty, and security of the person.

The role of the courts is central to Eddy's analysis, as it is for Small and Currie. Eddy focuses upon the important case of *Gosselin v. Quebec*,[12] where the Supreme Court of Canada addressed the question of whether the right to social assistance payments at the subsistence level could be derived from either of the *Charter* protections contained in section 36(1). Eddy's analysis of this case is a normative critique from the perspective of political theory rather than an assessment of the legal merits of the decision. Her question is whether Canadians *should* have constitutional welfare rights and not whether they are in fact provided for by the *Charter* as it stands. She addresses two arguments for welfare rights as they arose in the *Gosselin* case: one that contends that they can be derived from considerations of *equality* and one that points to the state's responsibility to alleviate *unmet need* as part of its duty to provide for its citizens.

In her discussion of *Gosselin*, she points out that one problem with the equality approach is that it makes the argument for welfare rights precarious. The risk is that all people might be equally mistreated without the principle of equality being offended; in other words, there is no breach of constitutional rights when the dignity and physical empowerment of all welfare recipients comes under threat in the same way. Like Currie and Small, Eddy focuses upon the poverty of an approach that is wedded too much to a thin version of formal equality. To avoid this, she advocates a more contextualized rendition of the equality argument, by which welfare rights are grounded in the state's overarching duty to respect the equal worth of its citizens and their human dignity, something that cannot be met simply by formal equality. For her, in order for the principle of equality to be meaningful, a substantive level of dignity must accompany equality.

The Canadian effort to establish a state that takes full account of, and that in fact seeks to define itself in terms of, its cultural diversity has been a long and difficult journey. As this collection demonstrates, it is a journey that can never be completed. The accommodation of difference leads to new claims from minority groups for further accommodation, and in this changing climate claims presented by one group will often clash with those posited by other groups seeking alternative models of constitutional change or reinterpretation. In Canada, the multicultural model of the state can only become more complex as more demands are articulated and as the nature of these claims mutate in light of the evolving Constitution, changing global conditions, and shifting ideological patterns. The Canadian experience of multicultural policy and the embodiment of a commitment to diversity in so many areas of the Constitution highlight several important questions. For example: in historical perspective, how and why has Canada adopted the approach it has taken? To what extent has the success of Canadian multiculturalism been the consequence of a fortuitous environment rather than deliberate policy choices? Has a suitable balance been arrived at between multiculturalism and Canada's federal heritage? And which version of liberal democracy best suits a country with such a deep cultural mix as Canada: is it one that tries to leave culture to the private sphere, guaranteeing only formal equality within the public space, or is it one that must look beyond formalism to engage with the aspirations of groups for official recognition of their distinctiveness? Attempts to answer these and related questions will remain central to the ongoing engagement, on the part of policy makers and scholars, with the country's complex demotic composition. It is hoped that the contributions contained in this book offer us fresh perspectives with which to address these complex issues.

Notes

1 Will Kymlicka, *Multicultural Citizenship: A Liberal Theory of Minority Rights* (Oxford: Oxford University Press, 1995), 108.
2 Charles Taylor, *Sources of the Self: The Making of the Modern Identity* (Cambridge, MA: Harvard University Press, 1989), 89.
3 Patriation was the process culminating in the passage of the *Canada Act*, 1982, by the Parliament of the United Kingdom, which severed all remaining constitutional and legislative ties between the two countries.
4 *Baker v. Canada (Minister of Citizenship and Immigration)*, [1999] 2 S.C.R. 817.
5 Ibid., 861.
6 *Hunter v. Southam*, [1984] 2 S.C.R. 145.
7 *R. v. Sparrow*, [1990] 1 S.C.R. 1075.
8 Ibid., 1093.
9 *R. v. Keegstra*, [1990] 3 S.C.R. 697.
10 *R. v. S. (R.D.)*, [1997] 3 S.C.R. 484 (hereinafter *RDS*).
11 *Mahe v. Alberta*, [1990] 1 S.C.R. 342.
12 *Gosselin v. Quebec* (Attorney General), [2002] 4 S.C.R. 429.

Part 1
The Evolution of Multiculturalism and Federalism in the Canadian Constitution

1

Trudeau as the First Theorist of Canadian Multiculturalism
Hugh Donald Forbes

My thesis is the simple one that the most illustrious and influential proponent of multiculturalism as a Canadian identity, Pierre Elliott Trudeau, took multiculturalism seriously and knew what he was doing. For him, contrary to what some have suggested, multiculturalism was not just a political expedient to be used for a few years to fend off attacks on official bilingualism and then to be forgotten. Nor was it, as others have suggested, something incompatible with basic liberal principles and therefore something that a principled liberal like Trudeau could never really have endorsed. I shall try to show, instead, that Trudeau had a broad understanding of multiculturalism, that he saw clearly what it meant, that he explained it as clearly as necessary, and, therefore, that Canada's current multicultural identity is not just an accidental effect of his policies but, rather, the intended result of his actions. I confine myself to a quick review of what Trudeau said and did up to the time of his retirement from office in 1984, but I think the conclusions I draw could be supported by a more extensive analysis of events and developments up to the present day.

Official Multiculturalism

Canada's official multiculturalism began with a statement that Trudeau made in the House of Commons on October 8, 1971. "A policy of multiculturalism within a bilingual framework commends itself to the government as the most suitable means of assuring the cultural freedom of Canadians," Trudeau declared.[1] I shall say something presently about the occasion for this statement and Trudeau's explanation of what multiculturalism would require in practice, but let me begin by focusing on "cultural freedom." What does this expression mean?

The aim of the new policy, Trudeau explained, was "to break down discriminatory attitudes and cultural jealousies." Such divisive attitudes and jealousies are rooted in cultural insecurity, he said, and they can be reduced by ensuring that individuals are free to be whoever they choose to be culturally. Only when everyone is given this freedom, it seems, will they all have the confidence they need to respect the identities of others and to share "ideas, attitudes, and assumptions" with them on a footing of equality. This social-psychological theory or conjecture, sometimes called "the multiculturalism hypothesis," was put forward as the basic justification for a "vigorous policy of multiculturalism" designed to create the confidence necessary for a meaningful and secure national unity. By increasing cultural freedom – that is, by affirming or recognizing the equal legitimacy of all cultures in Canada – prejudice would be reduced. There might be two official *languages* in Canada, Trudeau conceded, but there was no official *culture*, nor did any ethnic group take precedence over any other. In a supplementary document, he went further: "Indeed, we believe that cultural pluralism is the very essence of Canadian identity. Every ethnic group has the right to preserve and develop its own culture and values within the Canadian context. To say that we have two official languages is not to say we have two official cultures, and no particular culture is more 'official' than another."[2]

Trudeau was evidently endorsing the goal of creating a state or society that would strive to be as neutral with respect to all traditional national or ethnic cultures as the modern liberal state tries to be with respect to particular religions. Such a state or society would not deliberately impose any particular culture on its members: it would not favour the culture of its majority group (or groups) or of any of its ethnocultural minorities. Nor would it try, directly or indirectly (by deliberate action or by apparently benign neglect), to disrupt and destroy the cultures of any of its smaller, less powerful groups. Instead it would try to deal fairly or equally with all cultures. But this is not to say that it would be a divided society or an anarchic one, suffering from what is sometimes called cultural relativism. Despite its lack of any favoured or official culture, the state or society Trudeau envisioned would have laws, customs, conventions, purposes, and ways of educating its young: it would just not favour any *particular* culture.

Here as often elsewhere, the word "particular" carries a lot of weight. It seems to mean traditional as opposed to modern and partial as opposed to universal. Trudeau's aim, one could say, was to give every individual the freedom to adopt a modern outlook and the modern practices that had emerged from the interaction of many traditional cultures, if that was their choice, as well as the freedom to adhere to older ways of life, if that was what they were more comfortable doing. He wanted to ensure that individuals in a modern society could remain reasonably faithful to the old and familiar ways of their ancestors. They should be free to consume the mass-produced culture and entertainment of modern mass scientific societies, if they wished, and to participate in the large impersonal institutions of such societies, if necessary; but those who found living on the cutting edge of progress unsettling and unsatisfying should also be free to retreat to a more protected life within smaller and more traditional groupings that were better able to satisfy their need for a sense of belonging and distinct identity. As Trudeau said, "Ethnic pluralism can help us overcome or prevent the homogenization and depersonalization of mass society. Vibrant ethnic groups can give Canadians of the second, third, and subsequent generations a feeling that they are connected with tradition and with human experience in various parts of the world and different periods of time."[3] In short, then, no one should be compelled to make any particular choices among the cultural options available. Individuals should be free to practise their traditional ways, or those of others, or to shift to the new ways, or to mix and match as they pleased. Culture, often thought to be a matter of fate, should ideally be something chosen and tailored to fit the individual.

Trudeau concluded his short statement by emphasizing "the view of the government that a policy of multiculturalism within a bilingual framework is basically the conscious support of individual freedom of choice."[4] Needless to say, he knew that there had to be some limits on this freedom. He had no illusions about the possibility of absolutely unfettered freedom of choice – with respect to the side of the road that people would drive on, for example, or the units they would use when weighing or measuring. (They would drive on the right and measure their speed and progress in kilometres.) Moreover, he surely recognized that free choices get their meaning from the purposes they serve and the standards by which they are judged. But these purposes and standards can be questioned, and there are many areas of life where uniformity is unnecessary. Many different customs or conventions could easily coexist, were it not for the intolerance of cultural zealots. As Thomas Jefferson pointed out long ago, "it does me no injury for my neighbour to say there are twenty gods, or no god. It neither picks my pocket nor breaks my leg."[5] The real problem is the zealots. As John Stuart Mill explained in *On Liberty*, their intolerance can make a mockery of a merely formal or legal freedom of individual choice. So a state or society trying to empty itself of any particular cultural content – one aspiring to give its members as much freedom as possible to create their own individual cultures – would have to take some responsibility for neutralizing the private social pressures that might compel some of its members to conform to the demands of others, contrary to their real preferences. "We are free to be ourselves," Trudeau said. "But this cannot be left to chance. It must be fostered and pursued actively. If freedom of choice is in danger for some ethnic groups, it is in danger for all. It is the policy of this government to eliminate any such danger and to 'safeguard' this freedom."[6]

The practical meaning of these broad generalizations was spelled out in four points. First, Trudeau promised that there would be some new subsidies for the cultural activities of all groups, the small and weak as well as the large and highly organized, provided they were able to demonstrate their need for assistance in order to contribute to the development of Canada. The idea was not to put dying cultures on life-support systems but, rather, to recognize the vitality of the larger and more demanding ones with some modest subsidies. Second, the government would provide assistance to "members of all cultural groups to overcome cultural barriers to full participation in Canadian society." Third, there would be official promotion of "creative encounters and interchange among all Canadian cultural groups in the interest of national unity." Finally, financial assistance would be provided for "immigrants seeking to acquire at least one of Canada's official languages in order to become full participants in Canadian society."[7] Thus, from a practical standpoint, official multiculturalism was to have both preservative and assimilative elements: individuals and groups were to be helped to preserve their distinctive identities, but they were also to be helped to blend into the larger Canadian whole, or at least into one or the other of its two linguistic halves.

In Trudeau's historic statement, preservation was put before assimilation for reasons best understood by considering the background to it. The occasion for the statement was the publication almost two years earlier of some recommendations from the Royal Commission on Bilingualism and Biculturalism, which had been appointed in 1963 by Trudeau's predecessor, Lester Pearson, "to inquire into and report upon the existing state of bilingualism and biculturalism in Canada and to recommend what steps should be taken to develop the Canadian Confederation on the basis of an equal partnership between the two founding races." The commission's main task had been to work out a practical response to the growing threat of separatist nationalism in Quebec, but it was also directed, when doing so, to take into account "the contributions made by the other ethnic groups to the cultural enrichment of Canada and the measures that should be taken to safeguard that contribution." Book IV of its final report dealt with these "other cultural groups" and how their contributions should be safeguarded.

Formally, Trudeau's statement was the official endorsement by his government of the commission's sixteen specific recommendations in Book IV of its report. But it was also, in effect, a rewriting of the commission's terms of reference. Bilingualism should no longer be paired with biculturalism, Trudeau was saying. Language and culture were to be decoupled, so to speak, and, in the future, bilingualism would provide the "framework" for multiculturalism because, as Trudeau said, "biculturalism does not properly describe our society; multiculturalism is more accurate."[8]

Trudeau's immediate practical problem was to strike a workable, defensible balance between the conflicting demands for recognition of Canada's "two founding races," British and French, and its other ethnocultural groups, not just its various "ethnic" minorities, particularly in the West, but also its Inuit and Indian communities, or "First Nations." Two years earlier, in accord with the Royal Commission on Bilingualism and Biculturalism's major recommendations about bilingualism, Trudeau had taken a big step towards blunting the appeal of the separatist movement in Quebec by responding to the linguistic grievances of French-speaking Canadians in Quebec and elsewhere. His government had passed an extremely controversial "Official Languages Act" designed to put English and French on a footing of equality in the federal government and public service. Most of the opposition to it came, not surprisingly, from English-speaking Canadians, whose privileges were being revoked and whose sense of special status, and indeed whose conception of the country as essentially an English-speaking British dominion, was being attacked. Many resented these changes but hesitated to complain because of the gravity of the separatist threat. Many felt that they could reasonably object only to the *dualistic* definition of Canada that the *Act* seemed to embody. Canada, it seemed to be saying, was leaving behind its British colonial identity only to become a country of only *two* "races," or nationalities, with all its other races and nationalities subordinated to them, and this was unacceptable.[9]

Also in 1969, Trudeau's minister of Indian affairs and northern development, Jean Chrétien, had issued a White Paper proposing a basic change in the government's relation to Aboriginal communities. The old *Indian Act*, 1874, still largely in force, had started from the assumption that Aboriginal Canadians were dependent peoples, like children, in need of parental care and supervision. It was openly Eurocentric and paternalistic: it made "Indians" and "Eskimos" wards of the Canadian state. The White Paper proposed a radical break from this old pattern. In the near future, it said, Aboriginals should become full citizens, with the same rights and privileges as all other Canadians. This proposal, too, was extremely controversial, perhaps not surprisingly, but in this case the immediate outcry was from the supposed beneficiaries of the new approach, Aboriginal peoples, and not from those who were in theory losing status, non-Aboriginal Canadians. Aboriginal opposition was intense and widespread, however, so the White Paper was soon withdrawn. But the negative reaction to it showed the limitations of equal citizenship and non-discrimination as a formula for resolving conflicts of culture and identity. Aboriginal peoples were being offered a promotion to full and equal citizenship, it seemed, but they were rejecting it, even though their guardians had been careful to acknowledge their distinct identities and the value of their cultural contributions.[10] Still, it seemed they preferred to remain wards of the state! In the future, it would be necessary to solve the Aboriginal "problem" by somehow making them "citizens plus."[11]

The more immediate challenge, however, was to overcome the objection to bilingualism based on the claim that it made second-class citizens of all but the English and the French. A "plus" had to be added to the citizenship of "ethnic" Canadians, particularly Ukrainian Canadians, to balance the "plus" of bilingualism for the French. This was the immediate challenge Trudeau met in 1971, with his statement on multiculturalism.

Theoretical Clarification

Trudeau was indisputably the founder of Canadian multiculturalism in the limited "official" sense just explained, but this is not to say that his 1971 statement provides a clear explanation of the principles of multiculturalism or gives them a solid philosophical justification. Of course, he could reasonably have left these tasks to the theory professionals – political theorists, legal theorists, critical cultural theorists, and the like. But in fact, Trudeau was an unusually thoughtful and articulate politician, so perhaps it should not be a surprise that he did his own theorizing. He gave Canada's new multicultural identity as clear an explanation and justification as anyone has up to the present, even though it is not to be found in his 1971 statement on multiculturalism.

The only theory in that short statement is the rather rudimentary and contestable psychological theory or hypothesis already outlined. To paraphrase Trudeau, only if people are confident in their own identities will they be able to deal generously and respectfully with others. This confidence will exist only if governments stop favouring some identities. They must affirm all identities equally and try to get their citizens to do the same. People must be told that they are all free to be themselves. If this freedom is in danger for some, it is in danger for all. None can really be recognized unless all are. All must be affirmed or all will be oppressed.

These edifying generalizations were a first line of defence against the widespread suspicion that official multiculturalism was really just low electoral politics, nothing more than "a sop to the ethnics," just the squandering of public money to win votes for the Liberal party. By invoking a vague but familiar theory about something obscure but apparently deep and important – psychological identity – Trudeau shrouded his very practical new policy in a hazy glow of theoretical bafflegab. We all need secure identities, he seemed to be saying, and we will all have these only if the federal government officially recognizes all cultures.

Anyone unsatisfied with this explanation of the new policy and seeking a more persuasive justification of it has to look elsewhere in Trudeau's speeches and writings. In fact, some articles about nationalism that Trudeau published in the early 1960s, when he was still just a law professor and the editor of a small monthly magazine, are the best sources for something relevant.[12] These articles aimed to discredit the separatist nationalism that was gathering force in Quebec at the time, and they consolidated Trudeau's reputation as a sophisticated political thinker, both in English Canada and Quebec. Indirectly, they also provide a justification for multiculturalism and they suggest a revealing way of describing it.

Nationalism is a notoriously ambiguous term. It can refer to intense or extreme loyalty or patriotism, and nationalists in this sense are vulnerable to the criticism that collective egoism – dedication to the interests of one's own state or nation without regard to the interests of others – is little better fundamentally, despite its potentially self-sacrificing element, than simple selfishness and self-absorption. But nationalism can also refer to a principle or theory about political life, an *ism*, like federalism or egalitarianism. Nationalists in this sense – advocates of the so-called principle of nationalities – maintain that the boundaries of sovereign states should be aligned with the boundaries of ethnic or cultural nations. Such nationalists assume that a distinction can be made between nations as cultures and nations as states, or, in other words, that cultural nations (distinguished by language, religion, history, etc.) can exist "pre-politically," or apart from any organized political life, and not just as political groups formed or "constructed" politically. Depending on circumstances, such nationalists may be separatists, or irredentists, or partisans of a national unification movement, or just defenders of an existing nation-state. They are united only in their belief that political life is best organized on a national scale, with each cultural nation having the status of a separate sovereign state.

Trudeau objected to nationalism in both these senses. He was scathingly critical of the extreme patriots among the French Canadians in Quebec, but he also had hard words for English Canada's cultural chauvinists. The French had legitimate grievances against their English-speaking compatriots, Trudeau conceded. Indeed, he thought that French-Canadian nationalism was best understood as a defensive reaction against the aggressive nationalism of British-oriented Canadians. But the solution Quebec's newest nationalists favoured, political independence for the province, would be costly, regressive, and inherently unjust. These nationalists, or separatists, talked bravely about their openness to the world and their commitment to progressive causes, but Trudeau described them as fearful and reactionary, and he rejected the principle of nationalities to which they appealed.[13] He did not contend, as many do now, that the familiar nation-state distinction cannot be sustained because ethnic nations are "constructed," like political states; instead, he attacked the arguments advanced by nationalists in defence of their theory of peaceful diversity and republican politics – essentially that conflicts can be reduced (since good fences make good neighbours) and dedication to the common good increased (since blood is thicker than water) by creating sovereign states that are also ethnic nations. The principle can never be applied without difficulty, Trudeau pointed out, since "national" territories are always somewhat mixed ethnically and the boundaries between them are fuzzy at best. Hence, any attempt to apply the principle generates new, unnecessary conflicts and injustices. And even if it could be applied without difficulty, it would, because of the way it would link military power and the interests of the military class to the ethnic passions and prejudices of ordinary citizens, still just produce a world dangerously disposed to war.

Trudeau suggested that the solution to the problem of national differences and national rivalries must lie in a different direction altogether. The aim should not be to create a world of homogeneous nation-states, their differences carefully preserved or even augmented by governments disposed to foster a sense of opposition to the alien "Others" beyond their boundaries; rather, the aim should be to mix the populations of existing states even further, with a view to ultimately separating state and nation altogether, thus undermining the psychological basis for an intense and exclusive state patriotism and preparing the way for the necessary transition to a world of semi-sovereign states (or provinces) under some form of global governance. Only in this way could the terrible destructive potential of modern scientific warfare ultimately be brought under control.

What role could Canada play in promoting this long-term political transformation? As a large, wealthy country with a small but deeply divided population emerging from a colonial past, Trudeau thought that it could show other countries the way to create a society based, not on nationality, but on what he called "polyethnic pluralism." He dismissed the old "British North America" dream of making Canada a purely English or British country: French Canada was simply too large and too stubbornly united in defence of its language and culture to be assimilated. Moreover, "Britishness" no longer had much appeal as an identity, even to the English in Canada. To be sure, the English and the French could separate, as Quebec's *indépendantistes* proposed, and each linguistic nation would then be free to rid itself of the remnants of the other that remained within its boundaries, but Trudeau condemned this option as regressive and unjust. Even national unity based on a dualistic conception of Canada, such as the Royal Commission on Bilingualism and Biculturalism had been established to promote, while admittedly a more defensible option, was not, in itself, a very exciting one. It would be no great achievement, late in the twentieth century, merely to overcome the historic rivalry between anglophones and francophones and Protestants and Catholics. A two-nations Canada would be at best a simplified Switzerland, peaceful but boring and of no great interest to others. The aim of both English and French Canadians should rather be to make Canada as a whole neither English nor French, nor even a peaceful combination of the two, but a truly pluralist and polyethnic state. As Trudeau said:

> The die is cast in Canada: there are two main ethnic and linguistic groups; each is too strong and too deeply rooted in the past, too firmly bound to a mother-culture, to be able to engulf the other. But if the two will collaborate at the hub of a truly pluralistic state, Canada could become the envied seat of a form of federalism that belongs to tomorrow's world. Better than the American melting-pot, Canada could offer an example to all those new Asian and African states ... who must discover how to govern their polyethnic populations with proper regard for justice and liberty. What better reason for cold-shouldering the lure of annexation to the United States? Canadian federalism is an experiment of major proportions; it could become a brilliant prototype for the moulding of tomorrow's civilization.[14]

Indeed, Canada could provide a model not just for backward Asian and African states with their feverish ethnic hatreds but also for sophisticated Europeans dismayed by their atavistic tendency to plunge into murderous violence, and even for the world as a whole, facing the prospect of a nuclear holocaust because of its untamed imperial rivalries. Canadians should think big, Trudeau was suggesting. If English and French could put aside their old suspicions and animosities, overcoming the temptation of trying to regress to a simpler past, they (or their leaders) could make their country the "brilliant prototype" for creating a new and safer global order.

As a critic of nationalism, then, Trudeau gave Canadian multiculturalism a deeper and more persuasive theoretical justification than the one he had outlined in his 1971 statement. He offered Canadians an exciting vision of their future. He advised them to embark on a big political experiment, on the same scale as the American experiment in liberal democracy or the Russian experiment in egalitarian social planning, but one with even greater contemporary relevance. The aim of the experiment would be to test and refine a theory about how to overcome national or ethnic conflict. Canadians were much better suited than were most other countries for such an experiment. Trudeau put multiculturalism on a solid psychological foundation by treating it as a new, distinctively Canadian national identity.

Practical Implementation

If the basic aim of multiculturalism is cultural freedom with a view to the incorporation of diverse nationalities under a common political authority of a classless or democratic character (to demonstrate the possibility of a global order that would not be just the imperial domination of some nations over others), then the most important practical measures to be adopted in pursuit of this goal would seem to be:

1 measures to increase immigration from parts of the world not adequately represented in the base population of the multicultural society;
2 measures to suppress the negative or discriminatory reactions of the dominant or majority group to the increasing presence of Others; and to this end,
3 measures to reduce the political power and discretion of elected representatives, combined with other measures to increase the responsibilities of judges and other independent authorities.

A country does not become a welcoming home for representatives of all the world's peoples simply by proclaiming its intention to have this status. Good intentions must be matched by appropriate actions, that is, by the development of policies and institutions to effect the desired change from the exclusive practices and ethnocentric assumptions of the past to the openness and enlightenment of the future. This is a long and complicated process, which Trudeau began but which he obviously did not complete. Nor did he say much about the necessary measures in his historic statement on multiculturalism.

If the "multiculturalism hypothesis" from that statement were simply true, nothing would need to be done to overcome the prejudices of the dominant group (or groups) in Canada beyond providing them with as much public recognition and approval as the most sensitive among them thought was their due. This would increase their confidence in their own identity, and out of this increased confidence would grow greater respect for the identities of others. Simply by nurturing the pride of the larger groups, one could undermine their tendency to deal unfairly with the smaller ones. There may of course be a grain of truth in this hypothesis, as I suggested above, but neither Trudeau nor anyone else with a serious interest in promoting diversity has ever been willing to rely very heavily on this strategy for fighting prejudice and discrimination. Canadians are often praised for their remarkable tolerance, but they also need to be reminded from time to time of their shameful past and threatened with fines or imprisonment if they do not mend their discriminatory ways.

In his 1971 statement in the House of Commons, Trudeau spoke rather vaguely about "overcoming cultural barriers to full participation in Canadian society." In the accompanying document, he explained more clearly what he had in mind. He acknowledged that some reliance could be placed on anti-discrimination law to overcome discrimination – "the law can and will protect individuals from overt discrimination" – but "there are more subtle barriers to entry into our society" that cannot simply be outlawed. This makes it necessary, he said, for "every Canadian" to take responsibility for helping to eliminate these barriers, that is, their own and their compatriots' tendency to favour their own. "Every Canadian must contribute to the sense of national acceptance and belonging."[15]

Anti-discrimination legislation tries to penalize the most egregious breaches of this norm. Under the *Constitution Act*, 1867, it appears to be a provincial responsibility, under Property and Civil Rights. By 1971, several provinces had adopted more or less stringent human rights codes. The first recommendation of the Royal Commission to which Trudeau was responding was that "any provinces that have not yet enacted fair employment practices, fair accommodation practices, or housing legislation prohibiting discrimination because of race, creed, colour, nationality, ancestry, or place of origin, do so."[16] But the federal government could also legislate in this area, at least with respect to its own agencies, and Trudeau reported that his government "had the whole question of human rights under consideration."[17] This consideration ultimately produced two significant pieces of federal legislation, the *Human Rights Act*, 1977, and the *Employment Equity Act*, 1986. Even though this second *Act* was passed after Trudeau had retired and Brian Mulroney had become prime minister, Trudeau must be given some of the credit for it since it was under his direction that the process of developing an affirmative action strategy for Canada began.[18]

An earlier and in some ways clearer indication of Trudeau's commitment to human rights and the fight against prejudice and discrimination were the reforms of the Criminal Code that he sponsored as minister of justice in 1967 and that became law in 1969, after he had become prime minister. These reforms included the rarely remarked addition of a provision (section 319) outlawing the expression of hatred against identifiable groups. This addition implemented the principal recommendation of an earlier advisory committee of which Trudeau himself had been a member. It had suggested that the Criminal Code be amended to make "every one who by communicating statements, wilfully promotes hatred or contempt against any identifiable group" guilty of an indictable offence and liable to imprisonment for two years. To justify this novel and controversial new legislated limit on freedom of expression, the committee's members had reasoned that there existed "a clear and present danger" that "in times of social stress" individuals and groups promoting hatred "could mushroom into a real and monstrous threat to our way of life." In short, the advisory committee had seen the possibility, in a country like Canada, that sometime in the indefinite future "hate promoters" might have such an effect on "uncritical and receptive minds" that they would require forceful suppression.[19] Very little use has been made of this legislation since 1969, but it has helped to popularize the new concept of a hate crime, and it remains on the books as a reminder of every citizen's obligation to promote a positive sense of national acceptance and belonging.

The application of legislation employing very broad, ill-defined concepts such as "hatred" and "identifiable groups" requires delicate political judgment, not unlike the judgment required when applying legislation against "blasphemy" or "obscenity" or when deciding whether a particular violation of individual rights is reasonable in a free and democratic society. Thus any prosecution under section 319 requires the approval of a provincial attorney general before it can go before a court, and it must, of course, ultimately be decided in a court of law. This reliance on legal as well as political reasoning to settle difficult political questions is in accord with the basic trend of the past generation – the shift in the responsibility for defining the equal rights of all citizens from elected politicians and their officials to lawyers and judges more or less independent of government. This trend began more than forty years ago, with the passage of John Diefenbaker's largely symbolic "Canadian Bill of Rights" legislation in 1960. By far the most important step was taken twenty-one years later, with the acceptance (apart from Quebec) of Trudeau's immensely popular (even in Quebec) *Charter of Rights and Freedoms*. Trudeau's constitutionally entrenched bill of rights gave the judiciary a firm legal basis for resisting any actions by governments that might encroach on the rights of Canadians in an unreasonable way. The power to decide whether any particular encroachment was a reasonable one, consistent with the basic values of a free and democratic society, or an unacceptable one that should be struck down, was taken out of the hands of elected politicians and put in those of highly trained legal experts appointed by the politicians. Not only are these experts much better educated than are most ordinary politicians, but they are also better insulated from popular pressures and presumably more capable of understanding the long-term needs of a society striving to become genuinely multicultural.

Finally, such a society – a future home for all the world's peoples – must evidently have a door through which those peoples can enter. A discriminatory immigration policy, or even one that blocked all immigration, regardless of race or nationality, would clearly contradict whatever formal commitment to multiculturalism such a country professed. In the not-so-distant past, Canada openly tried to prevent the entrance of non-white migrants from Asia, Africa, and the Caribbean. The basic decision to reform this policy was taken in the early 1960s, before Trudeau entered federal politics, but the "points system" for selecting immigrants on a non-discriminatory basis was worked out after 1965, when responsibility for immigration policy was in the hands of Trudeau's friend and political mentor, Jean Marchand. The new immigration policy of which it was a crucial element was finally put into the form of a new immigration law in 1976. During this period, Canadian immigration offices were opened in various Third World countries to facilitate the processing of applications, and the number of immigrants coming from these "non-traditional sources" increased dramatically. Thus, in recent years, as many as 60 percent of Canada's new immigrants have come from Asian countries. (This compares with 58 percent from continental European countries other than France in the period between 1946 and 1959, and another 38 percent from the British Isles and the United States during the same period.)[20] Official multiculturalism obviously depends on this deliberate diversification of the Canadian population for much of its substance. Had the policy been limited by Canada's pre-1971 demography to making minor adjustments in the status relations of European nationalities in Canada – the vision of multiculturalism that some of its most vocal proponents seem to have entertained, forty years ago – then it would obviously have been much less relevant to the problems of the world as a whole than it is today. It is surely because Canadian multiculturalism now promises a way of incorporating the Third World into the First World without domination or oppression that it is attracting the kind of favourable international attention that Trudeau promised.

Conclusions

Before any lessons can be drawn from Canada's management of cultural pluralism, that is, its practice of multiculturalism, the principles inherent in that practice must be clarified. The intention guiding the development of the Canadian model of diversity must be put into words. In short, Canada's official multiculturalism must be theorized, and this may seem to be the exclusive responsibility of the professional theorists who spend their time theorizing things or deconstructing the theorizations of others. The practitioners of other arts, such as politicians, may seem to be too distracted by their practical obligations to think very clearly about what they are doing and to "articulate it theoretically." My contention, however, is that the politician who initiated Canada's official multiculturalism, Pierre Elliott Trudeau, also provided the clearest explanation so far of its fundamental principles. He was the first and remains the most authoritative theorist of Canadian multiculturalism, so if we wish to understand what it is, we should turn our attention to his thought and actions, keeping in mind the difference between a narrower and a broader understanding of multiculturalism.

Narrowly defined, official multiculturalism has to do with the activities of a few dozen civil servants in Ottawa and a few regional centres who spend a budget of $50 to $100 million a year. Multiculturalism in this narrow sense began with a mandate usually described as "cultural preservation"; then in the early 1980s, it became, to the dismay of many of its early enthusiasts, a program that gave priority to fighting racism. More recently, after the Liberals returned to power in 1993, its budget was cut (apparently because of its unpopularity with native-born Canadians) and its mandate changed to emphasize the promotion of good citizenship.[21] Multiculturalism in this narrow sense derives directly from Trudeau's 1971 statement. It was probably never of great interest to him, however, as those have seen who say that he used it for a short while and then forgot about it.

Multiculturalism more broadly understood (understood as I have been suggesting it should be) began before 1971 and underwent no fundamental change when it became "official." It has never had a serious "preservative" purpose, despite what has often been said by people who should have known better; rather, it was designed from the start to promote "integration" (sharply distinguished from "assimilation," despite their similarity) by fighting prejudice and discrimination (or racism), thus making it possible for new and old Canadians to meet and mingle (and intermarry) on a footing of equality. An essential element of this design has been the promotion of the public acceptance of certain markers of distinct identities, such as distinctive cuisine or religious headgear; but there was never any intention of reinforcing the structures of authority, independent of the Canadian state, that might exist within immigrant communities and that might try to impose traditional practices on their members. The distant goal of multiculturalism in this broader sense is the creation of a new relation between ethnic nationalities and our ever-expanding systems of governance, national and international. The ideal citizen, from its perspective, is not the zealous patriot ready to fight and die for his nation but, rather, the rational voter and dutiful taxpayer with a "cooler" relation to the political authorities over him, not completely alienated from them (because they are oppressing his nation) but not too identified with them either (since their nation is not really *his* nation).

Theorists trying to theorize multiculturalism invariably draw back from the cultural bureaucrat's narrow practical understanding of it, but they typically leave out of their accounts two crucial elements that seem to me to be part of the broader picture; namely, immigration policy and, for lack of a better term, foreign policy. They treat multiculturalism as a domestic policy designed to deal directly with the conflicts and tensions of a given population rather than as a long-term policy for transforming that population with a view to overcoming problems in international relations. They deal with it as though the alternative to multiculturalism were best described as liberalism, individualism, or monoculturalism rather than as nationalism or the principle of nationalities. Consequently, their accounts often strike me as rather unrevealing compared to the broader understanding suggested by considering the thought and actions of Trudeau. This is true even of the theory that seems to me to be closest to Trudeau's in its underlying assumptions and basic understanding of multiculturalism; that is, Will Kymlicka's well known theory about multicultural citizenship.[22] It features a distinction between internal restrictions and external protections that clarifies what Trudeau meant when he said that multiculturalism was "basically the conscious support for individual freedom of choice." Liberal multiculturalism requires group rights of a limited kind, as Kymlicka explains, but it does not diverge from the basic principles of the liberalism Trudeau represents. Similarly, Kymlicka makes a basic distinction between national and immigrant minorities that throws some light (perhaps too much light for practical purposes) on what Trudeau meant when he said that the formula for Canada should be "multiculturalism within a bilingual framework": all are equal but not all are the same. Nonetheless, Kymlicka, despite his interest in nationalism and its relation to liberalism, does not address the alternatives to the principle of nationalities as clearly and straightforwardly as did Trudeau.

Charles Taylor's justly famous reflections on "The Politics of Recognition" offer, among other things, a very erudite examination of the intellectual roots and conceptual puzzles of the psychological hypothesis that Trudeau invoked in his 1971 statement.[23] Why do we think that it is important for personal identities to be publicly recognized or affirmed? And how can everyone be affirmed without some being untrue to themselves in the very act of affirming others? Doesn't the so-called "ethic of authenticity" make impossible demands? What about authentic bigots and authentic thugs? These are intriguing puzzles, and they draw one's attention away from immigration policy and foreign policy.

The full reality of Canada's official multicultural identity will be seen, I have been arguing, only when it is seen from the perspective of its founder, as an experiment in creating a nation designed to show the world how to overcome nationalism and war. The confusing difficulty Trudeau faced was the need to foster a certain nationalism in the very act of trying to overcome it. Given the prevailing national organization of political life, any appeal to Canadians to embark on the experiment he favoured had to be cast as an appeal to their national pride and ambition. For a variety of reasons, many Canadians have obviously been receptive to his challenge, but perhaps others elsewhere, pondering the lessons to be learned from the Canadian experience with multiculturalism, should keep Trudeau's appeal to national feeling in mind when trying to decide how applicable the Canadian model may be in other, less favourable, circumstances.

Notes
1 Canada, *House of Commons Debates* (October 8, 1971), VIII, 8545.
2 Ibid., 8580-81.
3 Ibid., 8580.
4 Ibid., 8546.
5 Thomas Jefferson, *Notes on the State of Virginia*, Query XVII, in *Writings*, ed. Merrill D. Peterson (New York: Library of America, 1984), 285.
6 *House of Commons Debates*, 8546.
7 Ibid., 8546.
8 Ibid., 8581.
9 The classic statement of this objection is a speech by a senator of Ukrainian ancestry, Paul Yuzyk, in the Senate of Canada, *House of Commons Debates* (March 3, 1964), 50-58. The

descendants of the Ukrainian and other Eastern European pioneers who settled the Prairie provinces before the First World War tended to think that they, too, like the British and the French, were "founding races" who had brought civilization to an empty or savage land.

10 The White Paper had begun with the following declaration: "To be an Indian is to be a man, with all man's needs and abilities. To be an Indian is also to be different. It is to speak different languages, draw different pictures, tell different tales and to rely on a set of values developed in a different world ... To be an Indian must be to be free – free to develop Indian cultures in an environment of legal, social and economic equality with other Canadians." *Statement of the Government of Canada on Indian Policy, 1969* (Ottawa, 1969), 4.

11 See Alan C. Cairns, *Citizens Plus: Aboriginal Peoples and the Canadian State* (Vancouver: UBC Press, 2000), for a detailed analysis of the background to the White Paper and subsequent developments.

12 Most of these writings have been reprinted in English in Pierre Elliott Trudeau, *Federalism and the French Canadians* (Toronto: Macmillan, 1968).

13 See, in particular, Trudeau's "La Province de Québec au moment de la grève," in *La grève de l'amiante,* ed. Pierre Elliott Trudeau, 1-91 (Montreal: Editions du Jour, 1956); and Pierre Elliott Trudeau, "Nationalist Alienation," in *Canadian Political Thought,* ed. H.D. Forbes, 333-37 (Toronto: Oxford University Press, 1985).

14 Pierre Elliott Trudeau, "New Treason of the Intellectuals," in *Federalism and the French Canadians,* 178-79. "Brilliant prototype" is *outil génial* in the original.

15 *House of Commons Debates* (October 8, 1971), 8581.

16 Royal Commission on Bilingualism and Biculturalism, *Final Report,* Book IV: *The Cultural Contributions of the Other Ethnic Groups* (Ottawa, 1970), 64-65.

17 *House of Commons Debates,* 8584.

18 For an illuminating account of the long and complicated process of policy development that eventually produced the *Employment Equity Act,* see Annis May Timpson, *Driven Apart: Women's Employment Equality and Child Care in Canadian Public Policy* (Vancouver: UBC Press, 2001), chaps. 5-7. Timpson makes clear the crucial roles played by Trudeau's minister of employment and immigration, Lloyd Axworthy, and the person he chose to head the Royal Commission on Equality in Employment, Judge Rosalie Abella. The commission was appointed in June 1983 and submitted its report in October 1984.

19 *Report to the Minister of Justice of the Special Committee on Hate Propaganda in Canada* (Ottawa, 1966), 24-25, 69-70. The committee endorsed the following broad principle: "The Canadian community has a duty, not merely the right, to protect itself from the corrosive effects of propaganda that tends to undermine the confidence that various groups in a multicultural society must have in each other."

20 These figures are drawn from Royal Commission on Bilingualism and Biculturalism, *Final Report,* Book IV, table A1. Of the remaining 4 percent of the total, half came from France.

21 For a brief account of these changes, see Yasmeen Abu-Laban and Christina Gabriel, *Selling Diversity* (Peterborough: Broadview, 2002), chap. 4.

22 Will Kymlicka, *Multicultural Citizenship: A Liberal Theory of Minority Rights* (Oxford: Oxford University Press, 1995); Will Kymlicka, *Liberalism, Community, and Culture* (Oxford: Clarendon Press, 1989).

23 Charles Taylor, "The Politics of Recognition," in *Multiculturalism: Examining the Politics of Recognition,* ed. Amy Gutmann, 25-73 (Princeton: Princeton University Press, 1994).

2
Multicultural Rights, Multicultural Virtues: A History of Multiculturalism in Canada
Michael Temelini

I would like to explore the etymology of multiculturalism in Canada, which is to say the historical context in which the word was accepted into widespread public use. The claim I wish to defend is that multiculturalism cannot be understood primarily as a rule of law. It is not exclusively an aspect of what Pocock calls the "jurisdic," or law-centred paradigm, and what Foucault calls the "juridical edifice" of legal thought and action. It cannot be described solely in terms of what Tully calls the complex of "juridical practices" of governing, being governed and contesting government by rights and duties, sovereignty and constitutionalism.[1] Multiculturalism is not essentially a liberal theory of minority rights.

It would be foolish to deny the importance of multicultural rights. Constitutional guarantees recognizing and protecting ethnic and national identities are remarkable contributions to Canadian civilization. Nevertheless, to define multiculturalism essentially as a right is to privilege an exclusively juridical vocabulary and to screen out other possible meanings. Pocock reminds us, for example, that, in addition to the juridical language of right, there is also a distinct civic humanist language of virtue. While the word 'virtue' has a great variety of meanings, nevertheless, there is a sense in which it is "discontinuous with the language of right" because these two vocabularies of political thought "premise different values, encounter different problems" and "employ different strategies of speech and argument." Pocock concludes that "virtue cannot therefore be reduced to the status of right" or "assimilated to the vocabulary of jurisprudence."[2]

Pocock's distinction helps explain cultural pluralism in Canada, where multiculturalism was originally defined not only in terms of exclusively juridical vocabulary but also with a civic humanist language and practice of virtue. The word 'multiculturalism' did not gain entry into the Canadian public's lexicon as a full-blown rights theory. The idea originated· neither from constitutional negotiations nor from legislation nor from the courts; rather, its definition was a work in progress developed over time in the context of widespread public debate and championed by an organized political movement. The idea of multiculturalism was articulated in the parliamentary debates on the creation of Canada's Royal Commission on Bilingualism and Biculturalism as well as the widespread, popular, and sometimes spontaneous political reaction to the commission's terms of reference, reports, and recommendations. What this movement articulated was two different languages of multiculturalism: rights multiculturalism and a civic multiculturalism of virtue. Because of this political movement, the word itself was accepted into common use and then it was adopted as a federal policy on October 8, 1971.

The virtues this movement promoted cannot be reduced to what Rawls defines as "political virtues" because multiculturalism was seen by many of its advocates as precisely the comprehensive doctrine to which Rawls objects[3] – a civic virtue presupposing a way of life belonging to a comprehensive moral and philosophical conception of the good. Furthermore, this process did not really follow what Rawls calls "the steps to overlapping consensus" nor did the movement advance "a reasonable political conception of justice" shared by all "free and equal" citizens.[4] A better explanation of these historical events is that multiculturalism began as a popular political protest movement of citizens excluded by an emerging public consensus and who rejected the prevailing definitions of democratic freedom and equality. Moreover, contrary to the "stages" view Rawls describes, it was subsequent to the articulation of multiculturalism as a good that it was adopted as an official policy and then entrenched in the *Canadian Charter of Rights and Freedoms*. A proper understanding of this historical context clarifies the difference between juridical multiculturalism and civic multiculturalism, reveals the priority of multicultural virtue, and sheds light on the variety of ways to address the challenges of cultural pluralism in a democratic state.

Multicultural Rights

One of the finest expressions of the juridical language of multiculturalism is Kymlicka's thesis that it is essentially a liberal theory of minority rights. Multiculturalism is subsumed under a vocabulary of "the rights of ethnocultural minorities" (or "minority rights") and a debate about the justice of minority claims.[5] His argument is that one's position on multiculturalism depends on and is derived from three different "stages" of an ongoing philosophical debate about minority rights: between liberals and communitarians, among liberal individualists and liberal culturalists, and about a new way to characterize the liberal democratic state. Kymlicka accepts the terms of the third stage of the debate: multiculturalism must be understood as a response to majority nation building. Virtually all modern liberal democratic states, Kymlicka argues, have engaged in "nation building" – the diffusion of "a

single societal culture throughout all of its territory" and "a process of promoting a common language and a sense of common membership in, and
equal access to, the social institutions based on that language."[6] Such efforts create disadvantages for and injustices to minorities in the sense that
"mainstream institutions are biased in favour of the majority, and the effect
of this bias is to harm important interests related to personal agency and
identity."[7] Kymlicka's solution to the injustices of majority nation building
is to accommodate "enduring cultural differences" by way of a "comprehensive theory of justice in a multicultural state" that includes "both universal rights, assigned to individuals regardless of group membership," and
certain "group-differentiated rights or 'special status' for minority cultures."[8]
This position assumes that minority rights cannot be subsumed under the
category of human rights. Even if the state ensures basic individual rights to
all human beings without reference to membership in ethnocultural groups,
the state is obligated to treat immigrants and national minorities differ-
ently. Different treatment means that certain ethnic groups or national
minorities should be given a permanent political identity or constitutional
status in the form of "self-governing rights" or "polyethnic rights" or "special representation rights." In effect, political accommodation means granting national minorities the same constitutional powers of nation building
as the majority culture. Such accommodation may also entail recognizing
immigrants' demands for "fair terms of integration" in the form of culturally sensitive state policies. These minority rights cannot be seen as unjust
or as unfair special privileges or invidious forms of discrimination but, rather,
as a response to "perceived injustices that arise out of nation-building policies" and as "compensation for unfair disadvantages."[9] Kymlicka's juridical
paradigm is therefore as follows: citizens are essentially and primarily rights-
bearing subjects; the challenge of recognition is understood in terms of
being governed (a relationship between this subject and her government);
multicultural diversity is essentially a conflict between majorities and minorities; accommodation is justified as a duty to compensate and amounts to
legal guarantees that grant special status. And all this is framed in terms of
getting the right "comprehensive theory of justice." In any case, juridical
practices ground multiculturalism.

Several aspects of Kymlicka's account require amendment: first, the concept of multiculturalism emerged as a political protest in Canada at a much
earlier stage than Kymlicka suggests – namely, between 1962 and 1971. Second, there was a series of disputed issues that differed from those described.
In the context of Quebec's Quiet Revolution, and with the rise of French-
Canadian nationalism and secessionism, the word 'multiculturalism' was
mobilized in a contest among anglophones, French Canadians, Québécois,
and the established "other ethnic groups" (Canadian citizens of cultural

origins other than British or French). A multiplicity of issues was disputed: whether French Canadians and Québécois were distinct nations (compact versus unitary theories of Confederation); whether to accommodate Quebec with special linguistic and cultural guarantees or distinct status (symmetrical versus asymmetrical federalism); and whether the other ethnic groups deserved comparable guarantees (assimilation versus multiculturalism). Third, the concept of multiculturalism had a practical purpose during the Quiet Revolution in that it challenged the emerging consensus among Canadians of French and British origins regarding an essential biculturalism. In this sense, multiculturalism was a political strategy not of new immigrants but of the established ethnic groups who shared francophones' fears of loss of identity and their aspirations for cultural survival.[10] Troper warns that it is "unfair and incorrect to dismiss multiculturalism as simply an ethnic spin-off of French Canadian national resurgence." While the influence of the Quiet Revolution cannot be denied, the roots of multiculturalism "weave back through a tangle of historical forces," including the global movements of ethnic self-awareness as well as the decline of Britain's power and prestige and its anglophone-conformist model of assimilation.[11] We must also take into account the search for an authentic Canadian identity amidst the growing political and economic influence of the United States.

By neglecting this context in which the concept first entered into common usage, the important non-juridical aspects of multiculturalism go unnoticed. Over time, multiculturalism did resemble features of Kymlicka's interpretation, which sheds light on critically important aspects of multiculturalism that emerged after the 1971 announcement. But multiculturalism did not originate as, and was not exclusively justified with reference to, a theory of minority rights. It was also promoted as a qualitatively superior alternative to various contested images and forms of Canadian life. Kymlicka's interpretation must therefore be accompanied by the distinctly non-juridical vocabularies and practices and non-constitutional dialogues that were employed to promote multiculturalism. This ideal of multiculturalism and the language of multicultural virtue first appeared in the debates of Canada's 25th and 26th Parliaments.

The Parliamentary Debates: "We Shall Then Become Better Citizens"
In response to André Laurendeau's editorials in *Le Devoir*, various members of Parliament in the Canadian House of Commons launched a campaign between fall 1962 and spring 1963 for a royal commission on bilingualism.[12] Prime Minister J.G. Diefenbaker refused. One aspect of the campaign was, in the words of Gilles Gregoire, "respecting the rights of one another." But Gregoire and a number of other members of Parliament also stressed the importance of "a full understanding" and "a perfect understanding"

between the English-speaking and French-speaking Canadians.[13] One notable intervention was that of the leader of the Opposition, Lester B. Pearson, on December 17, 1962. Pearson expressed concern about the "serious crisis of national unity," and he defended an interpretation of Canadian Confederation as "the rejection not only of political and economic annexation of the United States, but also of the American melting pot concept of national unity." Instead, Pearson saw Canada as "an understanding or a settlement" made on the basis of "an acceptable and equal partnership" in which "national political unity would be achieved and maintained without the imposition of racial, cultural or linguistic uniformity."[14]

Throughout his speech, Pearson completely rejected uniformity and embraced a distinctly non-juridical vocabulary of cultural pluralism. He described the national unity crisis as a "misunderstanding" and as "difficulties in relations" based on "different interpretations" over "the meaning of confederation."[15] To solve this crisis of meaning and understanding Pearson did not appeal to a language of rights, and he did not propose formal intergovernmental constitutional negotiations; instead, he called for open public dialogue.[16] A number of members of Parliament reiterated Pearson's plea. Lionel Chevrier, for example, recommended "self-examination" and a "spiritual retreat."[17] He remarked: "we must learn, on both sides, not only to remain ourselves and better to live our own culture, but also to become a little like the other, and to participate more actively in the culture of the other." His idea was that "we shall then become better citizens, and we shall form a richer and more united nation."[18] Perhaps Stanley Knowles stated most clearly and succinctly the new way of life his colleagues were trying to articulate when he declared that the effort to establish "mutual respect and equality" was "not only a matter of according rights and adjusting certain grievances that have grown up, but that it [could] add to the richness of life in this country if we [could] further the binational, bicultural and biethnical heritage which [was] already ours."[19]

These speeches imply at least three related areas of disagreement. One topic of dispute concerned the vocabulary with which to properly characterize the political situation. Another quarrel was about the means by which to resolve the situation since conventional constitutional approaches were called into question. And this was also a fundamental disagreement about Canada's national identity. Prime Minister Diefenbaker's position is illustrative. He disagreed that this was a crisis of understanding. Consequently, in response to Opposition calls for a royal commission, he stalled, redefined the problem along customary terms, and proposed the conventional Canadian practice of ethnic conflict resolution: intergovernmental constitutional negotiations.[20] The Opposition did not renounce this conventional practice of negotiation and justified the royal commission as a complementary approach.[21] But intergovernmental negotiations were rejected as a sufficient strategy on the grounds that such negotiations could not exclusively reconcile the misunderstanding.

The debates of the 25th Parliament of Canada ended with the defeat of the Diefenbaker government on February 5, 1963, on a general non-confidence motion and with its replacement by the Pearson government following the April 8, 1963, election. In the May 16, 1963, Speech from the Throne, the new government announced to the 26th Parliament of Canada a commission "to study ... how the fundamentally bicultural character of Canada may best be ensured and the contribution of other cultures recognized."[22] When Laurendeau and Davidson Dunton accepted Pearson's invitation to be co-chairmen, the Royal Commission on Bilingualism and Biculturalism was created by an Order-in-Council of July 19, 1963.[23] Following the announcement of its terms of reference and personnel on July 22, 1963, widespread support was declared on the grounds that it could lead to "greater understanding, co-operation and spirit of unity."[24]

It is important to note that the word 'multiculturalism' was not used in these House of Commons debates. Furthermore, these speeches reveal that some defenders of cultural pluralism were promoting a strictly dualistic sense of this ideal. This, and Pearson's reference to "other cultures," has led some commentators to characterize multiculturalism as simply an "afterthought."[25] It is true that, in the struggle for recognition, many expected the commission to restrict its focus to the specific contest between Canadians of French and British origins. The co-chairmen themselves endorsed this limited focus, defending literally the commission's terms of reference and expressly rejecting the word 'multiculturalism.' For example, in an interview broadcast on CBC television in August 20, 1963, journalist Norman DePoe asked the newly appointed co-chairmen about the other ethnic groups in Canada: "Well is this then a commission on biculturalism or is it a commission on multiculturalism?" While expressing his desire to hear from other ethnic groups, Dunton reiterated the terms of reference and reaffirmed the dualist mandate of the commission. DePoe replied: "So it's a bicultural commission with some multicultural aspects." Laurendeau rejected the suggestion. "It's a bicultural commission because the country as a whole is bicultural but at the same time takes into account the fact that many groups are here which bring with them their own culture which is something ... we must not put aside."[26]

Despite the insistence on dualism, some members of the other ethnic groups immediately and vehemently refused to accept such narrow terms of debate.[27] They were joined by some members of the commission and members of the Parliament of Canada who promoted instead a multiple concept of pluralism. For example, in debating the Speech from the Throne,

Sylvester Perry Ryan suggested that, without "the recognition of the stimulating contribution of other cultures, this nation cannot flourish as it should." Furthermore, Ron Basford urged his colleagues "not to forget in our consideration of biculturalism" the thousands of people "who have come to Canada to build new homes and new lives."[28] The most politically significant challenge to dualism was delivered by Canadians of Ukrainian ancestry and their most prominent spokesperson Senator Paul Yuzyk.[29] The senator was the first to employ the word 'multiculturalism' in parliamentary debate and was among the first to acknowledge publicly the changes that were already occurring in Canada. Yuzyk was appointed to the Senate on February 4, 1963, on the eve of Diefenbaker's defeat. In his maiden speech on March 3, 1964, Yuzyk mobilized the 1961 census data to deliver a magnificent survey of population statistics and trends, a history of immigration, and the cultural contribution of the British, the French, and "all other ethnic groups," particularly Ukrainians. Yuzyk attacked as a "misnomer" the very idea of biculturalism. "In reality Canada never was bicultural ... Canada has become multicultural," a principle which meant "continuing diversity" and "unity in diversity" and "unity with variety."[30] Yuzyk then defended "the Canadian system of multiculturalism," which marked perhaps the first occasion in which this word was used in the Parliament of Canada. Yuzyk borrowed the word from a 1963 speech delivered by University of Alberta sociology professor Charles Hobart. Quoting Hobart, Yuzyk remarked that Canada's "system of multiculturalism" was an aspect of the Canadian identity that had "obvious advantages over the American melting-pot concept which produces a mixture in which there is loss of identity and peculiar genius."[31] Yuzyk invoked two languages of multiculturalism in his speech. He described it as a "rule of governance" that entailed "full equality of rights for all Canadian citizens wherever they were born." He also described it as a practice of "good Canadian citizenship" that would make "good Canadians" and a form of life that "enriched" Canada.[32]

Multicultural Virtues

This survey of the debates of the 25th and 26th Parliaments of Canada reveals a contest between two strategies to address the nationalist and secessionist challenges of cultural pluralism. Those who saw this as an exclusively intergovernmental crisis promoted solutions in conventional methods of constitutional negotiation such as cooperative federalism and elite accommodation. Those who saw it as a crisis of understanding launched a political movement challenging conventional notions of citizenship and democratic pluralism, and they promoted the unconventional idea that a solution had to be found in a conversation of ordinary citizens. The latter prevailed, and their approach can be explained by Aristotle's injunction in

Politics that anyone who is going to make a proper inquiry about the best form of constitution must first decide what is the most desirable way of life.[33] Aristotle's view is shared by contemporary thinkers in the civic humanist tradition, such as Charles Taylor, who makes an analogous claim regarding the politics of identity recognition. Taylor argues that the accommodation of cultural differences requires more than the acceptance of some principle of procedural justice or the uniform application of a rule without exception; rather, "there must be some substantive agreement on value" or else the formal principle "will be empty and a sham."[34] Taylor's historical approach is insightful because it entails giving an account of the new multicultural identity which makes clear what its appeal was, what gave it its moral authority, why people found (and find) it convincing, and what visions of good inspired and moved people to demand it.[35]

In the various debates surveyed here, the vocabulary employed is noteworthy. To speak of "better" and "richer" citizenship participation, of the necessary conditions in which a polity can "flourish," and in seeking "understanding" and "the richness of life," Canadian parliamentarians were articulating visions of what Taylor calls "a strongly valued good," which is "some action, or motive, or style of life, which is seen as qualitatively superior." A 'good' is anything considered valuable, worthy, or admirable and whatever is marked out as "incomparably higher in a qualitative distinction."[36] For Taylor, the good is always primary to the right not "in that it offers a more basic reason ... but in that the good is what, in its articulation, gives the point of the rules which define the right."[37] In Canada, multicultural rights actually followed the articulation of multiculturalism as a good, and this articulation did give, as Taylor suggests, the point of the rules that defined minority rights. In the course of debate, the majority of elected and appointed members of Canada's 25th and 26th Parliaments recognized that the challenges of cultural pluralism could not be solved first and foremost or exclusively by constitutional guarantees, human rights legislation, or federalism. Instead of looking for some uniform principle of justice, they launched an open public dialogue, the goal of which was "to learn from one another." It was in the context of this public dialogue that the word 'multiculturalism' was introduced and then adopted into widespread public use. It was described as a valuable and indispensable way of life that would contribute to the flourishing and enrichment of the polity. They defended dialogical cultural recognition on the grounds that it would strengthen the bonds of civic solidarity, build allegiance to Canada, and bolster citizenship. In this respect, there is nothing "new" about what Kymlicka calls the "second front in the multiculturalism wars." Even at its genesis, the multicultural ideal was seen as a civic virtue that would ensure rather than erode, undermine, or destabilize "long-term political unity and social stability."[38]

Aristotle is routinely cited and widely recognized as an authoritative philosophical source of the language of virtue. In his celebrated *Nichomachean Ethics*, he defines virtue as excellence of character constituted by customary social practice and signifying a devotion to the public good.[39] The good is that which "makes life desirable and in no way deficient," and because we are social animals a good life necessarily includes family and friends.[40] Friendship, Aristotle writes, "is a kind of virtue, or implies virtue" and constitutes a civic bond having "more importance to it than to justice."[41] In his *Politics*, Aristotle explains that, because we are political animals, a good life cannot exist without active participation in a political community in which we take turns at public service, "deliberating" and "judging" with fellow citizens.[42] These customary, social, and political aspects of a virtuous good life are critically important. A virtuous life cannot come from a rule or theory but,[43] rather, is inculcated through training and good habits that begin at an early age, through living under the guidance of right laws, and through ongoing civic participation. Therefore, an intellectually and morally virtuous life is achieved with time and life experience,[44] and in dialogue with others. The goal of politics, he explains, is "not to know what goodness is, but how to become good," otherwise this knowledge "would be useless." Therefore, "we must apply our minds to the problem of how our actions should be performed."[45]

It is necessary to recognize these civic humanist principles, and the Aristotelian variety in particular, because they resonated in the first debates on multiculturalism and might, in fact, be considered as organizing principles of the Royal Commission itself. At the Preliminary Hearing, November 7 and 8, 1963, André Laurendeau invoked Aristotle in describing the commission's purpose:

The equal partnership, l'égalité culturelle: this is not a notion that compels recognition by itself, even in deference to the most profound studies. For such an idea to flourish it must have the voluntary support of the people in a free society. And that is why the discussions between the Commission and the public will have to be continuous, intimate and free ... Aristotle wrote that friendship is the soul of the city. Today social sciences affirm that a nation exists where you find a collective "wish to live" among its members. Basically the two ideas are the same, and give our task some singularly profound perspectives.[46]

Laurendeau went on to define the Royal Commission as a "dialogue."[47] The commission's dialogical approach and Laurendeau's explicit reference to Aristotle conspicuously illustrate my point. For Laurendeau, the commission's purpose was not theoretical knowledge, and he mentions neither rights nor compensation; rather, its purpose was to promote a new practice of citizenship. Its goal was to persuade Canadians to follow Aristotle's advice to live in friendship.

The commission's other purpose was to convince Canadians to talk. In fact, in addition to the typical practice of receiving expert research, one of the commission's most remarkable innovations was the extent to which it sought to "encourage discussion" and "active participation by as many citizens as possible" by means of an unprecedented number of public hearings such as regional meetings.[48] From March 18 to June 16, 1964, twenty-three meetings were held across Canada, with over 11,800 participants.[49] Addressing the Empire Club of Canada on April 9, 1964, Laurendeau and Dunton outlined the significance of the regional meetings, which Dunton described as an attempt to try something "quite new for Federal Royal Commissions." The aim of the meetings was to attract "a considerable number of people from many different occupations and backgrounds." The participants were asked to "discuss the problems as they see them – and we listen." Dunton described these discussions as "highly successful," offering the commission "frank spontaneous views from ordinary Canadians" and "vivid, contrasting impressions."[50] Spontaneous and contrasting indeed. A May 6, 1964, report of CBC television described the participation as "surprising." Audiences ranged in size from one hundred to seven hundred people, and "a measure of the interest shown," according to the report, was "the fact that a Vancouver crowd demanded more time for discussion when the Commission tried to adjourn its evening meeting."[51]

Throughout the commission's "continuous, intimate and free" discussions, the participants defended at least four competing images of the Canadian identity: dualistic, unitary ("melting pot"), Aboriginal, and multicultural. These disputed images were rooted in "widely differing conceptions of the Canadian state and society" as well as contested interpretations of history.[52] Many francophones, for example, endorsed the duality expressed in the commission's terms of reference on the basis of a conception of Canada as a compact of two founding nations. Other participants defended this image as a bulwark against "union [with] or dependence" on the United States.[53] Alternatively, many rejected the compact theory of Confederation. They fell into three categories. Some defended assimilation and the unitary conception of statehood – "the necessity of unity of language and culture within one country." In this category, the commission noticed a "coincidence of opposites": anglophone conformists promoting the example of cultural uniformity of the United States, and francophones promoting either "a new and distinct political status for Quebec" or "the idea of a fully independent Quebec."[54] Other participants who rejected duality were Aboriginal peoples and their supporters, who protested their lack of representation on the commission and who demanded recognition. The commission refused to study the question of Canada's Aboriginal population "since the terms of reference contain[ed] no mention of Indians and Eskimos."[55]

The most influential opponents of duality were members of "the other ethnic groups," who categorically rejected the terms of reference. The commission reported that dualism "aroused fears" among these groups that, "in the developing dialogue" and "power-play" between Canadians of French and of British origin, they would be forgotten or considered "second-class citizens." They were concerned that "their place in Canadian society might be endangered."[56] These groups, therefore, lodged "the strongest possible protest," promoting instead "a multiplicity of cultures" and "unity in diversity: the harmonious co-operation of all ethnic groups in the Canadian country as a whole."[57] In their Preliminary Report, completed on February 1, 1965, the commissioners documented this protest as follows:

37. What image of Canada would do justice to the presence of these varied ethnic groups? This question preoccupied western participants especially, and the answer they often gave was "multiculturalism," or, more elaborately, "the Canadian mosaic." They asked: if two cultures are accepted, why not many? Why should Canada not be a country in which a multitude of cultural groups live side by side and yet distinct from one another, all contributing to a richly varied society? Certainly, it was stated, the mosaic idea was infinitely preferable to the "melting pot."[58]

The Royal Commission on Bilingualism and Biculturalism did not announce a theory of multiculturalism. While multiculturalism was generally understood to be synonymous with cultural retention and antithetical to assimilation, there was no consensus on whether it was primarily an individual right or a group-based claim. For some, multiculturalism complemented bilingualism. For others, it entailed multilingualism: constitutional guarantees for languages other than English and French. Senator Yuzyk and Commissioner J.B. Rudnyckyj were among those who supported this view. In his March 3 speech, Yuzyk defended constitutional guarantees for French and English as well as for other "mother tongues."[59] Rudnyckyj agreed, arguing for linguistic accommodation "in regions where there is a concentration of speakers of a particular mother tongue." Consequently, Rudnyckyj recommended amending section 133 of the *British North America Act* to recognize English and French as the two official languages and to guarantee "regional languages," which would be "any language other than English and French used by 10 per cent or more of the population."[60] The majority of commissioners rejected Rudnyckyj's proposals and steadfastly defended "the basically bicultural character" of Canada in Volume I of the Final Report, completed on October 8, 1967. Biculturalism was recognized on the premise that "the two dominant cultures in Canada are embodied in distinct societies." This recognized "a distinct French-speaking society in Quebec" and also "elements of an autonomous society" elsewhere, such as New Brunswick.[61]

Despite widespread objections to the conclusions of Volume I on the part of the spokespeople of other ethnic groups, the growing political movement for multiculturalism did not sway the commission.[62] In Volume 4 of the Final Report, completed October 23, 1969, the commissioners disagreed with the objections to dualism and simply reiterated their defence of biculturalism as originally stated in Volume I, expressly rejecting the claim that Canada was "officially bilingual but fundamentally multi-cultural."[63] Moreover, they declared that other ethnic groups did not exist "in any political sense" and that they were "more or less integrated with the Francophone and Anglophone communities." They argued, therefore, that it was "within one of these two communities" that their cultural distinctiveness "should find a climate of respect and encouragement to survive."[64] While avoiding any endorsement of multiculturalism, Volume 4 was groundbreaking in supporting its underlying ideal:

> [I]n adopting fully the Canadian way of life ... those whose origin is neither French nor British do not have to cast off or hide their own culture. It may happen that in their determination to express their desire to live fully in this mode, their culture may conflict with the customs of their adopted society. But Canadian society, open and modern, should be able to integrate heterogeneous elements into a harmonious system, to achieve "unity in diversity."[65]

The commission declared that the "presence in Canada of many people whose language and culture are distinctive by reason of their birth or ancestry represents an inestimable enrichment that Canadians can not afford to lose." And then it endorsed the "basic human right" of other cultural groups "to safeguard their languages and cultures."[66]

On October 8, 1971, Prime Minister Pierre Trudeau announced in the House of Commons that his government "accepted those recommendations of the Royal Commission on Bilingualism and Biculturalism which are contained in Volume 4 of its reports." The policy of "multiculturalism within a bilingual framework" was premised on the fact that, "although there are two official languages, there is no official culture, nor does any ethnic group take precedence over any other."[67] There are two notable aspects of Trudeau's announcement. First, "preserving human rights" was only one and not the principal justification for the policy. Trudeau placed greater emphasis on reinforcing Canadian unity, assuring cultural freedom and traditions, "developing the Canadian identity" as well as "strengthening citizenship participation" and "encouraging cultural diversification within a bilingual framework."[68] To promote these objectives the government did not introduce human rights legislation but did announce six new programs.[69] The second notable aspect of Trudeau's 1971 announcement is that not one of the sixteen recommendations of Volume 4 mentions the word 'multiculturalism.'[70] As for multilingualism, the commission did recommend that the teaching of languages other than English and French be incorporated "as options" but only "where there is sufficient demand." However, Commissioner Rudnyckyj's proposal was denied.[71] So Trudeau's government, while accepting the recommendations for bilingualism, in fact rejected the commission's claims in Volumes I and 4 that Canada was "basically bicultural."

If "multiculturalism within a bilingual framework" was not one of the sixteen recommendations, why, then, was it adopted? One answer to this question is that the commission was simply wrong in reporting that other ethnic groups did not exist "in any political sense." The policy was adopted because of successful public pressure, particularly from organized ethnic groups in western Canada. The political success of this movement is also partly due to the fact that it attracted the support of prominent federal parliamentarians, like Senator Yuzyk, and the governments of several provinces.[72] This movement's political success is also attributable to the fact that its goals complemented those of Pierre Trudeau, who became its most famous champion. Trudeau mobilized an individualist interpretation of multiculturalism in his political campaign against both Quebec nationalism and asymmetrical federalism,[73] and, in particular, against the Royal Commission's recognition of Quebec as a distinct society as well as the two-nations theory of Confederation sanctioned by the various reports. Trudeau also shrewdly embraced multiculturalism to appease western Canadians in their lingering resentment over the *Official Languages Act* and their perception of special treatment for Quebec.[74]

Conclusion: Cultivating Multicultural Virtues

This survey suggests that the juridical paradigm, while an important aspect of multiculturalism, does not exclusively capture its meaning. A careful examination of the historical context in which the word was first employed sheds light on the civic humanist sense in which the concept was originally used. This approach opens our eyes to the ways in which multiculturalism became what Tully calls a "constitutive good" and a "civic attitude."[75] This nonjuridical perspective was articulated by the Canadian parliamentary debates that established the Royal Commission on Bilingualism and Biculturalism as well the political movement for multiculturalism that emerged in response

to the commission's mandate, reports, and recommendations. This historical survey clarifies the difference between these two languages of multiculturalism. What is revealed here is that multiculturalism is neither simply a
rule of law nor derivative of the language of rights liberalism; thus, the
concept cannot be properly understood if it is reduced to this idiom. In this
sense, whether the other culture is in the minority or majority is irrelevant
because multiculturalism is not exclusively a procedure for according group
differentiated minority rights. It is also a virtue in the sense of being an
ongoing practice of understanding that is acquired in dialogue and that
shapes our character and makes us become better citizens.

Canada's journey to multiculturalism originated in the context of a national unity crisis rooted in our linguistic and cultural duality and its contested definitions of citizenship. The Royal Commission on Bilingualism
and Biculturalism was supposed to reconcile the dispute; instead, the contest was rendered more complicated when participants refused to accept
the terms of the debate and proposed a new competing definition. What's
significant is that this new self-understanding was constituted in dialogue
rather than in a theory. Moreover, it was promoted as a strongly valued
good: a desirable and qualitatively superior form of civic life. It was justified
primarily as a necessary democratic practice and a comprehensive moral
commitment that adds to the richness of the polity. In adopting the 1971
multiculturalism policy, the federal government implicitly recognized that
it could not remain neutral concerning the virtue of multiculturalism. The
aim of the new policy was to promote a new way of life presupposing this
comprehensive conception of the good. It was in 1982, eighteen years after
Yuzyk's speech, and eleven years after the adoption of the policy, that multiculturalism was entrenched in the *Canadian Charter of Rights and Freedoms*.
To paraphrase Taylor, articulating the good of multiculturalism was primary
to entrenching multicultural rights because this articulation expressed the
purpose of the rules that define these rights.

One of the implications of this civic humanism is that it offers important
lessons on how to promote enduring political unity and social stability in a
culturally plural state. One lesson is that education itself is of primary significance in a multicultural society. The connection here is obvious,[76] especially considering the fact that many of the commission's recommendations
addressed educational reform. Civic humanists promote education not only
as the essence of virtue (the attainment of the highest human excellence)
but also as the foundation of civic life and the common good.[77] This civic
humanist philosophy of education is significant because it suggests that
cultural recognition is "not only a matter of according rights and adjusting
certain grievances" (as Stanley Knowles said) but also an attitude that needs
to be cultivated and a practice that trains us to value what is both similar
and different in others. This civic humanist meaning of multiculturalism

must therefore be taken seriously, particularly if the aim is to promote unity and cross-cultural understanding. To see that multiculturalism is about virtues as well as rights means that, in a culturally plural state, long-term political unity and social stability must be based on something more than a constitution that guarantees the equal rights of all its citizens. It must also be based on an ongoing multicultural dialogue and what Aristotle called "a right training for goodness from an early age."[78]

Acknowledgments
This chapter is based on a paper delivered at the University of Edinburgh School of Law and Centre for Canadian Studies conference entitled "Constitutionalism and Cultural Pluralism: Lessons from Canada," April 28-29, 2004. Earlier versions of this chapter were presented at the Università degli studi di Genova, Fourth Annual Seminar in Atlantic History, 14-15 April, 2003, and the Association for Canadian Studies, annual conference, May 24-25, 2003. I would like to thank all the participants for their helpful discussions of these issues.

Notes
1 J.G.A. Pocock, *Virtue, Commerce and History: Essays on the Political Thought and History Chiefly in the Eighteenth Century* (Cambridge: Cambridge University Press, 1985); James Tully, *An Approach to Political Philosophy: Locke in Contexts* (Cambridge: Cambridge University Press, 1993); Michel Foucault, "Two Lectures," in *Power/Knowledge: Selected Interviews and Other Writings, 1972-1977*, ed. Colin Gordon, 92-108 (New York: Pantheon Books, 1980).
2 Pocock, *Virtue, Commerce and History*, 41-43.
3 John Rawls, *Political Liberalism* (New York: Columbia University Press, 1996), 173-211.
4 Rawls presents a "two stages" argument to explain how principles of justice are accepted in an overlapping consensus: the first stage begins as a modus vivendi and ends with a constitutional consensus. In the second stage, the constitutional consensus gives rise to a political (overlapping) consensus. See Rawls, *Political Liberalism*, 133-72.
5 See p. 169, and note 1, p. 172, Will Kymlicka "The New Debate over Minority Rights," in *Canadian Political Philosophy: Contemporary Reflections*, ed. Ronald Beiner and Wayne Norman, 159-76 (Don Mills: Oxford University Press, 2001).
6 Kymlicka, "New Debate," 164-65.
7 Will Kymlicka, *Contemporary Political Philosophy: An Introduction*, 2nd ed. (Oxford: Oxford University Press, 2002), 367.
8 Will Kymlicka, *Multicultural Citizenship: A Liberal Theory of Minority Rights* (Oxford: Clarendon Press, 1995), 4-33.
9 Kymlicka "New Debate," 167-69; Kymlicka, *Political Philosophy*, 365-66.
10 Harold Troper, "An Uncertain Past: Reflections on the History of Multiculturalism," *TESL Talk* 10, 3 (1979): 13. Jean Burnet has pointed out that the strongest advocates for multiculturalism were not immigrants but, in fact, the predominantly Canadian-born ethnic groups who had received few immigrants for many years. Jean Burnet, "Multiculturalism, Immigration, and Racism: A Comment on the Canadian Immigration and Population Study," *Canadian Ethnic Studies/Etudes ethniques du Canada* 7, 1 (1975): 35-39.
11 Troper, "An Uncertain Past," 7-13; Jean Burnet, "Ethnicity: Canadian Experience and Policy," *Sociological Focus* 9, 2 (1976): 200-1.
12 Laurendeau authored several editorials calling for an inquiry to address the concerns about the status of the French language in Canada. The first, entitled "Pour un equête sur le bilinguisme," was published by *Le Devoir* on Saturday, 20 January, 1962. Following the infamous "Donald Gordon Affair" and in response to a defence of Gordon by the *Globe and Mail*, Laurendeau authored an editorial entitled "Un caste?" published on Saturday, December 15, 1962, calling yet again for a royal commission. The idea gained momentum as other newspaper editors and increasing numbers of parliamentarians endorsed the inquiry.

13   Canada, *House of Commons Debates Official Report*, 1st Session, 25th Parliament (vol. 3, 1962, comprising the period from December 3, 1962 to February 5, 1963, Ottawa, 1963), December 17, 1962, 2721.

14   Ibid., 2723.

15   Ibid.

16   Pearson called for "a deep, responsible and understanding examination of basic situations" by means of a "review" of the "bicultural and bilingual situation in our country" in which there could be "every opportunity and every encouragement for Canadians, individually or in their associations, and organizations, to express their ideas on this situation" (ibid., 2725).

17   Ibid., 2749.

18   Ibid., 2750.

19   Ibid., 2738.

20   For example, ibid., January 21, 1963, 2929. Responding to T.C. Douglas, Diefenbaker remarked: "I at no time said that I would make a statement on a royal commission on biculturalism. I said I would make a statement on the problem as we saw it and the need for convening a federal-provincial conference" (ibid., January 30, 1963, 3265).

21   Pearson agreed that the provincial governments would have to be consulted and "associated" in some way with the wider inquiry (ibid., 2725).

22   The government declared that "the character and strength of our nation are drawn from the diverse cultures of people who came from many lands," and "the greater Canada that is in our power to make will be built not on uniformity but on continuing diversity, and particularly on the basic partnership of English speaking and French speaking people." Canada, *House of Commons Debates Official Report*, 1st Session, 26th Parliament (vol. I, 1963, comprising the period from May 16, 1963, to June 12, 1963), May 16, 1963, 6.

23   The first meeting was not held until September 4, 1963. The eighty-third and final meeting was held eight years later on February 27, 1971.

24   Still, members of the Progressive Conservative party, the official Opposition, expressed doubts concerning the commission's utility, and Diefenbaker continued to insist that no "effective action" could be taken "until there has been agreement between the dominion government and the provincial governments on the question of the amendment of the constitution." Canada, *House of Commons Debates Official Report*, 1st Session, 26th Parliament, vol. III, 1963 (comprising the period from July 10, 1963, to August 2, 1963), July 22, 1963, 2440-42.

25   J.L. Granatstein, *Canada, 1957-1967: The Years of Uncertainty and Innovation* (Toronto: McClelland and Stewart, 1986), 248.

26   Canadian Broadcasting Corporation, "Laurendeau and Dunton" *CBC Archives: The Road to Bilingualism*, http://archives.cbc.ca (viewed March 31, 2005).

27   Burnet, "Ethnicity," 202.

28   Canada, *House of Commons Debates Official Report*, 1st Session, 26th Parliament (vol. I, 1963, comprising the period from May 16, 1963, to June 12, 1963), May 23, 1963, 180, and May 24, 1963, 271.

29   For example, see Manoly R. Lupul, *The Politics of Multiculturalism: A Ukrainian-Canadian Memoir* (Toronto/Edmonton: Canadian Institute of Ukrainian Studies Press, 2005).

30   Canada, *Debates of the Senate Official Report, 1964-1965*, 2nd Session, 26th Parliament (February 18, 1964 to April 3, 1965) (Ottawa: Queen's Printer, 1965), 54-55.

31   Ibid., 55.

32   Ibid., 54, 57.

33   Aristotle, *Politics,* trans. T. A. Sinclair (London: Penguin Books, 1988), VII.i.1323a14.

34   Charles Taylor, *The Malaise of Modernity* (Concord, ON: House of Anansi Press, 1991), 51-52; Charles Taylor, "The Politics of Recognition," in *Multiculturalism: Examining the Politics of Recognition*, ed. Amy Gutmann, 25-73 (Princeton, NJ: Princeton University Press, 1994).

35   Charles Taylor, *Sources of the Self: The Making of the Modern Identity* (Cambridge, MA: Harvard University Press, 1989), 203.

36   Taylor, *Sources of the Self,* 89, 92.

37   Ibid., 89.

38 Kymlicka, *Political Philosophy*, 365-68; Kymlicka, "New Debate" 170-71.

39 Pocock, *Virtue, Commerce and History*, 41-42.

40 Aristotle, *Nicomachean Ethics*, trans. J.A.K. Thomson (London: Penguin Books, 1988), I.vii. Aristotle devotes Books VIII and IX of *Nicomachean Ethics* to the kinds and the grounds of friendship.

41 Furthermore, "Between friends, there is no need for justice, but people who are just still need the quality of friendship." Ibid.,VIII.i.

42 Aristotle, *Politics* I.ii.1253aI-a18; III.i-iv; III.vi.1278b15.

43 Aristotle, *Nicomachean Ethics* II.ii. Consequently, he says that "it is not enough to know about goodness; we must endeavour to possess it and use it, or adopt any other means to become good ourselves" (ibid., X.ix).

44 Ibid., I.ix-x.

45 Ibid., II.ii.

46 "Opening Remarks of Mr. André Laurendeau Co-Chairman of the Royal Commission on Bilingualism and Biculturalism, Preliminary Hearing – November 7 and 8, 1963," in Royal Commission on Bilingualism and Biculturalism, *A Preliminary Report of the Royal Commission on Bilingualism and Biculturalism*, (Ottawa: Crown Copyrights, February 1, 1965), 178.

47 Ibid., 178. The commission also described the hearings as "a great dialogue" (ibid., s. 12, p. 26).

48 A preliminary hearing held in Ottawa consisted of five meetings on November 7 and 8, 1963, when the commission heard "the opinions of 76 associations and individuals from seven provinces" representing "a wide range of institutions and groups, provincial governments, ethnic groups, the mass media, the Civil Service, universities, management and labour unions, political parties, artists, patriotic groups, etc." The commission finished its preliminary work in January 1964 and began the next phase of its work. The premiers of the ten provinces were consulted, in addition to provincial cabinet ministers and provincial representatives of business, education, journalism, and urban and rural organizations. "Thus they came into contact with over 500 outstanding Canadians from many backgrounds, cultures, beliefs and occupations. This was followed by regional meetings" (ibid., s. 4, p. 23; ss. 9-15, pp. 24-27).

49 Ibid., s. 29, pp. 158-59.

50 André Laurendeau and Davidson Dunton, "The Work of the Royal Commission on Bilingualism and Biculturalism," in *The Empire Club of Canada Addresses, 1963-1964*, ed. C.C. Goldring, 328-38 (Toronto: T.H. Best Printing, 1964).

51 Canadian Broadcasting Corporation, "A Thousand and One Opinions," *CBC Archives: The Road to Bilingualism*, http://archives.cbc.ca (viewed March 31, 2005).

52 *Preliminary Report*, s. 29, p. 45.

53 Ibid., ss. 30-33, pp. 45-48; ss. 43-44, pp. 56-57.

54 Ibid., s. 34, pp. 48-49; ss. 43-47, pp. 56-59.

55 Ibid., s. 35, pp. 49-50. See s. 4, note 1, in Royal Commission on Bilingualism and Biculturalism, *Report of the Royal Commission on Bilingualism and Biculturalism*, Book IV, *The Cultural Contribution of the Other Ethnic Groups* (Ottawa: Queen's Printer, 1970), 4. This publication is also entitled "Volume 4" and is sometimes cited as "Book 4."

56 *Preliminary Report*, s. 36, p. 50; s. 37, p. 51; s. 48, p. 59.

57 Ibid., s. 38, p. 52; s. 47, p. 59.

58 The commission also remarked that "the desire ... to be seen as a special element in Canadian life was strongest on the Prairies" (ibid., s. 37, p. 51).

59 *Debates of the Senate*, 56-57.

60 Rudnyckyj's recommendation was included as a "Separate Statement" in Royal Commission on Bilingualism and Biculturalism *Report of the Royal Commission on Bilingualism and Biculturalism*, Volume I (Ottawa: Queen's Printer, October 8, 1967), 155-69.

61 Ibid., ss. 35-47, pp. xxx-xxxiv.

62 For example, an association of ethnic groups called the Canadian Folk Arts Council convened a "Thinker's Conference on Cultural Rights" in Toronto from December 13 to December 15, 1968. Among those in attendance were Senator Yuzyk, Ontario education minister and future premier William Davis, and *Le Devoir* editor Claude Ryan. The conference

resolved, among other things, that Canada should adopt a policy of multiculturalism and that funds should be made available for the preservation of ethnic cultures and languages. An outstanding history of these events leading to the 1971 multiculturalism policy is offered in John S. Jaworsky, "A Case Study of the Federal Government's Multiculturalism Policy" (MA thesis, Carleton University, 1979), 54-55. I would like to thank Will Kymlicka for bringing to my attention this important work.

63   *Royal Commission,* vol. 4, s. 26, p. 12.
64   Ibid., s. 21, p. 10; ss. 231-32, pp. 86-87.
65   Ibid., s. 12, pp. 6-7.
66   Ibid., ss. 30-31, p. 14.
67   Canada, *House of Commons Debates Official Report*, 3rd Session, 28th Parliament, vol. VIII, 1971 (Ottawa: Queen's Printer, 1971), 8545.
68   Ibid., 8581.
69   They were: a multicultural grants program; a culture development program; an ethnic histories program; an investigation of the problems concerned with the development of a Canadian ethnic studies program; federal assistance to provinces for the purpose of teaching of official languages to children of immigrants; and funding for programs undertaken by federal cultural agencies (i.e., the National Museum of Man, the National Film Board, the National Library, and the Public Archives) (ibid., 8581-83).
70   *Royal Commission*, vol. 4, 228-30.
71   Ibid., s. 29, pp. 13-14. Yasmeen Abu-Laban and Christina Gabriel are incorrect, therefore, in claiming that, "if all the recommendations had been followed, a policy of both multiculturalism and multilingualism would have been the result" since neither were in fact recommended. See Yasmeen Abu-Laban and Christina Gabriel *Selling Diversity: Immigration, Multiculturalism, Employment Equity, and Globalization* (Peterborough, ON: Broadview Press, 2002), 108.
72   For example, the Alberta government announced a multiculturalism policy at an "Alberta multicultural conference" on July 16, 1971, and in September 1971, Ontario premier William Davis announced that his government might do the same. See Jaworsky, "A Case Study," 66.
73   "National unity if it is to mean anything in the deeply personal sense, must be founded on confidence in one's own individual identity; out of this can grow respect for others and a willingness to share ideas, attitudes and assumptions. A vigorous policy of multiculturalism will help create this initial confidence" (*House of Commons Debates 1971*, 8545).
74   Jaworsky, "A Case Study," 56-59. My argument differs with Jaworsky's in important respects. He argues that Trudeau embraced the policy of multiculturalism primarily due to "the atmosphere of change and innovation in Ottawa during the late 1960s," while I credit the success of multiculturalism as a social movement in promoting a vision of the good.
75   James Tully, *Strange Multiplicity: Constitutionalism in an Age of Diversity* (Cambridge: Cambridge University Press, 1995), 177-78.
76   Some have argued that multiculturalism is, in fact, a modern version of the classical civic humanist tradition of *studia humanitatis*. See Walter Temelini, "The Humanities and Multicultural Education," in *Multicultural Education: A Partnership*, ed. Keith A. McLeod, 53-64 (Toronto: Canadian Council for Multicultural and Intercultural Education, 1987). This may partly explain why voluntary educational associations (such as the Canadian Council for Multicultural and Intercultural Education and Teachers of English as a Second Language) are among the most vigilant defenders of multiculturalism.
77   Paul F. Grendler, *Schooling in Renaissance Italy: Literacy and Learning, 1300-1600* (Baltimore and London: Johns Hopkins University Press, 1989), 13-14. Quentin Skinner writes, for example, that during the Italian Renaissance "the first and fundamental move" humanists such as Petrarch made "was to spell out the sequence of assumptions underlying the Ciceronian concept of *virtus*": first that men are capable of attaining the highest kind of excellence, next "that the right process of education is essential for the achievement of this goal." See Quentin Skinner, *The Foundations of Modern Political Thought*, vol. I: *The Renaissance* (Cambridge: Cambridge University Press, 1980), 88-94.
78   Aristotle, *Nichomachean Ethics*, X.ix.

3
The Canadian Model of Multiculturalism in a Comparative Perspective
Will Kymlicka

One of the stated goals of Canada's foreign policy is to promote a greater understanding and appreciation of "Canadian values." Many of these values are, in fact, widely shared across the Western democracies, if not around the world – for example, human rights, peace, development, the environment. But some of these values are more distinctively Canadian than are others. Foremost amongst these is the value of diversity, or pluralism. When Canadian politicians and diplomats act on the international stage, they often emphasize that diversity is a defining characteristic of Canadian society and of Canadian identity. To understand Canada, it is said, one must understand the Canadian model of diversity. Moreover, this model is said to offer valuable lessons for other countries. While acknowledging that tensions remain among some of our ethnic, national, and linguistic groups, it is often suggested that Canadians have some special experience and expertise in accommodating diversity. We have some unique understanding of the benefits that diversity can bring and of the tools needed to manage it in a non-violent and cooperative way. Sharing this understanding is one of Canada's major contributions to the international community.

In this chapter, I explore this discourse of a "Canadian model" of pluralism and the way it is invoked in the international arena. I begin by noting some of the ways in which the Canadian government promotes this discourse internationally as well as its various motives for doing so. I then consider whether there really is anything distinctive about Canada's approach to diversity and, if so, whether it is successful and suitable for emulation elsewhere. While I support many aspects of Canada's approach to pluralism, I argue that the government discourse on diversity obscures as much as it reveals about the Canadian experience and its international relevance.

Promoting the Canadian Model Abroad
In various public speeches and documents, Canadian officials assert that Canada has been successful in accommodating diversity. By itself, this claim

is not unusual. The government of every country wants the world to believe that its citizens form a harmonious society in which the various ethnic, national, and linguistic groups respect each other's differences and get along well. Paeans to "unity in diversity" are ubiquitous when government officials speak in international contexts. These ritual pronouncements are not only intended to promote a positive and peaceful image of the country but also to uphold the state's legitimacy. For a state to admit that some groups are excluded, oppressed, or rebellious would put in question its legitimate authority to speak for those groups in international contexts.

While all countries claim to be harmonious, not all of them want this claim to be examined closely by the international community. In the Canadian case, however, these public pronouncements have been supplemented with efforts to encourage greater international knowledge of Canada's experience. The Canadian government actively funds academic research, conferences, and policy workshops that explore the international relevance of the "Canadian model."

Let me mention just three examples of government-funded support for studies of the international relevance of the Canadian model:

1 the Metropolis network on immigration, which is an international network of researchers and policy makers who share experiences regarding immigration and integration. The Canadian government played a vital role in establishing this network and has used its leadership role to ensure that the accommodation of immigrant diversity through Canadian-style multiculturalism policies is one of the major research areas of the network;

2 the Forum of Federations, which is an international intergovernmental organization bringing together all the federal states around the world in order to share experiences and knowledge. Here again, the Canadian government played a central role in establishing the organization and has used its leadership role to ensure that the accommodation of national/linguistic diversity through Canadian-style federal bilingualism is one of the Forum's major research areas;

3 the International Council of Canadian Studies, which funds academics and universities in other countries to teach courses on Canada, to purchase books on Canada, to visit Canada for research purposes, and to invite Canadian academics to lecture abroad. While, in principle, these funds can be used to explore any topic relevant to Canada, issues of diversity are clearly given a special focus and priority. Indeed, after CanLit, the Canadian model of diversity is the second most popular topic for Canadian Studies courses, study trips, visiting lectures, and workshops.

All three of these initiatives provide financial incentives and logistical support for researchers and policy makers in other countries to examine Canada as a model for accommodating diversity.[1]

This is, of course, just a partial list. One could also mention various international contexts within which the Canadian government presents itself as a world leader on indigenous issues and encourages other countries to study its policies.[2] And there are countless country-specific activities funded by the Canadian International Development Agency (CIDA) or local Canadian embassies that involve publicizing the Canadian model.

It might seem surprising that the Canadian government would spend so much time and effort encouraging people in other countries to study our policies on diversity, given that many of these policies are neither popular nor well understood at home. For example, virtually every study of multiculturalism in Canada has concluded that the policy has been "barely explained at all to the Canadian public," that "no serious effort was [been] made by any senior politician to define multiculturalism in a Canadian context," and that this has seriously jeopardized public support for the policy.[3] Much the same can be said about bilingualism or indigenous rights. Public opinion surveys repeatedly show considerable public confusion about the content and justification of these policies, and the government has done little to dispel this.[4] At times, the main public defence of these policies in the domestic context is simply to denounce critics as intolerant and un-Canadian.

Why would the government spend so much time and money promoting its policies on diversity to foreign audiences when so little time and effort is spent on the domestic Canadian audience? I think we can identify a few motives. First, there are humanitarian reasons. Many people in the foreign policy community genuinely believe that other countries would benefit by studying the Canadian model. Moreover, the perception that Canada is an even-handed respecter of diversity at home helps sustain its reputation as a potential honest broker in mediating conflicts abroad, further enhancing our capacity for humanitarian work.

A second motive is more self-interested. The more people abroad view Canada as a "diversity-friendly" country, the more likely they are to think of Canada as an attractive place to visit, study, do business, or even settle permanently. In a globalized world in which Canada is competing with many other countries for tourists, skilled immigrants, and foreign investors, the reputation for multicultural tolerance can give us a competitive advantage. When immigrants are choosing between Canada and Germany as a place to settle, or when foreign students are choosing between Canada and the United States as a place to study, our reputation for multicultural tolerance may tip the balance.

Third, and paradoxically, these international initiatives also have a domestic audience. Selling the Canadian model to foreigners can, indirectly, help to sell it to Canadians. In effect, the Canadian government hopes that, if international organizations and experts can be encouraged to describe Canada as a successful model of accommodating diversity, this will marginalize critics of the model within Canada. A good example is the government's role in creating the Forum of Federations. This organization was created (in part) in the hope and expectation that it could provide a setting for international statespeople to extol the global virtues of Canadian federalism. This hope was fulfilled in spades when, during the 1st International Conference of the Forum, held in the heart of Quebec at Mont Tremblant in 1999, then president Bill Clinton declared Canadian federalism a model for the world with regard to accommodating diversity.[5] This international praise serves to discredit Quebec separatists. If the rest of the world is declaring Canadian federalism a success in accommodating diversity, then Quebec separatists, who declare it an oppressive failure, appear as radical ideologues living in a nationalist myth disconnected from reality.[6]

I think a similar motivation underlies the Canadian government's role in creating the Metropolis network on immigration. This too was done, at least in part, in the hope and expectation that it would provide a setting for international policy makers and experts to extol the virtues of Canadian multiculturalism. This international praise serves to disarm right-wing critics of multiculturalism in Canada. If the rest of the world is declaring Canadian multiculturalism a model that should be adopted by other countries, then right-wing politicians or columnists who declare the policy to be a divisive and dangerous failure appear, at best, as ill-informed, and, at worst, as xenophobic demagogues. In these ways, government encouragement for an international discourse about the Canadian model can be seen as a way of discouraging domestic criticism of that model.[7]

In short, there is a mixture of motives behind the international marketing of the Canadian model of diversity: a humanitarian concern to help countries that are not dealing well with their own ethnic relations, an economic concern to attract foreign investment and skilled immigrants, and a political concern to delegitimize domestic critics of government policies. No doubt there are other motives as well.

Have any of these goals been achieved? The broad goal of enhancing Canada's international reputation as a diversity-friendly country has certainly had some success. Canada's reputation in this area has grown steadily over the past fifteen years. One striking example is the new Global Centre for Pluralism. In a recent visit to Canada, his Highness the Aga Khan, spiritual head of the world's 15 million Ismaili Muslims, declared that "Canada is today the most successful pluralist society on the face of the globe ... That is something unique to Canada. It is an amazing global human asset."[8] To help spread the good news about the Canadian model, he is spending $40 million to set up a "global centre for pluralism," headquartered in Canada, to serve as an international clearing-house of best-practices with regard to the accommodation of diversity.[9]

Similar ideas about Canada have also been invoked by a wide range of non-governmental, intergovernmental, and academic organizations around the world. Many international organizations today are expected to have a policy about multiculturalism and minority rights, to ensure that their activities recognize and accommodate cultural diversity. This is true, for example, of the United Nations; the United Nations Educational, Scientific and Cultural Organization; the International Labour Organization; the Council of Europe; and the World Bank, to name just a few organizations that have developed recommendations or declarations on respect for diversity. And, in formulating these recommendations, each has looked to Canada, in part because it is a "statistical outlier" in that it combines high levels of different types of diversity with peace, democracy, economic prosperity, and individual freedom.[10] International organizations are genuinely curious about how this works in Canada. A recent example is the 2004 UN Human Development Report, entitled *Cultural Liberty in Today's Diverse World*, which champions multiculturalism as a crucial component of successful development and which repeatedly cites Canadian examples.[11]

So Canada's reputation in this area is clearly growing. Whether or not this is due to the government's international marketing of the Canadian model is more difficult to assess. The idea of Canada as a global model was already circulating among experts in the field well before the Canadian government took an active interest in promoting it. In fact, I suspect that the establishment of the Metropolis network and the Forum of the Federations was, in part, a response to this pre-existing discussion rather than the initiator of it. Having noticed that experts were looking to Canada as a model for accommodating diversity, the government realized that Canada could benefit by creating high-profile international fora in which issues of diversity are discussed.[12] Moreover, it is precisely the fact that independent experts had already recognized Canada as a world leader in this area that gives credibility to the government's promotion of the Canadian model. If the government were not able to point to such independent judgments of Canada's success by credible third parties, its marketing efforts would be perceived as propaganda or national narcissism.

Thus, it is difficult to judge the extent to which the government's own marketing efforts are responsible for Canada's growing reputation in this field. It is even more difficult to judge whether this growing reputation, whatever its causes, has actually served the more specific humanitarian, economic, and political goals mentioned earlier. Has the marketing of the Canadian model abroad helped other countries deal with their ethnic problems? Has it inspired more people to visit, invest, or settle in Canada? Has it helped reduce domestic opposition to these policies?

So far as I know, there is no systematic evidence on any of these questions. (Indeed, it is difficult to know how precisely one could test these questions.) All we have are educated guesses. And my best guess is that there have been some important benefits, at least on the economic and political front.

On the economic front, there is anecdotal evidence that some immigrants and foreign students have chosen Canada over other countries because of our reputation for multicultural tolerance. (I think this is particularly true post-9/11 as many would-be foreign students and immigrants feel that the United States, and perhaps also Australia, have become less welcoming of newcomers.)[13] This evidence comes not only from discussions with immigrants in Canada but also from discussions with policy makers in other countries, who believe they are losing skilled immigrants to Canada for this reason. Defenders of multiculturalism in countries like Britain or Germany often say that adopting more visible multiculturalism policies would help ensure that they are competitive in recruiting the most desired immigrants.

On the political front, there are indications that the rise in Canada's international reputation for accommodating diversity has helped defuse some domestic opposition to these policies. As we see below, in Canada, unlike in some other countries, support for multiculturalism has rebounded in recent years, and I suspect that this is in part due to the awareness that Canada's track record in integrating immigrants is envied by much of the world. When the national newspaper runs articles entitled "Pluralism: The World Wonders How We Pull It Off,"[14] it is difficult for patriotic Canadians not to start taking pride in our record, even though, under other circumstances, such patriotism might have led them to be sceptical about multiculturalism. Moreover, the fact that international experts endorse the Canadian approach undercuts many of the traditional critiques of these policies. For example, multiculturalism used to be dismissed as simply a ploy by the Liberal party to win the ethnic vote. Yet, such domestic partisan considerations can hardly explain why foreign experts in international organizations would endorse Canadian multiculturalism. If nothing else, the awareness of international support for Canada's policies helps to shift the burden of proof in public debate, putting domestic critics on the defensive.

So I suspect that Canada's growing reputation as a model of diversity has had economic and political consequences. However, my main interest is in the humanitarian question, which is, after all, the main official justification for marketing the Canadian model abroad. In the rest of this chapter, therefore, I want to focus on the idea that Canada might provide a model for other countries when it comes to dealing with diversity.

Unpacking the Canadian Model

So far, I have been talking loosely about "the Canadian model" of accommodating diversity. But what exactly is this model, and what would it mean for other countries to adopt it? In reality, there is no single model or principle for dealing with diversity in Canada but, rather, a three-pronged approach to managing diversity that uses different strategies for different types of diversity. We can summarize these as:

1 multicultural citizenship (to accommodate ethnic communities formed by immigration);
2 bilingual federalism (to accommodate the major substate national[ist] group in Quebec); and
3 self-government rights and treaty relationships (to accommodate indigenous peoples).

Each of these has been described as a potential model for immigrants, substate nationalist movements, and indigenous peoples in other countries.

The idea that these three strategies could serve as global models rests on three central assumptions – namely, that in each case,

1 the Canadian approach to managing diversity is distinctive;
2 the Canadian approach is working well in Canada; and
3 other countries can learn from the Canadian experience.

In the rest of the chapter, I raise some questions about these assumptions and argue for a more modest view of the international relevance of the Canadian approach.

I should emphasize that my reservations are not about the second premise – that is, about how well the policies are working in Canada. Many critics, on both the right and the left, deny that these policies are working well in Canada, either because they are fragmenting and balkanizing the country and/or because the focus on accommodating cultural diversity obscures more serious issues of economic and political inequality. On their view, insofar as other countries can learn from the Canadian experience, the lesson is to avoid Canada's failed policies.

As I discuss below, I disagree with these critics. On virtually any relevant criteria for evaluating "success" in the accommodation of diversity, I think that Canada is a success, at least in comparison with earlier periods in Canadian history and in comparison with most other Western democracies.

However, I believe that the first premise about the distinctiveness of Canada's policies is false – or at least overstated. The policies that Canada has adopted with respect to its three main forms of ethnocultural diversity are broadly similar to those adopted by many other Western democracies, following the same basic trends over the past thirty years.

What is true is that these policies are often more successful in Canada than they are in other countries. Policies for accommodating diversity may be similar across many Western democracies, but they have worked more smoothly in Canada, with less of a backlash, with higher levels of public support (or at least public acquiescence), and with higher levels of comfort and security on the part of minority groups. If part of the goal of these policies is to encourage citizens to feel more comfortable with diversity in their personal and public lives, then there is strong evidence that these policies have indeed been more successful in Canada than in most other Western democracies and have, therefore, taken deeper root here than elsewhere.

This suggests that the success of the Canadian model lies not in its distinctive laws or policies (which are broadly similar to those in many other countries) but, rather, in the distinctive underlying circumstances that have helped facilitate the (comparative) success of these policies. And this, in turn, puts into question the exportability of the Canadian model: if the underlying conditions for their success are not present, then adopting these policies in other countries may not have the desired effect.

To illustrate my concerns, I primarily focus on the case of immigrant multiculturalism and offer only a brief discussion of federalism.

Immigrant Multiculturalism

The one component of the Canadian model that has been most strongly endorsed by international experts and organizations is our approach to immigrant integration, and the Canadian government actively promotes this as a model for other countries. I agree that immigrant multiculturalism has indeed been a striking success in Canada. However, in this section, I argue that the specific conditions that enabled its success in Canada also set limits on its likely exportability.

What is immigrant multiculturalism? It is best understood as a repudiation of the earlier policies of assimilation and exclusion. In the past, Canada, like other immigrant countries, had an assimilationist approach to immigration. Immigrants were encouraged and expected to assimilate into the pre-existing society, with the hope that, over time, they would become indistinguishable from native-born Canadians in their speech, dress, recreation, and way of life generally. Any groups that were seen as incapable of this sort of cultural assimilation (e.g., Africans and Asians) were prohibited from emigrating to Canada or from becoming citizens.

Since the late 1960s, however, we have seen a dramatic reversal of this approach. There were two related changes: first, the adoption of race-neutral admissions criteria (the "points system") so that immigrants to Canada are increasingly from non-European societies; and second, the adoption of a more "multicultural" conception of integration, one that expects that many immigrants will visibly and proudly express their ethnic identity and that accepts an obligation on the part of public institutions (like the police, schools, media, museums, etc.) to accommodate these ethnic identities.

These two changes are often described as a radical and bold experiment, unique to Canada but potentially exportable to many other countries with growing numbers of immigrants. In reality, however, the Canadian approach is not that distinctive. The same twofold change has occurred in virtually all of the traditional countries of immigration, like Australia, New Zealand, the United States, and Britain. All of them have shifted from discriminatory to race-neutral admissions and naturalization policies. And all of them have shifted from an assimilationist to a more multicultural conception of integration.[15] Even some countries that are not traditional countries of immigration, like the Netherlands and Sweden, have adopted versions of immigrant multiculturalism.[16]

So it is important not to overstate the distinctiveness of Canada's policies regarding immigrant multiculturalism. To be sure, Canada was a leader in this regard. Its formal declaration of a multiculturalism policy in 1971 was the first in the world, and it strongly influenced subsequent official declarations by Australia and New Zealand and shaped public debates and public policies in many other countries. But by the late 1980s, there was little, if anything, that was still unique or distinctive in the Canadian approach.

What is true, however, is that these policies have been more successful in Canada than in other countries. This success is attested by the higher level of public support for immigration and for multiculturalism in Canada compared to other countries; the virtual non-existence of a far-right backlash against immigrants; the high naturalization rates of immigrants; the fact that the perception that ethnic groups "get along well" is higher in Canada than in other Western democracies; the emergence of Toronto as "the most multicultural city in the world," without its losing its reputation as a clean and peaceful and prosperous city; and so on.[17] Earlier fears that multiculturalism would lead to balkanization, ghettoization, and increasing ethnic tensions have largely been disproved.[18]

By contrast, other countries have witnessed stronger backlashes against, and partial retreats from, their multiculturalism policies. France's recent ban on headscarves, and its earlier retreat from multicultural education, is perhaps the most prominent example. But we see similar debates in Australia, Britain, and the Netherlands. Multiculturalism has not taken root in these countries to the same extent as it has in Canada. In each case, there is not only widespread talk of a public backlash against multiculturalism but also of a government "retreat from multiculturalism" and a "return to assimilation."[19] This is true, for example, of Australia,[20] the Netherlands,[21] and Britain.[22]

What explains this differential success? I would highlight two contingent factors: timing and geography.

Timing

The way the story is usually told, there is assumed to be a connection between the adoption of race-neutral immigration admissions policy in the 1960s, which led to the arrival of large numbers of non-European immigrants, and the adoption of the multiculturalism policy in 1971. In other words, it is often implied that the latter was adopted in response to the former in order to accommodate "non-traditional" immigrants from the Third World. And this raises the question of why European countries can't also adopt such policies for their non-European immigrants.

However, it's important to remember that Canada's multiculturalism policy was not initially intended for non-European immigrants. It was initially demanded by, and designed for, European immigrant groups – the so-called "white ethnics" – particularly, the Ukrainians, Poles, Finns, Germans, Dutch, and Jews. And it was demanded under very specific conditions – namely, as a reaction to the rise of Québécois nationalism and the political reforms adopted to accommodate it. In response to growing Québécois nationalism in the early 1960s, including the rise of a separatist movement within Quebec, the federal government undertook a series of reforms aimed at enhancing the status of the French language, making the federal government genuinely bilingual, and increasing the representation of francophones in the civil service. More generally, the federal government sought to re-emphasize Canada's "duality"; that is, to re-emphasize the equality of English and French as the "founding nations" and to reaffirm "bilingualism and biculturalism." Understandably, white ethnic groups were nervous about all of this talk about "duality," "two founding nations," and "bilingualism and biculturalism," which seemed to render ethnic groups invisible. They worried that government funds and civil service positions would be parcelled out between British and French, leaving immigrant/ethnic groups on the margins. The white ethnics insisted that the accommodation of Quebec not be undertaken at their expense and that any strengthening of linguistic duality, therefore, be accompanied by recognition of ethnic diversity. The formula that gradually emerged – namely, multiculturalism within a bilingual framework – was essentially a bargain to ensure white ethnic support for the more urgent task of accommodating Quebec. And, indeed, it has proven to be a very stable bargain.

The key point here, for my purposes, is that, throughout this whole period from 1963 to 1971, when multiculturalism was first debated and adopted, the process was driven by white ethnics.[23] It was only much later – in the late 1970s and 1980s – that non-white immigrant groups became active players in the multiculturalism scene.

This is important because it means that a fundamental fear that many people have about multiculturalism, particularly in Europe, simply did not arise in Canada when multiculturalism was first adopted – namely, the fear that the logic of multiculturalism requires tolerating illiberal practices brought to the country by immigrant groups. For many people, a major risk of multiculturalism is that immigrant groups will invoke the ideology of multiculturalism to demand legal protection of illiberal practices such as female genital mutilation, forced arranged marriages, or honour killings. This idea never arose in the initial debates in Canada. After all, the white ethnic groups who were demanding multiculturalism had been present in Canada for several generations and were typically very well integrated. When they first arrived in Canada, some native-born Canadians expressed scepticism about their capacity to integrate into society and their capacity to adjust to liberal democratic values.[24] However, by the mid-1960s, these groups had proven their loyalty to Canada in the Second World War, were often fiercely anti-Communist during the Cold War, and were seen as proud and patriotic Canadians as well as being fully committed to the basic liberal democratic principles of the Canadian state. More generally, they were seen to share a common "Western" and "Judeo-Christian" civilization.

As a result, the idea that the multiculturalism policy might involve a "clash of civilizations" between Western liberal democratic values and conflicting religious or cultural traditions did not arise. The cultural differences between third-generation Dutch-Canadians and fifth-generation British-Canadians are simply not perceived that way.

By contrast, in many European countries, the accommodation of such "civilizational" differences is seen as a central dilemma of multiculturalism – indeed, it is seen as *the* central challenge of multiculturalism. For example, in a recent document explaining the idea of multiculturalism, the Dutch government has said:

> It is probably more fruitful to describe the conflicts concerning integration between autochthonous Dutch citizens and some groups of immigrants in terms of "clashing" norms and values. Against this background fundamental reflection is needed upon the norms and values that Dutch society wants to uphold in their policies, against the pressure of the norms and values of immigrants. Dutch tolerance is considered important, but the question is what are its limits and to what extent Dutch integration policy ... is consistent with [basic liberal values].[25]

Here we have the Dutch government telling its citizens that they should conceptualize multiculturalism as an issue concerned with how the liberal native-born Dutch majority should tolerate illiberal immigrants. Not surprisingly, Dutch citizens have responded by saying, "Well, if *that* is what multiculturalism is about, then we're not so keen on it," and there has been a predictable backlash and a retreat.

I believe that if multiculturalism had been viewed this way in Canada in 1971, then it would not have been adopted. If multiculturalism in Canada had initially been demanded by non-European groups who were perceived as having strong religious or cultural commitments to illiberal practices – say, by Somalis or Pakistanis rather than Ukrainians and Italians – and if their demand for multiculturalism was perceived as a demand that such illiberal practices be tolerated and accommodated, then I'm quite sure that multiculturalism would not have been adopted or taken root.

Gradually, over time, non-European immigrants to Canada have became more visible actors in the multiculturalism debate. Indeed, by the 1980s, they had become the main players, displacing the original white ethnic groups. Indeed, some white ethnics feel that the policy has been "hijacked" by visible minority immigrants and that they have become marginalized from a policy for which they fought. And so, inevitably, questions arose about "the limits of tolerance." Canadians started to ask how the state should respond to illiberal cultural practices, such as female genital mutilation or forced arranged marriages, and whether courts should accept the so-called "cultural defence," in which (for example) husbands attempt to excuse wife-beating by saying it is part of their culture.

As far as I can tell, this issue was first made prominent in Canada in a 1990 book by Reginald Bibby,[26] and it was then picked up in books by Bissoondath[27] and Gwyn,[28] not to mention innumerable columns and editorials – all in the first half of the 1990s. So, in this period at least, there was a major public debate, and, hence, public fear, about the possibility that multiculturalism would become a vehicle for the perpetuation of illiberal practices. Predictably, as in Europe, this led to a backlash. If we track public support for multiculturalism since its adoption in 1971, we find that it was at its lowest in the early 1990s.[29] In this period, there was a concerted effort by critics to persuade Canadians that multiculturalism was grounded in the idea of cultural relativism and, hence, that it required tolerating whatever practices immigrant groups brought with them to Canada. Had they succeeded, I think we would have seen not just a public backlash against the policy but also a government retreat from it.

However, this didn't happen. From its low point in the early 1990s, support for multiculturalism has not only rebounded to its original levels but, in fact, is now at historic highs: a recent poll showed 80 percent support.[30] There is an interesting untold story here: whereas other countries have witnessed the rise and fall of multiculturalism, Canada has seen its rise, decline, and revival.

I think there are three main reasons why critics' attempts to reframe multiculturalism as an issue concerned with tolerating illiberal groups failed.

First, the multiculturalism policy had been in place for twenty years before the issue of cultural relativism or the limits of tolerance emerged. It had become institutionally embedded not just in a particular federal government department but also in virtually every public institution – multiculturalism had been written into the mandate of the CBC, public schools, social services, museums, and so on – not to mention its inclusion in the Constitution in 1982.[31] More generally, an entire generation of Canadians had grown up with this idea, become comfortable with it, and viewed it as an important part of the Canadian identity. The idea of abandoning multiculturalism, after such deep institutional embedding, was simply inconceivable.

Second, by the time the question arose about whether non-European immigrants would use multiculturalism to demand accommodation of illiberal customs, it had already been answered in practice. After all, by 1990, when the question first arose in public debate, non-European groups had already, slowly and imperceptibly, taken their place within the larger framework of Canadian multiculturalism. Since the 1970s, visible minority ethnic organizations had begun to take a seat at the table, and so we already had a good idea about what sorts of demands they would make in the name of multiculturalism. And the reality is that no major immigrant organization had demanded the right to maintain illiberal practices. The Somalis had not demanded exemption from laws against female genital mutilation (FGM);[32] Pakistanis had not demanded exemption from laws against coerced marriages; and so on. If there was a danger that non-European immigrant groups would contest the basic principles of liberal democracy in the name of multiculturalism, it would have occurred by 1990. But it hadn't. These groups had already proven their willingness to work within the framework of a liberal (human rights-based) multiculturalism.[33]

A third reason concerns the role of Islam. So far, I have been discussing "non-European immigrants" as a single category; all of these immigrants are perceived as potential bearers of values and traditions at odds with the values of Western liberal democracy. But some non-European groups are seen by white Canadians as more of a threat to these values than others. In particular, throughout the West today, it is Muslims who are seen as most likely to be culturally and religiously committed to illiberal practices and/or supporters of undemocratic political movements. This is particularly the case after 9/11, but it has been true for several years now (I think it probably dates back to the Islamic revolution in Iran).

As a result, the fear that multiculturalism is a vehicle for perpetuating illiberal practices is linked to the size or proportion of Muslim immigrants. In most of Western Europe, the largest group of non-European immigrants are Muslims – up to 80 percent or 90 percent in countries like France, Spain, Italy, Germany, the Netherlands, and so on. And many of these Muslim immigrants are from parts of Africa or South Asia where traditions of FGM and arranged marriages persist and where Islamic fundamentalism is strong.[34] Racism and Islamaphobia combine to generate a perception of recent non-white immigrants as illiberal and, hence, a perception of multiculturalism as a threat to Western liberal values.

Even in Britain, where the immigrant intake is more mixed in terms of religion, issues of Islam have come to dominate the debate. The initial push for multiculturalism in Britain was spearheaded by (predominantly Christian) Caribbean blacks, but political mobilization and public debate is now dominated by South Asian Muslims, and the result has been a decided cooling of public support for multiculturalism. A recent article in the *Spectator* is entitled "How Islam Has Killed Multiculturalism."[35] The title and article are decidedly biased,[36] but it seems true that public support for multiculturalism has declined as Muslims have come to be seen as the main proponents or beneficiaries of the policy.

In Canada, by contrast, Muslims are a small portion of the overall population (less than 2 percent) and form only a small fraction of recent non-white immigration. Ninety percent of our recent immigrants are not Muslim. The two most visible immigrant groups in Canada are Caribbean blacks (particularly in Toronto and Montreal) and Chinese (particularly in Vancouver). Neither is Muslim, and neither is perceived as bringing "barbaric" or "illiberal" practices with them. There are certainly many prejudices and stereotypes about these groups, particularly with regard to Caribbean blacks. These include perceptions about criminality, laziness, irresponsibility, lack of intelligence, and so on – in short, old-fashioned racism.[37] But the idea that these groups have a religious or cultural commitment to offensive and illiberal practices is not particularly salient.[38]

In all of these respects, I believe that Canada has simply been lucky in its timing. Let me put it this way: if we wanted to ensure public support for multiculturalism as a framework for integrating non-European immigrants, what would be the best way of introducing it? I think the ideal sequence would be to first adopt the policy for groups that are seen as "safe" because they are part of the Judeo-Christian/Western civilization; then provide ample time (say, a generation) for this policy to become institutionally embedded and a part of people's identities before the perceived "hard cases" arise. And, finally, when the potential hard cases do emerge, ideally they would do so gradually and imperceptibly so that the ability and willingness of such groups to work within a liberal multicultural framework can become established in practice before it becomes a matter of heated public debate. As far as I can tell, the fact that Canada followed this sequence was entirely fortuitous rather than a matter of inspired political leadership or farsighted policy making. Unfortunately, as I discuss below, few other countries have had similar fortuitous circumstances, and their prospects for successfully and smoothly adopting multiculturalism are correspondingly lower than Canada's.

Geography

Let me turn now to the second major source of good fortune – namely, geography. A defining feature of the Canadian context is that we face no threat of large-scale influx of unwanted migrants from neighbouring poor countries – whether it be illegal immigrants or asylum seekers. The reason for this, obviously, is Canada's geographical position. Most Western countries are in geographic proximity to poor and/or unstable countries that are capable of producing large numbers of unwanted migrants seeking to enter the country either by land or sea. This is true, for example, of the United States with respect to Mexico (land) and Haiti (sea); and of Spain with respect to North Africa; and of Italy with respect to Albania. And given free movement within the (Schengen)-European Union, virtually all EU countries face the prospect of sizeable numbers of unwelcome migrants from the Balkans or Eastern Europe or North Africa. It is even true of Australia, which fears large numbers of sea-borne migrants from south Asia. In all of these countries, illegal immigrants and asylum seekers who wash up on shore form a sizeable percentage of the overall migrant population.

By contrast, it's virtually impossible for people from poor or unstable countries to get to Canada without government authorization. Canada has a land-border with only one country – the United States – which is richer, not poorer, than Canada. Very few people who manage to enter the United States have any desire to move to Canada.[39] On the contrary, the tendency is the reverse: many people who enter Canada do so with the ultimate goal of moving to the United States. So there is no threat of a large-scale movement of unwanted migrants across the land border. And it is essentially impossible for people from poor countries to get to Canada by sea. So, in effect, the only way for people from poor/unstable countries to get to Canada is by air, and it is impossible to board a plane to Canada without a visa. This means that, for all intents and purposes, virtually all migrants to Canada are people whom the government has chosen and/or authorized to come.

It is impossible to exaggerate the importance of this fact for the success of "the Canadian model" of immigrant multiculturalism. It has several profound implications. First, it reduces fear about being "swamped" by unwanted migrants, and it therefore lowers the temperature of debates and makes people feel that we are in control of our own destiny.

Second, in most Western countries, there is a strong moralistic objection to rewarding migrants who enter the country illegally or under false pretences (e.g., economic migrants making false claims about escaping persecution). Such migrants are seen as flouting the rule of law, both in the way they entered the country and often in their subsequent activities (e.g., working illegally). Most citizens have a strong moral objection to rewarding such illegal or dishonest behaviour. Moreover, such migrants are often seen as "jumping the queue," taking the place of equally needy or equally deserving would-be migrants who seek entry through legal channels. There is also a prudential objection to providing multiculturalism policies for illegal immigrants since this may encourage yet more illegal migration.

I think that much of what is called "anti-immigrant" feeling in the United States and Europe is in fact anti-*illegal* immigrant feeling. Citizens do not want to encourage or reward such illegal behaviour and so will not support multiculturalism policies that would benefit significant numbers of such migrants. I believe that this would be equally true in Canada were we to be faced with comparable levels of illegal immigration.[40]

Consider the hysteria that accompanied the appearance off the Canadian shore of four boats containing just under six hundred Chinese migrants in the summer of 1999.[41] There was overwhelming support in the Canadian public for forcibly repatriating them to China without allowing them to land and make asylum claims (which most Canadians assumed would be bogus).[42] I believe that Canadians are as opposed to illegal immigration as are the citizens of any other Western country. If such boats appeared on Canadian shores every week, as happens in Italy, Spain, and Florida, I have no doubt that there would quickly be a powerful anti-immigrant and anti-multiculturalism backlash.[43] In any case, one of the central risks associated with immigrant multiculturalism in most countries – namely, that it will reward and encourage illegal immigration – simply does not exist in Canada.

The fact that Canada faces no threat of a large-scale influx of unwanted migrants from a neighbouring poor country has other important consequences. It means that there is no danger that a single ethnic group will dominate the stock of immigrants. Because immigrants to Canada are selected by the government rather than showing up at the border uninvited, they are drawn from all corners of the world, and no single ethnic group forms more than 15 percent of the total immigrant intake. In the United States, by contrast, because of its land border with a poor country, almost 50 percent of immigrants come from Mexico. Similarly, North Africans dominate the immigrant intake in Spain and France.

This has many consequences for the integration process. In a situation in which immigrants are divided into many different groups originating in distant countries, there is no feasible prospect of any particular immigrant group's challenging the hegemony of the national language and institutions. These groups may form an alliance among themselves to fight for better treatment and accommodation, but such an alliance can only be developed within the language and institutions of the host society and, hence, is integrative. In situations in which a single dominant immigrant group originates in a neighbouring country, the dynamics may be very different. The Arabs in Spain, and the Mexicans in the United States, do not need allies among other immigrant groups. One could imagine claims for Arabic or Spanish to be declared a second official language, at least in regions where they are concentrated, and these immigrants could seek support from their neighbouring home country for such claims – in effect, establishing a kind of transnational extension of their original homeland into their new neighbouring country of residence. This scenario may sound fanciful, but native-born citizens may nonetheless see it is as a risk – one that has to be firmly prevented by restricting immigration and opposing multiculturalism.[44]

This fear is often compounded in situations where the immigrant group has historic claims against the receiving country, deriving from relations between the neighbouring countries. For example, in the Mexican-United States case, the American Southwest originally belonged to Mexico, and various minority rights were promised to the Mexicans even after it was forcibly annexed by the United States. Some Mexicans may believe, in light of this history, that they have a right to (re-)establish Spanish language institutions in this region and that the American government has no right to expect their integration into "Anglo" America.

In the case of Algerians in France, their country was forcibly colonized by France, and their language and culture were suppressed by French colonial officials. Algerian immigrants to France may feel, in light of this history, that they have the right to move to France without having to undergo yet another process of cultural adaptation. Having already had the French language and culture imposed on them in the past, Algerians may feel that the French government has no right to impose it again. This is a common perception among ex-colonial migrants to their imperial metropole.[45]

In Canada, by contrast, there is no single dominant immigrant group, and no sizeable immigrant groups from territorially contiguous states or from ex-colonies. As a result, no immigrant group has either the capacity or a territorial/historical basis to contest the basic assumption that immigrants should integrate into the institutions of the existing society. Here again, a basic risk that accompanies immigrant multiculturalism in many countries simply does not exist in Canada.

The fact that immigrants to Canada do not show up uninvited from neighbouring poor countries has a further important consequence – namely, it reduces the risk of creating an ethnic underclass. In countries in which most migrants enter illegally, and then often work illegally, without the protection of the law and without access to social benefits, there is a serious danger that a racially defined underclass will emerge and that the category of "immigrant" will come to be seen, in many people's minds, as "poor" and/or "criminal." This, in turn, can lead to a situation in which debates about the welfare state become racialized – that is, a situation in which native-born citizens withdraw support for welfare programs that are seen as disproportionately benefiting poor non-white immigrants. Canada has mercifully avoided this poisonous dynamic.[46]

Geography, in short, is pivotal. If we want to ensure public support for immigrant multiculturalism, the optimal conditions would be that immigrants be legal rather than illegal; that they come from distant countries rather than contiguous countries (particularly from contiguous countries with whom one has had a tense historic relationship); and that they come from multiple sources rather than a single dominant source. In all of these respects, Canada's geography serves us well. This is a matter of complete luck rather than of political virtue or maturity. Had our geographical circumstances been different – for example, if Mexico or China were twenty kilometres off the Canadian coast – I think it is much less likely that Canada would have adopted multiculturalism or that it would ever have taken root.

I believe that these two factors together – timing and geography – go a long way towards explaining the success of the Canadian model of immigrant multiculturalism. And, if we take these factors seriously, they suggest serious limits to the likely exportability of the Canadian model. To oversimplify, we can lump countries into three general categories:

First, there are countries that have the same general conditions regarding timing and geography as does Canada. I can think of two – namely, New Zealand and Australia – and these are precisely the two countries that studied and adapted the Canadian model back in the 1970s and 1980s.

Second, there are countries that did have some of the same fortunate conditions as did Canada when ideas of multiculturalism first arose, but whose circumstances have since diverged significantly. The two cases that come to mind are the United States and Britain. In these countries, the initial demands for immigrant multiculturalism came from legally admitted immigrant groups, originating in distant lands, who shared a Judeo-Christian religion (white Europeans in the American case, Caribbean blacks in the British case).[47] And so they too started down the multiculturalism road in the 1980s. But in these cases, unlike in the case of Canada, the debate over multiculturalism quickly became focused on groups that were either unwanted/illegal migrants from neighbouring poor countries (Hispanics in the United States) or perceived as illiberal (South Asian Muslims in the United Kingdom). And so the potential for adopting the Canadian model diminished.

Third, there are those countries in which the issue of multiculturalism was, from the start, tied up with groups that were either perceived as illiberal or as unwanted migrants from neighbouring poor countries or both. In many European countries, the largest group demanding multiculturalism has been illegal migrants from a neighbouring Muslim country – the very opposite of the Canadian situation. In these countries, ideas of multiculturalism have typically met maximal resistance. Yet, these are precisely the countries that are now being encouraged by the Canadian government to follow the multiculturalism model.

Put another way, by the time the Canadian government started to think seriously about promoting Canadian multiculturalism internationally through the Metropolis network in the mid-1990s, the golden age for exporting the Canadian model was already over. Those countries that shared some or all of the conditions underlying Canada's successful adoption of multiculturalism had already studied the Canadian model in the 1970s and 1980s and had adopted or adapted some of its features. It is not clear that there are new markets of willing buyers of Canadian-style multiculturalism waiting to be tapped.

Federalism and Québécois Nationalism

I believe that an analysis similar to that advanced in the preceding section can also be applied to Canada's experience with regard to accommodating Québécois nationalism. Canada's use of federalism and official bilingualism to manage a powerful substate nationalist movement is viewed by many international experts and organizations as a success, and the Canadian government promotes it as a model for other countries. I agree that bilingual federalism is a success in Canada. However, I suspect that here, too, there are special conditions that have enabled its success in Canada, and these conditions set limits on its potential exportability.

Federalism in Canada involves a complicated set of institutions, but if we focus on its role in accommodating Québécois nationalism, I would highlight three essential features:

1 territorial autonomy – that is, creating a federal subunit in which the Québécois form a local majority and so can exercise meaningful forms of self-government;
2 official language status for French;
3 institutional completeness – that is, the Québécois have access to a full range of public institutions (educational, media, political, legal) that allow its members to achieve a high degree of class mobility and professional accomplishment within their own community, without having to integrate or assimilate into the English-speaking community.

In my view, these three features can be seen to define a special sort of federal system – what we can call a "multination" federalism. Any federal system that exhibits these features is grounded, implicitly at least, on the principle that the substate national group will endure into the indefinite future and that its sense of nationhood and nationalist aspirations must be accommodated. Many aspects of such a "multination" conception of

Canadian federalism were present at Confederation but were more fully implemented in the 1960s and 1970s.

The adoption of this sort of multination federalism is sometimes seen as an achievement unique to Canada, although potentially exportable to other countries facing their own powerful substate nationalist movements. In reality, however, the Canadian experience is not particularly distinctive. We see the same basic trend throughout the established Western democracies. Virtually every long-standing Western democracy that has a powerful substate nationalist movement has adopted the same threefold package of federal or quasi-federal territorial autonomy, official language status, and institutional completeness. This is true of the Flemish and Walloons in Belgium, the French and Italian minorities in Switzerland, the German minority in South Tyrol in Italy, the Scots and Welsh in Britain, the Catalans and Basques in Spain, the Swedish minority in Finland, and Puerto Rico in the United States.

So it is important not to exaggerate the distinctiveness of the Canadian approach to substate nationalism. To be sure, Canada was a leader in this area. At the beginning of the twentieth century, only Switzerland and Canada had adopted this combination of territorial autonomy and official language status for substate national groups. Since then, however, partly inspired by the Swiss and Canadian examples, virtually all established Western democracies that contain sizeable substate nationalist movements have moved in this direction, and there is little if anything that is unique to the Canadian example.[48]

Moreover, unlike the case of immigrant multiculturalism, the basic elements of multination federalism seem to have taken root in all of these countries. There is no danger of a public backlash or government retreat from multination federalism in any of them (e.g., no established Western democracy would contemplate abolishing existing forms of territorial autonomy or stripping official language status from a minority). If multination federalism has been a success in Canada, it has equally been a success in all of these countries, providing a means of managing nationalist conflict while preserving peace, individual rights, democracy, and economic prosperity.[49]

So the market among the established Western democracies for Canadian-style multination federalism is already saturated. As a result, the focus of the Canadian government's efforts has been on promoting multination federalism farther afield, particularly in post-communist Eastern Europe and the Balkans, Asia, and Africa. This, indeed, is one goal of the Forum of Federations.

Unfortunately, there appears to be little appetite for multination federalism in these regions of the world. Consider the conflicts between majority Sinhalese and minority Tamils in Sri Lanka, between majority Macedonians and minority Albanians in Macedonia, between majority Arabs and minority southerners in Sudan, between majority Greeks and minority Turks in Cyprus, between majority Turks and minority Kurds in Turkey, between majority Serbs and minority Albanians in Serbia, and between majority Moldovans and minority Slavs in Moldova. In all of these cases, we have a minority group that, like the Québécois, is regionally concentrated, with a distinct language and culture, forming a significant percentage of the population, mobilized around a nationalist political movement, seeking a form of federal autonomy and official language status. Viewed from Canadian eyes, the idea of a bilingual federation seems the obvious solution. Yet, in all of these countries, the state has preferred to suppress rather than to accommodate minority nationalism and has rejected bilingualism and federalism. Indeed, they have all risked civil war rather than accept a negotiated solution based on bilingual federalism, and the result has been years or even decades of instability and violence.

What explains this differential receptiveness to multination federalism? Here again, I think there are two key factors – namely, geopolitical security and individual security.

Geopolitical Security

The treatment of minorities within a state is intimately linked to relations between neighbouring states. Where states feel insecure in geopolitical terms, fearful of neighbouring enemies, they are unlikely to treat their own minorities fairly. More specifically, states will never voluntarily accord self-governing powers to minorities that they view as potential collaborators with neighbouring enemies. In other words, they will not voluntarily accord rights and powers to groups that they view as a "fifth column" for a neighbouring enemy.

In all of the non-Western cases I just mentioned, this is precisely how states perceive their situation. These are all countries with one or more powerful enemies at or near their borders, and they believe that if these enemies invaded, or otherwise attempted to undermine the state, their minorities might well collaborate with the aggressor. One reason that minorities are assumed to be potential fifth columnists is that they often have religious, cultural, ethnic, or linguistic ties to the neighbouring state. The minority may view this neighbouring state as its "mother state" and may look to it for protection. Consider the Turkish minority in Cyprus (vis-à-vis Turkey), or the Albanian minority in Serbia and Macedonia (vis-à-vis Albania), or the Russian minority in Moldova (vis-à-vis Russia), or the Serbian minority in Croatia (vis-à-vis Serbia), or the Hindu Tamil minority in Sri Lanka (vis-à-vis India), or the Muslim minority in Kashmir (vis-à-vis Pakistan), to name just a few. Under these circumstances, it appears that states will only grant genuine autonomy to minorities if they are forced to do so as a result of minority rebellion and insurgencies (and/or external imposition).

In Canada, by contrast, there is no comparable fear that the Québécois will collaborate with Canada's neighbouring enemies. Part of the reason for this is that the only possible "mother state" for the Québécois (i.e., France) is thousands of kilometres away (and, partly for that reason, is no longer viewed as the "mother state" by most people in Quebec). In any event, France is Canada's ally, not its enemy. More generally, Canada has no neighbouring enemies with whom the Québécois might collaborate.

Of course, Canada does have some potential long-distance enemies, such as Soviet Communism in the past, Islamic jihadism today, and perhaps China in the future. But in relation to these long-distance threats, there is no question that the Québécois are on the same side as the Canadian state. If Quebec gains increased powers, or even independence, no one in the rest of Canada worries that it will start collaborating with Al Qaeda or China to overthrow the Canadian state.[50] Quebec nationalists may want to secede from Canada, but an independent Quebec would be Canada's ally, not its enemy, and would cooperate with Canada in NATO and other Western defence and security arrangements.

This geopolitical factor helps to explain the success of multination federalism not only in Canada but also throughout the established Western democracies. In the past, fears of disloyalty have sometimes been an issue in Western Europe. For example, prior to the Second World War, Italy feared that the German-speaking minority in South Tyrol was more loyal to Austria or Germany than it was to Italy and would, therefore, support any attempt by Germany/Austria to invade and annex South Tyrol. Similar fears were expressed about the German minority in Belgium and Denmark. These countries worried that Germany might invade in the name of "liberating" their co-ethnic Germans and that the German minority would collaborate with such an invasion.

Today, however, this is essentially a non-issue throughout the established Western democracies, at least with regard to national minorities.[51] It is difficult to think of a single Western democracy in which the state fears that a national minority would collaborate with a neighbouring enemy and potential aggressor.[52] Part of the reason for this is that Western states do not have neighbouring enemies who might invade them. NATO has been spectacularly successful in removing the possibility of one Western country invading its neighbours. As a result, the question of whether national minorities would be loyal in the event the state is invaded has been removed from the table.

Similarly, there is no doubt that national minorities would side with the state in any conflict with long-distance threats. In the event of some future "clash of civilizations" between the West and Islam, or between the West and China, there is no doubt about whose side the Scots, Catalans, and Puerto Ricans will be on. In all of these cases, national minorities are assumed to be allies, not enemies, and accommodating them poses no risk to the basic geopolitical security of the state.[53] This has been a crucial precondition for the successful operation of multination federalism in Canada and throughout the Western democracies, but it is absent in most of the rest of the world.

Individual Security

A second factor in the willingness of states to adopt multination federalism is confidence that self-governing minorities will respect the human rights of everyone living on their territory. In particular, states will not voluntarily grant self-governing powers to minorities if they fear that members of the dominant group who live on the minority's territory will be persecuted, expelled, or killed.

In the established Western democracies, this confidence is the product of a deep consensus across ethnonational lines regarding the basic values of liberal democracy and human rights. It is assumed that any powers of self-government that are granted to national minorities will be exercised in accordance with shared standards of democracy and human rights. Everyone assumes that these substate autonomies will operate within the constraints of liberal democratic constitutionalism, which firmly upholds individual rights. In virtually every case of multination federalism in the West, substate governments are subject to the same constitutional constraints as is the central government, and so they have no legal capacity to restrict individual freedoms in the name of maintaining cultural authenticity, religious orthodoxy, or racial purity.[54] In fact, these basic liberal freedoms and human rights are typically protected at multiple levels: regionally, nationally, and internationally.

Not only is it legally impossible for national minorities to establish illiberal regimes, but they have no wish to do so. On the contrary, all of the evidence suggests that members of national minorities are at least as strongly committed to liberal democratic values as are members of dominant groups, if not more so. Indeed, substate autonomies often adopt more progressive policies than those adopted at the central level. Policies on gender equality or gay rights, for example, are more progressive in Scotland than they are in the rest of Britain, more progressive in Quebec than in other parts of Canada, and more progressive in Catalonia than in other parts of Spain. Moreover, support for cosmopolitan values is also typically higher in these substate regions than in other parts of the country, including support for foreign aid and for strengthening the role of the European Court of Human Rights and other international human rights instruments.[55]

This may seem obvious, but it is a pivotal consideration as it removes one of the central fears that dominant groups have about multination federalism. In many parts of the world, there is the fear that, once national minorities acquire self-governing power, they will use it to persecute, dispossess, expel, or kill anyone who does not belong to the minority group. (Think about the recent fate of the Serbs in Kosovo.) In the established Western democracies, however, this is a non-issue. There is no fear that self-governing minorities will use their powers to establish islands of tyranny or theocracy. More specifically, there is no fear that members of the dominant group who happen to live on the territory of the self-governing minority will be subject to persecution or expulsion. The human rights of English residents of Scotland are firmly protected not only by Scottish constitutional law but also by European law, and this would be true even if Scotland seceded from Britain. The human rights of English-Canadian residents of Quebec, or of Castilian residents of Catalonia, are fully protected, no matter what political status Quebec or Catalonia ends up having.[56]

I believe that these two factors – the lack of geo-political security concerns regarding minority rights, and the protection of human rights – have been crucial to the successful operation of multination federalism in Canada and other established Western democracies. And, if we take these two factors seriously, they suggest serious limits on the likely exportability of the Canadian model. If we ask which countries around the world share these two conditions, the answer is very few. More specifically, the countries that share these two conditions are precisely the countries that have already adopted some version of multination federalism. In most countries in Eastern Europe, Africa, the Middle East, and Asia, one or both of these conditions is absent. Yet, it is precisely in these countries that the Canadian government is now promoting multination federalism.

In short, by the time that the Canadian government started to aggressively promote its model of multination federalism internationally in the mid-1990s through the Forum of Federations, the golden age for exporting it was already over. Those countries that shared some or all of the conditions underlying Canada's successful adoption of multination federalism had already studied the Canadian model and had adopted or adapted some of its features. Here again, it's not clear that there are any untapped markets for Canadian-style multination federalism.

Conclusion

If the analysis I've given is correct, then we should be more modest in our expectations about exporting the Canadian model of diversity. As most countries lack the fortunate circumstances that have underpinned Canada's comparative success in this field, we have little basis for expecting them to voluntarily adopt the Canadian model. Indeed, we have little reason to assume that the model would work in their very different and more diffi-cult circumstances. The Canadian experience provides no lessons about how to manage the sort of diversity that arises from large-scale illegal migration, or from irredentist national minorities, or from many of the other ethnic problems that beset countries around the world. Whether immigrant mul-ticulturalism and bilingual federalism would be useful in these contexts simply cannot be predicted on the basis of the Canadian experience.

I hasten to add that I am not recommending that Canada abandon its humanitarian desire to protect minorities around the world or that it should turn a blind eye when countries adopt assimilationist or oppressive policies towards minorities. On the contrary, I firmly believe that a robust set of minority rights is needed to achieve justice in multiethnic states and that the international community has a responsibility to help achieve justice for minorities. I hope that Canada will be a world leader in strengthening the international protection of minorities.

But it is naïve (and narcissistic) to suppose that the only or best way to protect minorities is by marketing the Canadian model of diversity abroad. More attention should be paid to strengthening international norms of minority rights and improving mechanisms for their protection. And, inso-far as we do market the Canadian model abroad, we need to think more critically about what we can do to promote the underlying conditions that sustain it, such as reducing the geo-political security fears that can erode support for minority rights. Promoting the Canadian model abroad with-out attending to these conditions may help us to attract a few new immi-grants, but it is unlikely to do much good for the supposed beneficiaries of our "amazing global human asset."

Acknowledgments
This chapter originated as the Standard Life Visiting Lecture at the University of Edin-burgh, April 29, 2004. An earlier, abbreviated version was published in *International Journal* 59, 4 (2004): 829-52.

Notes
1 In the interests of full disclosure, I should note that my own work has been supported, directly or indirectly, by all of these organizations, including the Forum of Federations, Metropolis, the ICCS, and several Canadian embassies.
2 For example, Canada uses its position in the Arctic Council to promote its policies regard-ing the Inuit; and it uses its role at the UN to promote its policies regarding the appropriate use of treaties with status Indians.
3 Freda Hawkins, *Critical Years in Immigration: Canada and Australia Compared* (Montreal: McGill-Queen's University Press, 1989), 221.
4 For example, the federal government has made no attempt to explain the principles under-lying the major Aboriginal rights court cases to the public (Fred Bennett, "Aboriginal Rights Deliberated," *Critical Review of International Social and Political Philosophy*, forthcoming).
5 William Clinton, "President Clinton's Federalism Speech," Forum of Federations Confer-ence, October 8, 1999, Mont-Tremblant, Quebec (available at http://www.uni.ca/library/clinton99.html).

6 That this was indeed part of the motivation is made clear by the fact that the Forum was funded out of the so-called "secret" national unity fund.
7 The complex relationship between the humanitarian/foreign considerations and strategic/ domestic elements is illustrated by the government's ambivalent approach to the codification of international norms of minority rights – for example, its objections to the 1993 UN Draft Declaration on the Rights of Indigenous Peoples and its refusal to ratify the 1990 UN Convention on the Protection of the Rights of All Migrant Workers. Ratifying these international norms might serve the humanitarian goal of protecting minorities around the world but it would have no domestic pay-off; consequently, it is not part of current efforts to market the Canadian model abroad.
8 Michael Valpy, "The World of the Aga Khan," *Globe and Mail*, February 2, 2002; John Stackhouse and Patrick Martin, "The Aga Khan Extols Canada's Virtues," *Globe and Mail*, Focus interview, February 2, 2002.
9 John Ibbitson, "Pluralism: The World Wonders How We Pull It Off," *Globe and Mail*, February 6, 2004.
10 Leslie Laczko, "Canada's Pluralism in Comparative Perspective," *Ethnic and Racial Studies* 17, 1 (1994): 20-41.
11 UNDP (United Nations Development Programme), *Cultural Liberty in Today's Diverse World: Human Development Report 2004* (New York: UNDP, 2004). I should note that I was involved as an advisor to this report, although not as the source of the Canadian examples, which were drawn from a variety of international consultations and background reports.
12 This must have been particularly desirable, given that Canada has been falling behind in its traditional areas of foreign policy strength (e.g., peacekeeping, foreign aid, the environment). Canada needed a new high-profile issue that would enable it to be seen as a world leader, and establishing these new international fora helps to give diversity that high profile. It also fits easily into Axworthy's "human security" framework.
13 For example, my own university, Queen's University, had a sudden upsurge in foreign students after 2001. On the other hand, it's also important to note that many immigrants feel frustrated by the difficulties in getting their professional credentials recognized, and some, in fact, leave Canada as a result. Our reputation overseas does not always survive the reality of day-to-day life in Canada.
14 *Globe and Mail*, February 6, 2004.
15 There are differences in how formal this shift to multiculturalism has been. In Australia and New Zealand, as in Canada, it was officially marked by the central government's declaration of a multicultural policy. But even in the United States, we see similar changes on the ground. The United States does not have an official policy of multiculturalism at the federal level, but if we look at lower levels of government, such as states or cities, we find a broad range of multiculturalism policies. State-level policies regarding the education curriculum, for example, or city-level policies regarding policing or hospitals, are often indistinguishable from those in Canada. As Nathan Glazer puts it: "We are all multiculturalists now." See Nathan Glazer, *We Are All Multiculturalists Now* (Cambridge: Harvard University Press, 1997). Similarly, in Britain, while there is no nation-wide multiculturalism policy, the same basic ideas are pursued through a race relations policy. See Adrian Favell, *Philosophies of Integration: Immigration and the Idea of Citizenship in France and Britain* (New York: St. Martin's Press, 2001). All of these countries have accepted the same twofold change that lies at the heart of the Canadian model: (1) adopt race-neutral admissions and naturalization policies and (2) impose on public institutions a duty to accommodate immigrant ethnocultural diversity.
16 In general, however, this trend towards immigrant multiculturalism applies to "countries of immigration"; that is, countries that legally admit immigrants as permanent residents and future citizens. It is a different story in those countries that do not legally admit immigrants, such as most countries of northern Europe. These countries may well contain large numbers of "foreigners" in the form of illegal economic migrants, asylum seekers, or "guest-workers," but these groups are not admitted as part of an immigration policy, and the state does seek to include them in society either though assimilation or multicultural integration.

17 For relevant evidence, see Andrew Parkin and Matthew Mendelsohn, *A New Canada: An Identity Shaped by Diversity* (Centre for Research and Information on Canada, Montreal, CRIC paper no. 11, October 2003); "Canada's Welcome Mat," *Globe and Mail*, 31 May 2004, A12; Irene Bloemraad, "The Naturalization Gap: An Institutional Approach to Citizenship Acquisition in Canada and the United States," *International Migration Review* 36, 1 (2002): 194-229; Irene Bloemraad, *Becoming a Citizen: Incorporating Immigrants and Refugees in the United States and Canada* (Berkeley: University of California Press, 2006); Will Kymlicka, *Finding Our Way: Rethinking Ethnocultural Relations in Canada* (Toronto: Oxford University Press, 1998); and Will Kymlicka, *Multicultural Odysseys: Navigating the New International Politics of Diversity* (Oxford: Oxford University Press, 2007). The old Reform/Alliance party was often described in the Canadian context as an "anti-immigrant" party, but its expressed policy goal of reducing the intake of immigrants by half would have left Canada with the second largest per capita intake of immigrants in the world. Now that Reform/Alliance has merged with the Conservative party, it appears to have dropped any talk of reducing immigration levels. This is nothing like the anti-immigrant programs of Le Pen or the British National Party or other neo-fascist, white-supremacist parties in Europe.

18 For examples of these fears, see Neil Bissoondath, *Selling Illusions: The Cult of Multiculturalism in Canada* (Toronto: Penguin, 1994); and Richard Gywn, *Nationalism without Walls: The Unbearable Lightness of Being Canadian* (Toronto: McClelland and Stewart, 1995). For overviews of these debates, see Yasmeen Abu-Laban and Daiva Stasiulus, "Ethnic Pluralism under Siege: Popular and Partisan Opposition to Multiculturalism," *Canadian Public Policy* 18 (1992): 365-86; and John Biles, "Everyone's a Critic," *Canadian Issues* (Association of Canadian Studies), Special Issue, "30 Years of Multiculturalism" (February 2002): 35-38. A new fear is that the ideology of multiculturalism enables terrorist organizations to use Canada as a base for their activities. See Stewart Bell, *Cold Terror: How Canada Nurtures and Exports Terrorism around the World* (Toronto: John Wiley, 2004). Yet, terrorist organizations often set up shop in countries like Germany, Spain, or Italy – countries that do not have multiculturalism policies. Indeed, they may prefer such countries since the members of ethnic/religious communities in these places are less integrated into the larger society and less connected to the state. Multiculturalism policies, by contrast, encourage immigrant groups to engage with the state, and some observers view this as helping to reduce the terrorist threat in Canada. See Edna Keeble, "Immigration, Civil Liberties, and National/Homeland Security," *International Journal* 60, 2 (2005): 359-61.

19 Rogers Brubaker, "The Return of Assimilation?" *Ethnic and Racial Studies* 24, 4 (2001): 531-48.

20 Stephen Castles, "Migration, Citizenship, and Education," in *Diversity and Citizenship Education: Global Perspectives*, ed., James Banks, 17-48 (San Francisco: Jossey-Bass, 2004).

21 Hans Entzinger, "The Rise and Fall of Multiculturalism in the Netherlands," in *Toward Assimilation and Citizenship: Immigrants in Liberal Nation-States*, ed. Christian Joppke and Ewa Morawska, 59-86 (London: Palgrave, 2003).

22 Les Back, Michael Keith, Azra Khan, Kalbir Shukra, and John Solomos, "New Labour's White Heart: Politics, Multiculturalism and the Return of Assimilation," *Political Quarterly* 72, 4 (2002): 445-54; Christian Joppke, "The Retreat of Multiculturalism in the Liberal State: Theory and Policy," *British Journal of Sociology* 55, 2 (2004): 237-57. Some of this talk of a retreat from multiculturalism is misleading. Relatively few policies or programs have been eliminated; instead, they have been supplemented and/or qualified with (often heavy-handed) "nation-building" policies, such as mandatory language classes in the Netherlands. For more on the link between multiculturalism policies and nation-building policies, see Keith Banting and Will Kymlicka "Introduction," in *Multiculturalism and the Welfare State: Recognition and Redistribution in Contemporary Democracies*, ed. K. Banting and W. Kymlicka, 1-45 (Oxford: Oxford University Press, 2006).

23 For the role of white ethnic groups in the process, see Linda Blanshay, "The Nationalisation of Ethnicity: A Study of the Proliferation of National Mono-Ethnocultural Umbrella Organisations in Canada" (PhD diss., University of Glasgow, 2001); John Jaworsky, "A Case Study of the Canadian Federal Government's Multiculturalism Policy" (MA thesis, Carleton University, 1979); Manoly Lupul, *The Politics of Multiculturalism: A Ukrainian-Canadian Memoir* (Edmonton: Canadian Institute of Ukrainian Studies Press, 2005).

24 Howard Palmer, "Reluctant Hosts: Anglo-Canadian Views of Multiculturalism in the Twentieth Century," in *Readings in Canadian History: Post-Confederation*, ed. Douglas Francis and Donald Smith, 143-61 (Toronto: Harcourt, Brace, 1994).
25 Quoted in Odile Verhaar, "Principles and Pragmatism in Dutch 'Multicultural Policy,'" paper presented at the International Conference on Ethics and Public Policy, Netherlands Organization for Scientific Research, Utrecht, May 2003.
26 Reginald Bibby, *Mosaic Madness: The Poverty and Potential of Life in Canada* (Toronto: Stoddart, 1990).
27 Bissoondath, *Selling Illusions*.
28 Gywn, *Nationalism without Walls*.
29 Donna Dasko, "Public Attitudes towards Multiculturalism and Bilingualism in Canada," in *Canadian and French Perspectives on Diversity: Conference Proceedings*, ed. Margaret Adsett, 119-25 (Ottawa: Department of Canadian Heritage, 2005).
30 Parkin and Mendelsohn, *A New Canada*.
31 For examples of this institutional embedding of multiculturalism in a range of public institutions in Canada, see Dorothy Zolf, "Comparisons of Multicultural Broadcasting in Canada and Four Other Countries," *Canadian Ethnic Studies* 21, 2 (1989): 13-26 (on the media); Peter Li, "A World Apart: The Multicultural World of Visible Minorities and the Art World of Canada," *Canadian Review of Sociology and Anthropology* 31, 4 (1994): 365-91 (on the arts); Sarah Wayland, "Religious Expression in Public Schools: Kirpans in Canada – Hijab in France," *Ethnic and Racial Studies* 20, 3 (1997): 545-61 (on the schools); Federation of Canadian Municipalities, *Dealing with Diversity: Multicultural Access to Local Government*, Race Relations Series no. 2 (Toronto: Municipal Race Relations Program, Federation of Canadian Municipalities, 1988) (on municipal government); McInnis Consulting, *Multicultural Change in Health Services Delivery Project: Final Report* (Vancouver: Ministry Responsible for Multiculturalism and Immigration, Government of British Columbia, 1997) (on health care); Mohammad Qadeer, "Pluralistic Planning for Multicultural Cities: The Canadian Experience," *Journal of the American Planning Association* 63, 4 (1997): 481-94 (on urban planning).
32 In 1995, the Canadian government gathered together representatives of the various ethnic groups from countries where FGM is traditionally practised in order to discuss how this issue should be dealt with. See Government of Canada, *Female Genital Mutilation: Report on Consultations Held in Ottawa and Montreal*, Research, Statistics and Evaluation Directorate, WD1995-8e (Ottawa: Department of Justice, 1995). There was unanimous agreement that the practice should not be allowed in Canada, and the discussion quickly moved to questions of how best to inform people within these groups about the law and the reasoning behind it. See Alissa Levine, "Female Genital Operations: Canadian Realities, Concerns and Policy Recommendations," in *Ethnicity, Politics and Public Policy*, ed. Harold Troper and Morton Weinfeld, 26-53 (Toronto: University of Toronto Press, 1999); Ontario Human Rights Commission, *Policy on Female Genital Mutilation* (Toronto: Ontario Human Rights Commission, 1996). The fact that ethnic organizations disavow these illiberal practices does not mean that individual members of the group do not attempt in private to maintain them or to avoid punishment for them. But they have not been able to use multiculturalism as a justification or shield for such practices, and there is nothing in Canada like the debates in the United Kingdom regarding forced arranged marriages (see Anne Phillips and Moira Dustin "UK Initiatives on Forced Marriage: Regulation, Dialogue and Exit," *Political Studies* 52, 3 [2004]: 531-51), or in France regarding FGM (see Marie-Benedicte Dembour, "Following the Movement of a Pendulum: Between Universalism and Relativism," in *Culture and Rights: Anthropological Perspectives*, ed. Jane Cowan, Marie-Benedicte Dembour and Richard Wilson [Cambridge: Cambridge University Press, 2001], 56-79), or even in the United States regarding "the cultural defence" (see Alison Dundes Renteln, *The Cultural Defence* [New York: Oxford University Press, 2004]).
33 On the broad consensus across racial/religious lines regarding a human rights-based liberal multiculturalism in Canada, see Rhoda Howard-Hassmann, *Compassionate Canadians: Civic Leaders Discuss Human Rights* (Toronto: University of Toronto Press, 2003). For example, no one has attempted to invoke the multiculturalism clause (s. 27) of the Constitution to

defend the practice of FGM, and any such attempt would certainly be rejected by the courts. Indeed, Canada was one of the first countries in the world to accept that a girl could be granted refugee status if she faces a risk of being subject to FGM if returned to her country of origin (Levine, *Female Genital Operations*, 40). Since, for the purposes of refugee determination, Canada views FGM as persecution, it can hardly permit it to be practised within the nation.

34 The popular view in the West that FGM is a "Muslim" practice is doubly incorrect: FGM is practised by Christians, Jews, and animists as well as Muslims in parts of sub-Saharan Africa, and it is strongly disavowed by many Muslim leaders. Yet, this popular misperception is very strong.

35 Rod Liddle, "How Islam Has Killed Multiculturalism," *Spectator*, May 1, 2004, 12-13.

36 Note that Liddle says it is Islam, not Islamaphobia, that has killed multiculturalism.

37 Frances Henry, *The Caribbean Diaspora in Toronto: Learning to Live with Racism* (Toronto: University of Toronto Press, 1994).

38 I should emphasize that I am talking here of perceptions, which may or may not correspond with reality. See Susan Okin, *Is Multiculturalism Bad for Women?* (Princeton: Princeton University Press, 1999) for a discussion of illiberal practices among some (non-Muslim) Southeast Asian immigrant groups in the United States. And, indeed, one could find examples from all cultures. Yet it remains true that, in terms of perceptions, East Asians are not widely perceived as being committed to illiberal practices.

39 There was one small exception to this rule – namely, some Latin American refugees who preferred to make their asylum claims in Canada rather than in the United Sates. However, that exception has now been removed by the recent US-Canada agreement.

40 In principle, one might imagine an attempt to preserve multiculturalism policies for legally admitted immigrants while denying access to these policies for illegal immigrants or failed asylum seekers. But it is in the very nature of these policies that they benefit all people with the same ethnocultural background. For example, there is no way to prevent illegal immigrants from enjoying minority-language media or gaining access to minority-language public documents.

41 Sean Hier and Joshua Greenberg, "Constructing a Discursive Crisis: Risk, Problematization and Illegal Chinese in Canada," *Ethnic and Racial Studies* 25, 3 (2002): 490-513.

42 And, in all likelihood, most such claims were unfounded. Most of these migrants were classic economic migrants, not people fleeing persecution for their political or religious beliefs. As of July 2000, of the 501 refugee claims that had been decided, only sixteen had been accepted. See Hier and Greenberg, "Constructing a Discursive Crisis," 506.

43 The same hysteria accompanied the arrival of 174 Sikhs on the shore of Nova Scotia in 1987. In response to this "crisis," the federal government recalled Parliament for an "emergency session." See Janet Hiebert, "Determining the Limits of Charter Rights: How Much Discretion Do Governments Retain?" (PhD diss., University of Toronto, 1991), 282-99. This shows that most Canadians are "pro-immigration" and "pro-multiculturalism" in the sense of supporting the legal admission of significant numbers of government-selected immigrants and of fairly accommodating them once admitted. But Canadians are violently (and hysterically) "anti-immigration" in the sense of opposing illegal immigration and would almost certainly oppose any multiculturalism policies that benefited such migrants. I suspect that this is true of the citizens of most Western countries. The difference is that Canada, for reasons of brute luck, does not face the problem of large-scale illegal immigration, and so the antipathy to that form of immigration does not erode support for the multicultural accommodation of legally selected immigrants.

44 For an example of this sort of fear, invoking the facts about the contiguity and numerical dominance of Hispanic immigrants in the United States, see Samuel Huntington, "The Hispanic Challenge," *Foreign Policy*, March 2004, 30-45.

45 Some Jamaican immigrants to Britain view themselves as "more British than the British," and, given that they were born and raised in societies whose legal, political, and educational institutions were designed by their British imperial masters, they resent the implication that they need to be resocialized into British culture. See Yasmin Alibhai-Brown, *After Multiculturalism* (London: Foreign Policy Centre, 2000).

46   There is growing evidence that recent immigrants to Canada are taking longer to achieve parity in earnings with native-born Canadians and that many suffer an "ethnic penalty" in that they are underpaid in relation to their skills and qualifications. However, while these trends are disturbing, they are unlikely to generate an immigrant "underclass." Given the high education levels of many immigrants, they are not likely to suffer complete economic exclusion or intergenerational poverty, even if they are underpaid or underemployed in relation to their skills. For a balanced discussion, see the essays in Keith Banting, Thomas Courchene, and Leslie Seidle, eds., *Belonging? Diversity, Recognition and Shared Citizenship in Canada* (Montreal: Institute for Research on Public Policy, 2007).

47   I emphasize that I am focusing here on demands for *immigrant* multiculturalism. In the United States there were, of course, demands for multiculturalism from African-Americans. These demands involved different sorts of issues, often relating to historic injustice. In terms of immigrant multiculturalism, however, the initial demands were from white ethnics and then shifted to Hispanics.

48   France is the main exception as it refuses to grant autonomy to its main substate national-ist group in Corsica. However, legislation was recently adopted to accord autonomy to Corsica. The implementation of this law has been prevented by the Constitutional Court, but some amended version is likely to be adopted in the future.

49   The violence in the Basque Country is an obvious exception to this generalization, but it is important to remember that this violence predated the adoption of multination federal-ism in Spain and almost certainly would have been worse had federalism not been adopted.

50   Well, almost no one: a columnist in the right-wing *National Post* recently suggested that Quebec separatists were friends of Islamic terrorists. See Barbara Kay, "The Rise of Quebecistan," *National Post*, August 9, 2006.

51   Since 9/11, there are security concerns in some Western states about Muslim immigrants, but there is no comparable concern about long-standing national minorities.

52   If we move beyond the established Western democracies, Cyprus is an obvious case: the Turkish-Cypriot minority is seen by the Greek-Cypriot-dominated state as likely to col-laborate with aggression/intervention by Turkey. In this respect, Cyprus fits squarely into the larger Balkan pattern.

53   For a more extensive discussion of the "securitization" of minority rights – i.e., the ten-dency of states to invoke geo-political security concerns as a grounds for rejecting minority rights – see Will Kymlicka, *Multicultural Odysseys*, chaps. 3 and 6.

54   The partial exception concerns Indian tribal governments in the United States, which are exempted from some provisions of the American Bill of Rights. This exemption has al-lowed some tribes to adopt policies that violate liberal norms. But it is worth emphasizing that, while many tribal governments defend this partial exemption from the American Bill of Rights, they typically do not object to the idea that their self-government decisions should be subject to international human rights norms and international monitoring. See, on this, Will Kymlicka, *Politics in the Vernacular: Nationalism, Multiculturalism, Citizenship* (Oxford: Oxford University Press, 2001), chap. 4.

55   For some of the evidence, see Kymlicka, *Politics in the Vernacular*, chaps. 10-15.

56   This is an important issue even in contexts where the dominant group does not itself respect liberal democratic values and human rights. Indeed, it can be especially important in such contexts. In countries where the dominant group has habitually mistreated minor-ities, there is likely to be a particularly strong fear that the minority will take revenge on local members of the dominant group once it acquires self-government. Dominant groups do not want to give minorities an opportunity to do to them what they have done to minorities. In this context, it may be hypocritical for the dominant group to invoke "hu-man rights" as grounds for rejecting federalism; but fear regarding the treatment of their co-ethnics who are living on the minority's self-governing territory is nonetheless a power-ful factor.

4
The Death of Deference: The Implications of the Defeat of the Meech Lake and Charlottetown Accords for Executive Federalism in Canada
Ian Peach

It has become commonplace to speak of the decline of citizen deference towards political elites, not only in Canada but also in other Western countries.[1] As Nevitte notes, the weight of evidence points to the conclusion that significant shifts in political values have taken place, beginning in the 1980s, and that these shifts represent a generational change, not merely a transitory one.[2] The decline in deference seems particularly dramatic in Canada due to the image of the country as, formerly, a political community that was highly deferential to elite direction.[3] Indeed, one might reasonably go further and argue that deference to political elites is not merely in decline. It is not "pining for the fjords," as was allegedly the case with Monty Python's Norwegian Blue parrot, but, rather, is "pushing up the daisies." It is dead, and it was a lingering death, one that lasted from June 1987 to June 1990. Its deathbed was the Meech Lake Accord.

To take the analogy further, deference's funeral procession was the long, slow, and, for many of the participants,[4] painful march to the Charlottetown Accord; its burial was the defeat of that Accord in the October 1992 referendum. The implications of this death remain with us still, even if they are but poorly integrated into the practice of intergovernmental relations in Canada. They continue to challenge the supremacy of territorially based conceptions of group identity in national political discourse, to undermine the legitimacy and efficacy of traditional intergovernmental processes of national policy making, and to demand that governments find ways to integrate citizens into the decision-making apparatus.[5]

In Canada, the symbol for the death of deference – whether a reflection of the phenomenon, a cause of it, or a catalyst for its acceleration – is the *Canadian Charter of Rights and Freedoms*. While Nevitte rightly notes that it is difficult to argue that the *Charter* could have unleashed all of the value shifts seen in Canada in the 1980s, he also notes that its introduction "opened up new avenues for a qualitatively different form of political participation, avenues that rely less on the rugged political arithmetic of majoritarianism and give Canada's courts a more prominent role in resolving policy dis-agreements."[6] As Nevitte shows,[7] in Canada there has been a surge in the activity of groups promoting women's rights, gay and lesbian rights, con-sumers' rights, the environment, and a host of other concerns related to quality of life and the status of historically marginalized groups, and the *Charter* has provided them with a vehicle to bring their concerns into polit-ical discourse.

While the story of the 1982 constitutional amendment is often told as an intergovernmental war story, non-governmental actors also played a formal and influential role in the course of those events. One must under-stand the impact that equity groups had during the winter of 1980-81 on the substance of the *Charter* due to their advocacy in the Parliamentary Committee on the Constitution.[8] One must also understand the sense of empowerment that derived from the 1982 Constitution and people's at-tachment to it as a statement of fundamental human values. According to Johnston et al.:

> Groups hitherto excluded were mobilized through a public committee pro-cess to support the package and even to modify it. Subsequent changes behind closed doors seemed only to prove the consultative rule, as these changes were modified still further to accommodate a last-minute, mass mobilization by women's and Aboriginal interests. The lesson seemed clear: elite bargaining should *accommodate*, not supersede, deeply felt popular sen-timent. (emphasis in original)[9]

This new-found connection to the Constitution was not confined to some elite group of Ottawa-based social advocates. Thanks to television, in the late 1970s and early 1980s the course of Canada's constitutional debates was played out in the public eye, giving those watching a connection to the discussion that had not been available to previous generations of Canad-ians. For those who watched these events, the image of First Ministers Con-ferences is most likely that of a 1981 conference held in the railway station-turned government conference centre in Ottawa.

Since its entrenchment, the *Charter* has generated a remarkable degree of loyalty among Canadians in every province.[10] As Johnston, et al. note, the *Charter* both responded to and nurtured an emergent rights agenda, and it converted the 1982 settlement from a mere rectification of a "his-torical anomaly" into something valued for itself.[11] In 1983, Reg Whitaker commented:

> The British North America Act ignored individual Canadians ... almost all of the commentary ... on the nature and reform of the constitution has tended to ignore the question of the relation of people to government, or of

people to each other, in favour of persistent attention to the relation of government to government, or of Crown to Parliament, or of Canada to the British Parliament. This obsessive orientation has ... had the effect of making constitutional questions appear tedious and irrelevant to most Canadians.[12]

After 1982, however, Canadians were able to conceive of their Constitution as a culturally significant document rather than as the somewhat esoteric guide to the allocation of governmental authority that Whitaker described.

Then prime minister Brian Mulroney, with his desire to bring Quebec into the constitutional family "with honour and respect" and his apparent anger at former prime minister Pierre Trudeau for the dishonour he allegedly imposed on that province, failed to understand how profound a change the 1982 patriation of the Constitution had brought about in our processes of political accommodation. Thus, in 1987, when he launched the rapid, closed-door intergovernmental process for negotiating the Meech Lake Accord, he returned to the familiar model that had served him well in his previous career as a labour negotiator.

The ideas behind the Meech Lake Accord had arisen with the election of Robert Bourassa's Liberal party in Quebec in December 1985. Leading up to the 1985 election, the Liberal party had made constitutional reform an important part of its platform, and this continued once it formed government. The speech made by Quebec's minister of intergovernmental affairs, the Honourable Gil Rémillard, at Mont Gabriel, Quebec, in May 1986 is the best known statement of the Quebec government's position at the time. In his speech, M. Rémillard stated:

On 2 December 1985, the population of Quebec clearly gave us a mandate to carry out our electoral program, which sets out the main conditions that could lead Quebec to adhere to the *Constitution Act* of 1982.

These conditions are:

1 Explicit recognition of Quebec as a distinct society;
2 Guarantee of increased powers in matters of immigration;
3 Limitation of the federal spending power;
4 Recognition of a right of veto;
5 Quebec's participation in appointing judges to the Supreme Court of Canada.[13]

Further, the other premiers supported Quebec in its desire to embark on constitutional reform discussions. The communiqué for the August 1986 Annual Premiers Conference in Edmonton stated: "The Premiers unanimously agreed that their top constitutional priority is to embark immediately upon a federal-provincial process, using Quebec's five proposals as a basis for discussion, to bring about Quebec's full and active participation in the Canadian Federation."[14] This had not, however, been the subject of any extensive national discussion before the first ministers announced an agreement to amend the Constitution at Meech Lake, Quebec, in April 1987.

There were really two separate critiques of the Meech Lake style of intergovernmental decision making that, when combined, undermined the support that a critical mass of Canadians had for the Accord, increased their distrust of the political elites who negotiated it, and gave them cause to believe that their lack of deference to the decisions of those elites was well warranted. One critique was a democratic one; this was a critique of executive federalism itself, and it challenged governments to find more open, democratic, and deliberative (one might even say republican) ways of making constitutive decisions. The other was less a fundamental challenge to the processes of intergovernmental negotiation and more a challenge to the inadequacy of Mulroney's conception of who had a legitimate place in those negotiations. This challenge came most forcefully from territorial governments and Aboriginal peoples, though it was also heard from key interest group representatives. While, initially, public opinion was strongly in favour of the Accord, eventually, these two critiques became joined in the minds of many Canadians to destroy the legitimacy of the Meech Lake Accord and the process of executive federalism by which it was created.

It is likely that, when they sat down together at Meech Lake in April 1987, neither Mulroney nor the other first ministers thought much about the impact that either of these critiques could have on constitution making and executive federalism. With the Constitution having been patriated only five years earlier, citizens' attitudes were in flux, and there had not been much opportunity to test the public's level of deference to the traditional, elite accommodation model of intergovernmental negotiations. As they were to discover, though, first ministers misread people's attitudes at their peril. The short time-frame within which the Meech Lake negotiations were completed and the unwillingness of the first ministers to alter the Accord in response to public debate, except in the case of "egregious errors,"[15] locked them into a clash with the public that not only made the defeat of the Accord inevitable but also dealt a death blow to the willingness of many Canadians to defer to their elected leaders. Indeed, even the Special Joint Committee of the Senate and the House of Commons on the 1987 Constitutional Accord (the Tremblay-Speyer Committee) suggested that legislators and the public should be encouraged to participate in the process of constitutional change before, not after, the first ministers made their decisions.[16] Senator Lowell Murray, the federal minister of state for federal-provincial relations, likely summed up all that people objected to in intergovernmental politics when he told the Tremblay-Speyer Committee that the Meech Lake Accord was a "seamless web" that could not be changed.[17]

The image of "eleven white men in suits negotiating behind closed doors," as the first ministers negotiations were often described at the time, and the potential for the deal so negotiated to substantively affect the *Charter* led to intense opposition to the Accord. Initially led by legal academics and representatives of equality-seeking groups, and having limited impact on public support for the Accord, the opposition took on a new significance once the iconic figure of Pierre Trudeau returned to the public spotlight to oppose it. The level of public support for Trudeau's liberal democratic vision, in a country whose political history had been much more consistent with Mulroney's tory vision of elite accommodation, reflected just how much the public's deference to political elites had declined in five short years.

If the democratic challenges to the Meech Lake Accord from Trudeau and from equity groups and citizens committed to a liberal democratic vision of our constitutional politics (and the symbol of this vision, the *Charter*) was not enough, it was also assaulted by those who believed that the first ministers were attacking their evolving governance projects. Territorial governments, which had evolved into fully self-governing constituent parts of the federation with substantially the same powers as provinces, had been ignored, treated as though they were still merely administrative units of the federal government. Worse, the Accord made their aspirations to some day become provinces – aspirations that were particularly strong in the Yukon – effectively unachievable. The Meech Lake Accord would have subjected the creation of new provinces to the approval of all existing provinces (in contrast to the situation before 1982, when ordinary federal legislation was all that was required), a standard that has only rarely been achieved in Canadian history.[18] This led to such an intense critique of the Accord that the Yukon government challenged it in court,[19] and the Yukon Progressive Conservative Party changed its name to the Yukon Party, severing all ties to the federal Progressive Conservative (PC) party.

For their part, Aboriginal peoples saw the Meech Lake Accord as deeply offensive to their desire to become self-governing. They also considered their exclusion from negotiations at Meech Lake as an insult, coming as it did within weeks of the failure of the last of the four constitutionally mandated First Ministers Conferences on Aboriginal Constitutional Matters to make any progress with regard to their aspirations.[20] The opposition to the Meech Lake Accord, and to Aboriginal peoples' exclusion from the negotiations, generated a wave of sympathy among many members of the public. This opposition was personified by the chief of the Assembly of First Nations, Ovide Mercredi, and it further undermined support for the Accord.[21]

What may be most instructive in understanding what the defeat of the Meech Lake Accord says about national policy making today is how important a role democratic processes played in both the efforts to save the Accord in 1990 and in its ultimate defeat. The united front that the first ministers presented in support of the Accord was broken by the election of new governments in three provinces. First, on October 13, 1987, Frank McKenna's Liberals defeated the PC government of Richard Hatfield in New Brunswick, winning every seat in the Legislature. Then, on April 26, 1988, Gary Filmon's PCs in Manitoba defeated the New Democratic Party (NDP) government of Howard Pawley after the latter lost a vote on a non-confidence motion. One of the most notable aspects of this election is that, while the PCs were elected in enough ridings to form a minority government, the Manitoba Liberals, under leader Sharon Carstairs, one of Canada's strongest advocates for the Trudeau vision of the Constitution, went from one seat in the Legislature to twenty. Third, on April 20, 1989, the Liberal party in Newfoundland, under Clyde Wells, defeated the PC government of Tom Rideout (who had succeeded Brian Peckford upon his retirement).[22] These elections brought three premiers who had not signed the Meech Lake Accord, and, indeed, who were opposed to it, onto the national political stage at a time when Mulroney was trying to secure the unanimous provincial consent necessary to make the Accord law.

With these three new governments in place and public criticism of the Meech Lake Accord gaining strength, by 1990 it had become clear that saving the Accord would require governments to renew their commitment to democratic debate. Taking the first step in the effort to save the Accord, the New Brunswick government introduced a "companion resolution" on March 21, 1990.[23] This was an attempt by McKenna to respond to the harshest critiques of the Meech Lake Accord, but it was also an admission that a constitutional text that could not garner or retain public support was, in a democratic society, a flawed document. For its part, the federal government launched the Special Committee to Study the Proposed Companion Resolution to the Meech Lake Accord (the Charest Committee) on March 27, 1990. This parliamentary committee was designed to seek public input on the companion resolution in the hope of finding a way to accommodate the conflicting demands of the Quebec government, which insisted on the approval of the Accord as originally negotiated, and of the Accord's critics in the rest of Canada, who wished to see the Accord rejected. Mulroney then initiated last-ditch intergovernmental negotiations.

The defeat of the Meech Lake Accord also had its roots in concerns about the democratic legitimacy of the Constitution. New Brunswick, Newfoundland, and Manitoba, the three provinces that held up approval of the Accord, all did so principally on the basis of a democratic critique. Each province demanded more time to engage its legislature in a public hearing process. In Manitoba, the refusal of Elijah Harper, an Aboriginal member of the Legislative Assembly, to agree to changing the rules of the assembly to allow for Manitoba's approval of the Accord by the three-year deadline made unanimous approval impossible.[24] After Manitoba's Legislature adjourned on June 22 without approving the Accord, Newfoundland premier Clyde Wells cancelled the proposed free vote on the Accord and adjourned the Newfoundland Legislature.[25] On June 23, 1990, time ran out for the Meech Lake Accord, for the proposed companion resolution, and for intergovernmental politics as historically practised.

The aftermath of the defeat of the Meech Lake Accord was a period of radical experimentation in public engagement. At the time, one could have been tempted to believe that the death of the Accord had taught politicians a lesson. Between June 1990 and March 1992, Canadians were consulted by all provincial and territorial governments as well as by the Citizens' Forum on Canada's Future, two Parliamentary committees, and six "Renewal of Canada" conferences at the federal level. As Johnston et al. comment, "the failure of Meech seemed to deliver the message that the people at large would no longer tolerate being excluded from deliberation over their own constitution. This time they would be consulted, even if it was only to bore them to death."[26] A *Maclean's* Magazine/Decima Research poll conducted in November, 1991, confirms this view: in that poll, only one respondent in four supported the traditional intergovernmental processes of constitution making, while 73 percent of respondents nationally, including 65 percent in Quebec, favoured the involvement of "Canadians from across the country" in seeking a constitutional resolution.[27]

While some commentators suggested that the Citizens' Forum on Canada's Future (the Spicer Commission) "may have gotten silly the odd time,"[28] it was a remarkable process, both because of its wide-ranging agenda and because it experimented with new information and communications technologies in an effort to bring citizens from diverse locations and with diverse perspectives together in "virtual town hall meetings." The first of the two parliamentary committees, the Committee on the Process for Amending the Constitution (the Beaudoin-Edwards Committee) was also given a wide-ranging mandate to consult the public not merely on the formal constitutional amending formula but also on the broader question of what processes should be used to ensure that proposed amendments reflected the democratic will. It was this discussion that provided the federal NDP with the opportunity to advocate a constituent assembly as a more democratically legitimate way to generate constitutional amendment proposals, something that Newfoundland premier Wells was also advocating. This discussion would lay the groundwork for the later Renewal of Canada conferences.

The six Renewal of Canada conferences were the highlight of this period, even though they came about largely by accident. When the Parliamentary Committee on a Renewed Canada (initially known as the Castonguay-Dobbie Committee and, later, the Beaudoin-Dobbie Committee), which was itself supposed to include a significant public outreach component, collapsed in November 1991 amid mismanagement and the blatant patronage of its co-chair, Dorothy Dobbie, efforts began immediately to resurrect it. The Opposition parties initially demanded Dobbie's removal, as she was the person responsible for the fiascos that led to the committee's collapse. When, in the aftermath of Opposition Leader Jean Chrétien's public insistence that Dobbie be removed, the government refused to fire her, the NDP resurrected the idea of a constitutent assembly contained in its Beaudoin-Edwards minority report, which it believed offered a solution to the impasse. The NDP felt that, at a minimum, the work of the parliamentary committee had to be supplemented by a new, more legitimate process that was separate from the committee and thus not tainted by its history of patronage and mismanagement. In the end, the federal government agreed to the NDP's demand to undertake a series of miniature constituent assemblies in which members of the public would participate in constitutional reform discussions along with government officials, interest group representatives, and members of the parliamentary committee.

These conferences were truly remarkable events. The members of the public who participated were listened to closely and, thus, wielded influence well beyond their numbers. The participants proved that, if they were provided with the right forum, citizens could discuss issues intelligently and come to a considered resolution of difficult conflicts. The conferences also had a significant influence on the content of the Beaudoin-Dobbie Report. The best example of this is likely the Renewal of Canada Conference that was held in Montreal.[29] Its purpose was to discuss the Canadian economic union, but interest group representatives and members of the public developed an attraction to the social covenant proposal put forward by the Ontario government and the federal NDP. The economic union proposals would have prohibited any laws, programs, or government practices that constituted barriers to or restrictions on the mobility of goods, services, persons, or capital (with exceptions for reasons of national interest or the promotion of regional development and equalization) and would have provided Parliament with the power to make laws for the efficient functioning of the economic union (with the agreement of at least seven provinces, representing 50 percent of the population).[30] This agenda was supported (indeed, driven) by the business community, most notably the Business Council on National Issues, which had a close relationship with the Mulroney government. On the other hand, the social covenant was being driven by New Democrats in Ontario and the federal Parliament, along with a coalition of equality-seeking, anti-poverty, social policy, environmental, and union groups. It would have placed in the Constitution a commitment to provide comprehensive, universal, portable, publicly administered, and accessible health care throughout Canada; to provide adequate social services and benefits that would ensure reasonable access to housing, food, and other basic needs; to provide high-quality public primary and secondary education to all residents as well as reasonable access to postsecondary education; to provide for the rights of workers to organize and bargain collectively; and to protect and preserve the integrity of the environment (albeit in an economically sustainable manner). It also would have created a review agency to report on government performance with regard to meeting these goals.[31]

By insisting that the social covenant was, in effect, the other half of Canada's political union and that it be given at least equal time with the economic union, not only did the "non-elite" representatives at the conference turn the event into a discussion of the social union (the term more commonly used today) but they also locked the concept of a social union into the political discourse of the period. One of the final issues to be settled between the NDP and the PCs in negotiating the content of the Beaudoin-Dobbie Report was the fate of the government's economic union proposals. The social union was sufficiently secure that the PCs decided they had to accept the social covenant proposals, and they decided that the only way to save their economic union agenda from oblivion was to attach their economic union proposals to them. When it came to the Charlottetown Accord negotiations themselves, the social union and the economic union proposals continued to be linked as a statement of principles.[32] This, however, was a significant downgrading of the federal government's economic union proposals, which had originally called for a judicially enforceable constitutional commitment to the interprovincial free movement of goods, services, people, and capital. The roots of this negotiating dynamic can be traced directly back to that weekend in Montreal.

The record of the period leading up to the negotiation of the Charlottetown Accord in the spring and summer of 1992 would suggest that political elites realized, in the wake of the defeat of the Meech Lake Accord, that serious citizen engagement had become a mandatory part of constitutional renewal. Yet, as the intergovernmental negotiations that led to the Charlottetown Accord commenced, citizen engagement was effectively shoved aside. As a consequence, the Accord began slowly to diverge from the democratic consensus that had begun to develop through the previous processes.

At first, the divergence between politicians and the public that they had so carefully courted for the better part of two years was subtle. To their credit, people like Joe Clark (the federal minister for constitutional affairs) and Ontario premier Bob Rae tried to bring as much transparency as possible to the Charlottetown negotiations, as they recognized that this was the key to creating a climate of trust within an environment in which citizen deference to elite decision making, and trust in elite decision makers, was low. Rae effectively created the Charlottetown process when Mulroney was planning to take a constitutional reform package directly to a referendum as a way of forcing the premiers' hands. Rae also secured the full participation of the four leading national Aboriginal organizations in the negotiations; later, one of these groups, the Native Council of Canada (now the Congress of Aboriginal Peoples), invited some equity group representatives to take part in the negotiations as part of their delegation. The two territorial governments were also given seats at the negotiating table, in belated recognition of their status as part of the federation. Even with these additions to the negotiating table, though, the Charlottetown negotiations were challenged in court by the Native Women's Association of Canada (NWAC), which had been excluded from the process.[33] While NWAC eventually lost its case, its challenge was taken seriously and sent a ripple of concern through the negotiating rooms.

Clark, for his part, was committed to keeping people informed about the progress of the negotiations through daily press conferences involving all the ministers who participated in the negotiations.[34] After an intense spring and early summer of negotiations among ministers and the representatives of the national Aboriginal organizations, on July 7, 1992, Clark was able to announce that an agreement had been reached between himself, the provincial and territorial premiers (except for Quebec's Premier Bourassa, who had absented himself from this round of intergovernmental negotiations to await "acceptable offers" from the rest of Canada), and the leaders of the four national Aboriginal organizations represented at the negotiating table. Mulroney had left for that year's OECD summit in Europe prior to July 7, likely still believing that the Clark negotiations would end in failure; his enthusiasm for the July 7 agreement was notably absent when he was interviewed about it in Europe.

The negotiations did not, however, come to an end with Clark's success. While other ministers and first ministers believed that the July 7 agreement would be acceptable to both Quebec and the other provinces, Mulroney was convinced that Quebec would reject it.[35] He invited the provincial premiers to a "first ministers lunch" on August 4; however, in part to satisfy Bourassa, who had agreed to attend, he excluded the territorial premiers and the national Aboriginal leaders who had been part of the earlier negotiations. When Mulroney took over from Clark as the federal negotiator, the latter's efforts at transparency were shoved aside in favour of another Meech-like process involving quick, brokerage-style negotiations. It seemed to observers close to the process that Mulroney had learned nothing from the aftermath of the Meech Lake negotiations. As, between August 4 and

August 28, 1992, the July 7 agreement was changed in closed-door negotiations to accommodate Bourassa's demands, the public's distrust of the political class and elite accommodation models of decision making grew. People remembered their exclusion from the creation of the Meech Lake Accord, and their dislike of the particular politicians making the decisions behind the closed doors, particularly Mulroney, began to generate a deep suspicion about the Charlottetown Accord.[36] As Johnston et al. indicate, acceptance or rejection of the idea of Canada as a construction of founding peoples, and the acceptance of elite accommodation models of decision making inherent in this conception, constituted a critical division between the "Yes" and "No" voters in the referendum on the Accord.[37] In their words, "not only did voters reject a specific product of elite bargaining, but they also severely constrained prospects for future bargaining."[38]

The data from Johnston et al.'s study of voting patterns in the Charlottetown Accord referendum support two possible versions of the argument that a rejection of elite accommodation models of decision making, driven by a reduction in both trust and deference, was a significant factor in the rejection of the Charlottetown Accord. One argument supported by the evidence is that one's orientation to political parties, political leaders, and political institutions, those responsible for making the elite accommodation model work, exerted a powerful influence on one's response to the Accord.[39] The other, more indirect argument that the data could also support is one about the reaction to Quebec elsewhere in Canada. As Johnston et al. note, Canadians outside Quebec were not fearful about the unity of the country, possibly because their political elites had cried wolf too many times, but they were anxious that Quebec might "get too much" out of the Accord.[40] Of course, the history that left these voters with the impression that Quebec's demands were insatiable and that Quebec's agenda was constantly being pandered to is the history of intergovernmental decision making among political elites. Thus, the negative reaction to Quebec is, in many ways, a rejection of deference to elite accommodation.

The renewed public concern about the legitimacy of the Charlottetown Accord put Mulroney and the other first ministers in a bind; it made a national referendum on the Charlottetown Accord a necessity, despite the limitations of referenda as vehicles for democratic discourse, and it simultaneously made approval of the constitutional reform package that first ministers had negotiated more difficult.[41] The public's lack of trust in, and lack of deference to, political accommodations was a regular theme in the criticism of the Charlottetown Accord during the fall 1992 referendum campaign and was encapsulated in one of the two catchphrases from the referendum campaign for which Reform Party leader Preston Manning is remembered – "Know more." Indeed, the demand for legal text and the assertions that the lack of such text was proof that the first ministers were trying to hide something from the public is a prime example of the huge role distrust played in the referendum campaign and ultimate defeat of the Charlottetown Accord in October 1992.

How did politicians become so disconnected from the public they were supposed to represent? And why, in intergovernmental relations, does it keep happening, creating gaps to this day between the rhetoric of commitment to citizen engagement, such as that in the Social Union Framework Agreement,[42] and the actions of governments in making national policy? Writing soon after the defeat of the Charlottetown Accord, Susan Delacourt claimed that the style of the negotiations demonstrated a mutual, and destructive, lack of respect between politicians and the public.[43] There is much merit to this claim; however, even more, Meech and Charlottetown are about the strength of familiarity and faith in shared norms of behaviour.

Because of the structure of the pre-1982 Constitution, constitutional theory and politics in Canada focused on the allocation of powers between governments. Occasionally, human rights issues were addressed in constitutional law (as was the case with the Senate Persons reference[44] and local prohibition case),[45] but this was rare. Governments came to understand the rules of the game of federal-provincial politics, and bureaucrats in the field developed long-standing relationships and shared norms of behaviour. Nongovernmental organizations, citizens, Aboriginal peoples, and territories, which were suddenly part of our constitutional politics and part of intergovernmental politics more generally, were unfamiliar to the established players in Canadian intergovernmental politics. The new players did not feel bound by the rules of the intergovernmental relations game as they had had no role in establishing those rules. They also lacked the long-standing relationships with others whose opinions on particular issues may have been in conflict with their own. These relationships allowed conflicts to be managed and overcome for the sake of the parties' long-term interests, which was essential to the effective functioning of intergovernmental relations. Governments failed, and too often fail still, to understand that, with new actors in our national political discourse – whether they are territorial governments and Aboriginal peoples at the intergovernmental negotiating table or a much more attentive, astute, and less deferential public – their old, familiar ways had to either obtain democratic legitimacy in the eyes of these actors or change into something that could gain such legitimacy.

The events of this period hold important lessons for managing the federation today, the clearest of which is that many citizens care, possibly more than ever, about national policy and the potential effects of intergovernmental bargaining on the quality of national policies and programs. Canadians are not prepared to trust their politicians to decide on their behalf what constitutes good national policy: deference is dead, and its resurrection seems unlikely. The extensive citizen involvement in the Commission on the Future of Health Care in Canada (the Romanow Commission) over the course of 2002 supports this conclusion. The Romanow Commission provided citizens with several different means of input, and people took advantage of these opportunities in significant numbers. For example, 13,109 on-line workbooks were completed, along with 1,083 paper versions; approximately 13,500 issue surveys were completed; and approximately 14,000 letters, e-mails, and calls to the 1-800 number were received.[46] In addition, the commission, in partnership with the Canadian Policy Research Networks (CPRN), held twelve regional, day-long "deliberative dialogue" sessions, each of which brought together forty randomly selected Canadians. As well, of the 627 organizations and individuals who made presentations to the Romanow Commission in its twenty-one days of public hearings, 265 presentations were made by individuals.[47] As CPRN senior fellow and former president Judith Maxwell and several co-authors commented in reporting on the results of the Romanow Commission's citizens' dialogues:

> Much has been written in the past decade about the decline in deference for political institutions and weak participation in the political process ... Canadians' response to the Citizens' Dialogue on the Future of Health Care in Canada is a testament to [their] desire to participate. In their random telephone calls, Ekos Research Associates found it easy to interest potential participants in the project, even though people were asked to commit a full day on a weekend and in some cases to travel long distances ... Once engaged in the dialogues, they showed unfailing energy, over an eight-hour session with only one short break. They were sophisticated, passionate, spontaneous, thoughtful, and, in the end, logical and consistent in their conclusions ... Independent observers at the individual sessions were astonished at the quality of the engagement ... As [the participants] came to understand that the session was designed for their use, they facilitated their own small groups, and seized the opportunity to learn, to talk to each other, and to speak directly to the Commissioner through the video camera.[48]

The second lesson is that, if they are trusted and engaged by governments in the right fora and are given enough time to come to understand what, for the intergovernmental relations community, has become second nature, Canadians are quite capable of making the kinds of accommodations among differing positions that are so much a part of the intergovernmental bureaucratic machine. This is the lesson of the Renewal of Canada conferences and the Romanow Commission's Citizens' Dialogue on the Future of

Health Care in Canada. To quote Maxwell et al. regarding the Romanow Commission's dialogues:

> Participants struggled with the contradictions in their own values. It was relatively easy to construct a wish list of what they wanted from the health care system. It was more difficult to decide how to pay for it, and who should pay. In the end, they dropped things from their wish list, and relented on their aversion to tax increases. By the end of the dialogues, citizens agreed to make adjustments in their own behaviour, and to change the way they interact with the health care system in ways that would have been unimaginable 10 years ago. As they began to work through these more difficult choices, participants felt like "real citizens." They engaged.[49]

Canada is not the sum of its governments but, rather, a democratic polity that actually cares about the "big issues" of national policy and about finding the answer that will promote the legitimacy and integrity of our nation.

Some governments have shown a real interest in new ways of making constitutive decisions: British Columbia, with its Citizens' Assembly on Electoral Reform, is an excellent example, as was the Romanow Commission's effort at transparency and citizen engagement. But, on the whole, intergovernmental relations is still largely a "closed shop" of bureaucrats and politicians. In designing new mechanisms to make the governance of our federation more legitimate, governments must accept that, in a democratic society, legitimacy requires the public to have a role in shaping not only the terms of the debate but also the results of the debate.

Further, those who get to define who has access to intergovernmental negotiations (the federal and provincial governments) should remember the other lesson of the Meech Lake/Charlottetown period. The "junior governments," both territorial governments and national Aboriginal organizations, and possibly municipalities as well, have a valid claim to be at the intergovernmental table; they are, after all, representative bodies of polities with either a substantial degree of self-government today or an unassailable claim to a substantial degree of self-government in the future (and, one would hope, the near future). The territories and the national Aboriginal organizations also proved, in the Charlottetown process, that they can contribute responsibly to the conduct of intergovernmental relations and that they bring important perspectives to intergovernmental negotiations. These governments deserve to be more than simply consulted: they should be full partners in the federation. They certainly cannot be ignored.

In the end, to come back to where this commentary began, deference, like Monty Python's Norwegian Blue parrot, is dead; the world of constitution making, and of intergovernmental decision making generally, is a more democratic and pluralist world than it was in the decades prior to 1982. If this fact is ignored, the legitimacy of intergovernmental relations and federal governance will die, too. The fates of the Meech Lake Accord and the Charlottetown Accord continue to be reminders of this reality.

Acknowledgments

This chapter is based on presentations made at two conferences that took place in 2004: Constructing Tomorrow's Federalism: New Routes to Effective Governance, in Regina, Saskatchewan, and Constitutionalism and Cultural Pluralism, in Edinburgh, Scotland. I would like to thank the staff and fellows of the Saskatchewan Institute of Public Policy, various friends and colleagues, and the anonymous reviewers for taking the time to read earlier drafts of this text and to provide helpful comments. Any errors or omissions that remain are strictly mine.

Notes

1 The most thorough account of this development in a Canadian context is likely Neil Nevitte's *The Decline of Deference: Canadian Value Change in Cross-National Perspective* (Peterborough: Broadview Press, 1996); see also Peter C. Newman, *The Canadian Revolution, 1985-1995: From Deference to Defiance* (Toronto: Viking Books, 1995), esp. 279-81, for a thorough discussion of changing Canadian attitudes in the post-*Charter* era and the role of the *Charter of Rights* in inciting this "revolution."
2 Nevitte, *Decline of Deference*, 104, 305.
3 Ibid., 301.
4 I was one of those participants. Having been a law student specializing in constitutional law and a summer resident of Ottawa during the negotiation of, and debate over, the Meech Lake Accord, I found myself articling for the Constitutional Law Branch of the Ontario Ministry of the Attorney General and being involved in discussions of Ontario's position during the 1990 attempts to save that accord through a "companion resolution." Upon the completion of my articles and bar admission exams, I was hired to provide advice to, first, the Special Joint Committee of the Senate and the House of Commons on the Process for Amending the Constitution of Canada and, subsequently, the Special Joint Committee of the Senate and the House of Commons on the Renewal of Canada – two committees that set the stage for the negotiation of what was to become the Charlottetown Accord. I was then hired by the Executive Council Office of the Government of the Yukon to be part of the territory's negotiating team during the negotiation of the Charlottetown Accord and the accompanying draft legal text. Thus, the progress of Canada's constitutional debates was a central part of my intellectual and professional life for over five years.
5 For example, while the Social Union Framework Agreement included commitments to report on outcomes of social programs to the public, to use third parties to assist in assessing progress on social priorities, and to "ensure effective mechanisms for Canadians to participate in developing social priorities and reviewing outcomes," reporting was never consistent or rigorous, and the promised mechanisms for citizen inclusion in social policy development were never created. Ultimately, the Social Union Framework Agreement became largely irrelevant not only to the public but also to governments. See *A Framework to Improve the Social Union for Canadians: An Agreement between the Government of Canada and the Governments of the Provinces and Territories*, February 4, 1999, 3.
6 Nevitte, *Decline of Deference*, 104.
7 Ibid., 9.
8 See, for example, Roy Romanow, John D. Whyte, and Howard Leeson, *Canada ... Notwithstanding: The Making of the Constitution, 1976-1982* (Toronto: University of Toronto Press, 1984), 248.
9 Richard Johnston, André Blais, Elisabeth Gidengil, and Neil Nevitte, *The Challenge of Direct Democracy: The 1992 Canadian Referendum* (Montreal/Kingston: McGill-Queen's University Press, 1996), 44.

10 See, for example, Philip Saunders, "The *Charter* at 20," *CBC News Online*, April 2002, http://www.cbc.ca/news/features/constitution/; "The *Charter*: Uniting or Dividing Canadians," *CRIC Papers*, no. 5, April 2002, http://www.cric.ca/pdf/cahiers/cricpapers_april2002.pdf.
11 Johnston et al., *Challenge of Direct Democracy*, 44.
12 Reginald Whitaker, "Democracy and the Canadian Constitution," *And No One Cheered: Federalism, Democracy and the Constitution Act*, ed. Keith Banting and Richard Simeon (Toronto: Methuen, 1983), 240-41.
13 Peter M. Leslie, *Rebuilding the Relationship: Quebec and Its Confederation Partners* (Kingston: Institute of Intergovernmental Relations, 1987), 42.
14 Mollie Dunsmuir, *Constitutional Activity from Patriation to Charlottetown (1980-1992)*, Library of Parliament Backgrounder BP406, November 1995.
15 See *The Report of the Special Joint Committee of the Senate and the House of Commons on the 1987 Constitutional Accord* (Ottawa: House of Commons, 1987), 131-32. As noted by Mollie Dunsmuir in *Constitutional Activity from Patriation to Charlottetown*, once the Government of Quebec passed a resolution adopting the Meech Lake Accord, it became virtually impossible to change the accord even in the face of "egregious errors."
16 *The Report of the Special Joint Committee of the Senate and the House of Commons on the 1987 Constitutional Accord*, 141.
17 Ibid., 132.
18 Constitution Amendment, 1987, s. 9.
19 *Penikett v. Canada* (1987), 43 D.L.R. (4th) 324; (1987), 45 D.L.R. (4th) 108 (C.A.); leave to appeal to the Supreme Court of Canada refused [1988] 1 S.C.R. xii.
20 The fourth and final conference on Aboriginal constitutional matters was held on March 26 and 27, 1987, while the First Ministers Conference that led to the Meech Lake Accord was held on April 30, 1987. For a full chronology of the period, see Library of Parliament, *The Constitution since Patriation: Chronology*, http://www.parl.gc.ca/information/about/related/Federal/ConstPat.asp?Language=F.
21 For a discussion of how Aboriginal peoples effectively used the media to generate public sympathy with regard to their exclusion from the Meech Lake Accord, see David Taras, "Mass Media and Political Crisis: Reporting Canada's Constitutional Struggles," *Canadian Journal of Communications* (online) 18, 2 (1993). Available at http://www.cjc-online.ca/viewarticle.php?id=164.
22 "Liberal Resurgence on the Rock" *CBC Archives* (http://archives.cbc.ca/IDC-1-73-928-5476/politics_economy/elections_newfoundland/clip4, viewed January 17, 2005).
23 See *The Report of the Special Committee to Study the Proposed Companion Resolution to the Meech Lake Accord* (Ottawa: House of Commons, 1990), 69-71 for the complete text of the New Brunswick Companion Resolution.
24 Library of Parliament.
25 Ibid.
26 Johnston et al., *Challenge of Direct Democracy*, 51-52.
27 Chris Wood, "In a Mood for Compromise," *Maclean's*, 105, 1 (January 6, 1992), 46.
28 Roy MacGregor, "Dear Joe: Your Unity Committee Has Fallen Off the Rails" *Ottawa Citizen*, November 5, 1991.
29 The Renewal of Canada Conference: Economic Union, Montreal, January 31 to February 2, 1992.
30 Government of Canada, *Shaping Canada's Future Together: Proposals* (Ottawa: Minister of Supply and Services, 1991), 30-31.
31 *Report of the Special Joint Committee of the Senate and the House of Commons on a Renewed Canada*, February 28, 1992, 122-23. After this report was released, Lorne Nystrom, MP, and I met with the Ontario deputy minister of intergovernmental affairs to discuss the outcomes of the Parliamentary Committee process and the transition to intergovernmental negotiations. In a humorous moment at this meeting, the deputy minister jokingly chastised us for having secured such a rich social union commitment, including the right of workers to organize and bargain collectively, as it left the Ontario government with nothing more to "win" on the social union agenda through intergovernmental negotiation.
32 Draft Legal Text, October 9, 1992, s. 31.

33 *Native Women's Association of Canada v. Canada* [1992] 2 F.C. 462 (F.C. T.D.); [1992] 3 F.C. 192 (F.C.A.); [1994] 3 S.C.R. 627 (S.C.C.).

34 David Taras notes that Clark was adept at using the media to rally support for his positions. As one example of this, Taras points to the interview Clark provided to CBC Newsworld when the July 7 agreement was under attack in the federal cabinet. He felt that this appearance, and the media coverage it generated, seemed to strengthen Clark's credibility and may have given him some more power at the cabinet table. See Taras, "Mass Media and Political Crisis."

35 Susan Delacourt, *United We Fall: In Search of a New Canada* (Toronto: Penguin Books, 1994), 53. Interestingly, Bourassa's response to the July 7 agreement was non-committal rather than clearly oppositional.

36 Johnston et al. note that negative reaction to the Charlottetown Accord in the "Rest of Canada" appeared even before the Accord was concluded and that Mulroney's association with it was highly damaging. They suggest that, for many voters, the vote in the referendum on the Charlottetown Accord must have been a repudiation of the political class in general and of Mulroney's leadership in particular. See Johnston et al., *The Challenge of Direct Democracy*, 64, 137, 277. Given Mulroney's notable absence from the process up to July 7, and the relative popularity of Clark, the connection between the Accord and Mulroney is likely to have been a consequence of his involvement in the negotiations that took place between August 4 and August 28.

37 Ibid., 253.

38 Ibid., 251.

39 Ibid., 190.

40 Ibid., 113-14.

41 Johnston et al.'s analysis of the Charlottetown Accord referendum indicates that knowledge changes attitudes. It also indicates that many voters, for lack of knowledge, fail to make the connection between their own opinions and their choice of for whom (or what) to vote. This supports the idea that referenda are extremely poor mechanisms for making choices on complex issues in a democratic society. See ibid., 250.

42 *A Framework to Improve the Social Union for Canadians*.

43 See, for example, Delacourt, *United We Fall*, xviii-xix., 21, 26.

44 *Edwards v. Canada (Attorney General)* (1929), [1930] A.C. 124 (J.C.P.C.).

45 *A.G. Ontario v. A.G. Canada (Local Prohibitions)*, [1896] A.C. 348 (P.C.).

46 Roy J. Romanow, *Building on Values: The Future of Health Care in Canada* (Ottawa: Commission on the Future of Health Care in Canada, 2002), 295, 270.

47 Romanow, *Building on Values*, 271-72, 274-85.

48 Judith Maxwell, Karen Jackson, Barbara Legowski, Steven Rosell, Daniel Yankelovich, Pierre-Gerlier Forest, and Larissa Lozowchuk, *Report on Citizens' Dialogue on the Future of Health Care in Canada* (Ottawa: Commission on the Future of Health Care in Canada, 2002), 67.

49 Ibid.

5

Federalism in Canada: A World of Competing Definitions and Views

Marc Chevrier

Although the literature on federalism in Canada is abundant, the country's two political communities have no common set of criteria for defining the federal system. Overall, this literature has not really aimed at situating the Canadian federal regime among a general theory of federal systems; rather, it has been much more interested in exposing the specificity of the federal arrangement that was hammered out by local elites in the colonies of British North America. Some questions have thus become canonical, such as: Was the founding law of 1867 a unilateral imperial law of Westminster or a compact concluded between the founding colonies or peoples?[1] Was it a federal or a legislative union? A lot of focus has been put on determining whether the balance of intergovernmental power dynamics is tipping towards centralization or decentralization. Moreover, the mere existence of two linguistic communities that find it difficult to adopt a common language of coexistence within the Canadian ensemble has triggered inexhaustible reflections on how to reconcile diversity of languages and cultures as well as on how to approach the question of differentiated political status in a liberal society.

It is often forgotten that federalism is an old method of dividing powers in order to institutionalize political pluralism (and, indeed, other forms of pluralism) on a territorial basis.[2] By conceiving a federal republic large enough to suit a whole continent, the American founding fathers created a genuinely novel political formula – representative federalism – that relied on the pluralism of diverse minorities to establish democracy on firm ground.[3] Since the nineteenth century, Americans have taken pride in possessing a theoretical corpus that is seen as a common reference point for understanding their federal Constitution. In Canada, however, the merging of three colonies into a so-called federal union in 1867 was conducted in such a way that the founding fathers left no text as famous as the Federalist Papers, and, thus far, it seems that no one has yet filled this void with a work worthy of a Montesquieu.[4]

Is it necessary, however, for such a grand theory to accompany the analysis of the Canadian federal system? Although one might concede the virtual impossibility of giving federalism a universal definition,[5] it is difficult to analyze a political system, to compare it to another, or to come up with proposals for constitutional reform without having in hand a shared conception of federalism. Moreover, even if the observer wants to ground her/his analysis on anything but a normative assumption, the fact that political actors usually have their own normative conception of what a federation is about cannot be disregarded, particularly since such visions influence the interplay of institutions and the goals pursued by reforms. Nevertheless, it appears not only that there exists no common definition or theory of federalism but also that, in fact, there is a plurality of these conceptions, each of which expresses itself separately in the country's two linguistic communities.[6] This may partly be explained by the diversity of approaches found in political science, a phenomenon that is enhanced by the fact that the way in which political scientists look at Canada tends to be affected by their linguistic and cultural backgrounds. Furthermore, one should be aware of the strength of the legal profession in Canada. By their presence in every branch of the state, lawyers help shape the political discourse and build their own representations of the state according to the assumptions of their profession.[7] Thus, just as political scientists may disagree over the nature of Canada's federal union, depending on the linguistic community to which they belong, so constitutional lawyers may disagree over the nature of this union, depending on whether they practise common law or civil law.

The Study of Federalism in Canadian Political Science

Before the aforementioned differences can be demonstrated, some remarks should be made regarding the methods and approaches used by political science in its study of Canada's federal system. First of all, it seems that the political analysis of federalism proceeded from an anti-legalistic position. Many analysts of federalism grounded their comparative studies in works written by constitutional lawyers. The seminal work of K.C. Wheare, *Federal Government*,[8] first published in 1946, is often referred to and used as a springboard for further study, although it was soon criticized for having too narrow a perspective and for focusing too much on institutions and norms.[9] The desire of many political scientists to free themselves from legalistic analysis can be understood when one considers the need that Canadian political science felt to separate itself from the field of law and to establish itself as an autonomous field of study. Its willingness to dissociate itself from law was so strong that, from the 1930s to the 1960s, political science in Canada has pretty much defined itself in contrast to law, often to the point of excluding the latter from its field of investigations.[10] While they generally left the description of federal institutions and of constitutional norms to law, political scientists dedicated themselves to the study of governmental processes and to the interplay between state and society.[11]

Political science in Canada has thus sought to shed light on the informal processes of exchange, negotiation, and accommodation used by political actors to adapt institutions, to develop policies, or to reform the constitutional system. The prevalence of this non-formalistic approach has been obvious in the way the role of the Senate is treated. Many observers underline the strangeness of the second chamber, composed of appointed senators, which appears as an anomaly in comparison to other second federal chambers. However, the development of cooperative federalism in the 1960s, which flourished with institutionalized intergovernmental relations, was viewed as the consequence of the Senate's inability to channel the voices of the provinces in the federal Parliament.[12] Political scientists thus designed many new concepts to describe the informal processes taking place outside the parliamentary arena: for example, executive federalism,[13] along with intra- and interstate federalism.[14] By suggesting that intergovernmental federalism amounts to a form of internal confederalism, this new conceptualization went so far as to describe these intergovernmental exchanges as a kind of federal-provincial diplomacy.[15] Although Canada may look like an exception in terms of the general features associated with classical federal systems, the very fact that informal exchanges are taken into account serves to categorically situate the country among a variety of federations. It may even constitute a perfect expression of an interstate form of intergovernmental federalism. Starting as an exception, Canada then becomes a model. The same non-formalistic approach has dominated the analysis of constitutional reform. Due to the uncertainties of reform and the stalemate that has paralyzed the country since the failure of the Meech Lake and Charlottetown accords, studies have shifted their focus from formal processes associated with the amending formula to informal ones. This has proceeded in order to bring to light non-constitutional mechanisms for adjusting the distribution of powers and accommodating the claims put forward by Quebec and First Nations.

Many of the analysts of the federal question in Canada who were largely influenced by the works of the systemic school of thought – works such as those of David Easton and Karl Deutsch – have tried to situate their study within a more general theory of political systems. They aimed at enlarging the matrix of the explanatory factors that affect the working of the federal system in Canada in such a way as to include in their model elements like society, political culture, parties, and the economy. Consequently, the systemic approach moved the focus of federalist studies from institutions to society. Having become dominant in the United States after the Second World War, behaviouralism and systems analysis made a conclusive foray into Canadian territory. Systems analysis opened the door to the sociological analysis of federalism (which came to be conceptualized as the result of social forces underlying the state) and to studies that treated the federal system as both a dependent and an independent variable. It is thus not surprising that many political scientists in English Canada worked to determine the interrelation between the legal and institutional dimensions of federalism and its social and economic dimensions. Institutions, however, have not totally vanished in political science. They have been reintroduced through neoinstitutionalism, currently a major paradigm in the discipline.[16]

The study of federalism in Canada has also been influenced by the functionalist approach, much in use in political economy, which is based on the calculus of interest, utility, and the maximization of the state's macroeconomic functions. Seen through these lenses, the federal system appears as a bundle of constraints imposed on the decision-making processes that shape state policies, in particular, on the state's capacity to perform functions such as the regulation of the economic union, stabilization, and redistribution.[17] Other studies, less committed to economic efficiency, endeavoured to determine the limitations the federal system imposes on the design of social policies and/or on the access of social groups to governmental processes.[18] Finally, it took a long time before the historical and ideological genesis of the federal regime in Canada came to the fore in political science. It was only in the 1980s that thorough studies of the ideological foundation of the Dominion of Canada were published,[19] and it wasn't until the end of the 1990s that the pre-confederative debates that took place in British North American colonies attracted the attention of political scientists.[20]

Other observations may be drawn from the diverse approaches used in the study of Canadian federalism. The distinction between federalism and federation, implied in many works, has not always been explicitly stated.[21] In fact, the expression "Canadian federalism" appears conceptually ambiguous if the distinction is not made between, on the one hand, the constitutional system of the state, modelled after principles and techniques for distributing powers, and, on the other hand, the elements of pluralism emanating from society and interacting with the state and political parties. By confusing federalism and federation as conceptual tools, the dialectical dynamics that are associated with this particular political system are lost: indeed, these dynamics imply a tension between a political regime seeking to preserve its formal and ideological foundations and the conflicts arising from social and cultural pluralism. As a result, this mixture of concepts undermines the salience of the constitutional regime as a distinct aspect of the political system. This distinction between the two concepts was made by systems analysis theorists like David Easton, who is no longer referred to anywhere near as frequently as he was in the 1970s and 1980s. For Easton, what he called the "political regime" enjoyed relative autonomy as a component of the political system. Far from reducing the latter to its normative ingredients, Easton includes in his "matrix" official values and a particular structure of authority that allocates roles between political actors.[22]

The concept of a federal system has been widely used for studying federalism in Canada, and it is Ronald Watts, the pioneer of comparative federalism in Canada, who gave this concept its most extensive application. Watts created a typology of federal systems in which a federation appears as one type of political system among a variety of others. More specifically, it is singled out as the system in which constitutionalism plays the greatest role in distributing powers.[23] By putting the federation on an equal footing with political arrangements as diverse as political unions, confederations, leagues, and so on, the concept of federal systems ends up encompassing any form of intra- or interstate arrangement that contrasts with the classical model of the unitary, centralized, and symmetrical state. Moreover, this typology depicts a group of "common structural characteristics" of federations without indicating which method or theory the analyst employed to derive such characteristics.[24] The typology proposed by Watts reveals a kind of political science whose main concern is to compare the Canadian federal regime with a host of institutional arrangements and to work out sophisticated classifications without aiming at making explicit the normative implications of a federation as a political regime. Descriptive and taxonomic in scope, such an undertaking has a limited explanatory capacity as it does not offer a comprehensive understanding of the interplay between state, society, and ideology within a federal system.

Finally, as a result of this non-formalistic approach in political science, it becomes difficult to evaluate how federal institutions and practices conform to a set of minimal requirements that flows from the idea of a federation as a principle of organizing the state and as a moral ideal of political behaviour. In that sense, one can say that Canada, compared to other federal systems, is still a quasi-federation. However, the insistence on the compensatory role played by federal-provincial "diplomacy" and on the practices of accommodating regional interests through central institutions such as the cabinet, which would supposedly offset the absence of any formal participation of provinces in the federal process of decision making, has given substance to the idea that the Canadian formula is an accomplished form of federation among an array of many equivalent models.[25] Therefore, the deficit of legitimacy that burdens federal institutions is neglected, and the federalization of Canada is seen as a finished enterprise that is to be protected from centrifugal forces threatening the existence of the country.[26]

Let us more closely assess the approaches adopted by political scientists according to their linguistic and cultural backgrounds. French-speaking authors are generally more prone than English-speaking authors to remind us of the historical genesis of the Canadian federal system; many of them underline the fact that Canada has kept, over time, the unitary and imperial characteristics enshrined in its founding law.[27] They often point out the ambiguous nature of federalist discourse in Canada, claiming that such a discourse.describes institutions and loyalty to the country in a language that is more suitably applied to unitary countries.[28] Often placing more emphasis on the descriptive study of institutions than their English-speaking colleagues, French-speaking authors are less eager to do comparative analyses, though neither francophones nor anglophones have dared to develop an overall theory of federal systems.[29] Francophones are also less interested than anglophones in understanding the workings of the federal system in terms of economic efficiency or as a mechanism for limiting state power or for sustaining democracy as such; rather, they are keen on observing the dynamics relating to the distribution of powers between the two levels of government, especially with regard to bringing out the centralizing tendencies that threaten the federal equilibrium.[30] Whereas many anglophone political scientists tend to present Canada as among the most decentralized of known federations,[31] many francophone political scientists argue that, although provincial governments do enjoy a somewhat meaningful margin of freedom to govern, their autonomy is severely restricted by the federal government's preponderance in intergovernmental relations and by its financial and legal levers over the provinces. Indeed, contrary to the spirit of federalism, provincial governments are increasingly reduced to a state of de facto subordination. The many unilateral powers vested in the federal government give it a kind of imperial ascendancy over the provinces that is still reflected in intergovernmental relations and constitutional reform.[32] Like their anglophone colleagues, francophone analysts draw their analytical concepts from the huge Anglo-American literature; however, they also draw from the European literature – French, German, and Swiss – which happens to be more formalistic and theoretical than the Anglo-American literature.[33]

Both francophone and anglophone authors dedicate a large part of their analyses to exploring how to reform federal institutions in order to recognize linguistic and cultural diversity and to strengthen the cohesion of the federal system. However, while anglophone authors often view the objective of national unity and the aim of preserving the country's federal character as equivalent, francophone authors prefer to dissociate the two as national unity may be pursued at the expense of federalism altogether. Anglophone political scientists generally emphasize the risks of balkanization, which are claimed to result from the sovereigntist movement in Quebec or from the mounting alienation and discontent felt in western provinces or the Maritimes towards central Canada. For many francophone authors, the threats to Canada's federal system are to be found less in the centrifugal forces and more in the centripetal ones. The mitigated victory won by the "federalist" forces in the October 1995 referendum has reinforced a "defederalizing" process under the leadership of the federal government – now called the "national government" – for the sake of preserving the integrity of the Canadian nation.[34] In a study comparing Canada to Belgium and Spain, François Rocher, Christian Rouillard, and André Lecours describe what they conclude to be the dominant spirit of federalism emerging in Canada:

> But federalism seems to be mainly understood as an administrative arrangement in which only the principles of uniformity and homogeneity can guarantee a fair and equal treatment of every citizen. The logic of Canadian federalism is more congruent with a unitary representation of Canada than with the spirit of federalism which combines unity with diversity and seeks to recognize, preserve and promote distinct collective identities with a larger political partnership.[35]

Despite the differences of perspective and method between English- and French-speaking political scientists, both communities tend to point out that the political science literature lacks a comprehensive and theoretical analysis of federalism that captures the complex dynamic of federal systems. This is the conclusion of Richard Simeon's overview of more than seventy years of literature, mostly from English-speaking political scientists. Too much focus has been placed on the working of Canadian federalism and not enough on comparative analysis or on a grand theory.[36] In a foreword written for a thesis on Canadian federalism and Quebec's cultural identity, Guy Laforest bluntly admitted that Quebec's intellectuals have shown little interest in federalism over the last thirty years, favouring instead themes like sovereignty, nationalism, feminism, and globalization.[37] During this time, more systematic studies of federalism have been found in law faculties. According to Laforest, this is why, in the domain of political philosophy and intellectual history, there is still no major Quebec work that deals critically with the genesis of Canadian federalism and the differences between schools of thought found in Quebec and French Canada, on the one hand, and English Canada, on the other. This has been the case from the founding debates of 1867 up to the recent willingness of Jean Charest's Liberal government to renew federal practices.

This disquieting finding may help explain the new interest that many political scientists in Quebec have shown for a more normative and all-encompassing approach to the study of federalism.[38] This approach entails accepting the postulate that, before beginning empirical work, one cannot escape the necessity of making more explicit the normative content of federalism. Alain-G. Gagnon clearly adopts this approach in his study of asymmetrical federalism, in which he goes beyond the mere institutional aspects of implementing asymmetrical arrangements in order to dig out the values and ideologies that are inherent in this phenomenon.[39] Debates on asymmetrical federalism can thus be understood in light of three distinct normative justifications related to community, equality, and democracy, respectively. Dimitrios Karmis also addresses the revival of federalism in normative political theory.[40] According to him, an idea is never an end in itself and is often lost when applied to a particular institutional arrangement. It is not so much pragmatic considerations that determine the value and strength of a federal system as the latter's ability to fulfill certain normative objectives. However, the study of the normative conceptions of federalism is made all the more difficult by the fact that most of the history of political thought has been dominated by the defence of unitary states. According to Karmis, in Canada, three normative conceptions of federalism clash with one another: the universalist, the communitarian, and the pluralist.[41]

Relying on the conceptual framework developed by Watts and Blinder-bacher to sort out the structural characteristics associated with federal systems and identity, Jean-François Caron, Guy Laforest, and Catherine Vallières-Roland proposed a new conceptual tool designed to measure the health of Canadian federalism. The gap between these requirements and the functioning of institutions and practices observed in Canada is what they refer to as the "federal deficit." Although Canada seems to score well on many indicators, as compared to other countries, it fails to fulfill many requirements with regard to its Constitution, its federal institutions and practices, its political culture, and the coexistence of many national projects. François Rocher went further in explaining how French- and English-speaking analysts differed in their understanding of federalism, depending on their normative assumptions.[42] This difference of views is mainly due, he argues, to the fact that each linguistic community sees only one aspect of what federalism normatively implies. Francophones view federalism mainly as a means for securing a kind of autonomy that recognizes Quebec's specificity and thus guards it from any external interference or attempts to subordinate it to the federal government. The other major implication of federalism – the co-management of interdependence through processes that permit participation and solidarity among members of the federal state – is then neglected, if not discarded. Among anglophones, it is quite the opposite view that prevails. The pragmatic, managerial, and functional approach that Richard Simeon and Ian Robinson refer to as "modern federalism" leaves little room for provincial autonomy. Province building is then seen as a suspect, onerous, and unpalatable enterprise; hence, only the general sharing of governmental responsibilities monitored by so-called "national norms" is thought to be conducive to efficiency and legitimacy.

The Federal Question According to Lawyers

One might expect that an understanding of the workings of the Canadian federal system would be among the priorities of constitutional lawyers. However, it should be kept in mind that, in both civil law and common law, legal positivism has long prevailed in the study of constitutional law. Lawyers were not encouraged, nor did they want, to go beyond what positivism required of them, which was to make explicit the content of constitutional law and to put in order the different normative layers of this special domain of law. The main works in the field usually contain a preamble on the historical genesis of Canada's foundations, summarizing the events and motivations that led to the union of 1867. Allowing for some exceptions, one can say that constitutionalists have very little to say regarding federalism as a concept, relying instead on the classical distinctions between unitary, federal, and confederal forms of government. More recently, law professors Jean-François Gaudreault-Desbiens and Fabien Gélinas, in an essay that presents many theoretical and comparative contributions to federalism, dispensed with addressing the definition of federalism as such. They did, however, argue that one should overcome the "epistemological obstacle" of equating federalism as a whole with the form it happens to take in a particular country.[43]

There are sharp differences between the conclusions that various constitutionalists draw from the evolution of Canada's federal system. Constitutionalists from English Canada usually avoid dwelling on mere theory. In characterizing the nature of Canada's federal system, at least as it was in 1867, their analyses tend to rely on the premises established by K.C. Wheare. They willingly admit that, in that year, due to the numerous unifying elements contained in the founding act, the Dominion of Canada exhibited the features of a quasi-federal state. Nevertheless, they all conclude that contemporary Canada has evolved into a true federation. This is explained by the role that, until 1949, the British Judicial Committee of the Privy Council played in shaping the legal categories used for distributing powers. It is also explained by the fact that the unilateral powers vested in the federal cabinet, such as disallowance and reserve, fell into disuse.[44] Since a large community of lawyers accepts common law as a referential universe, constitutionalists in English Canada do not feel the need to go anywhere else for their doctrinal and theoretical sources. Nevertheless, Peter W. Hogg imported the concept of subsidiarity from Europe, believing that it is implied by the structure of the distribution of powers.

Furthermore, according to several constitutionalists, federalism does not offer a theoretical ground that is solid enough to support the foundations of Canada's federal system. Patrick Monahan, for instance, acknowledges that there is no normative theory of federalism that can legitimate Canada's federal system and explain its workings.[45] Legal discourse pertaining to federalism is, for him, a set of contradictory theories proceeding from radically different assumptions about the Canadian political community. According to Monahan, federalism, as a concept, is too indeterminate to offer any guidance in constitutional disputes. It has proved an unpredictable mechanism with regard to addressing the distribution of legislative powers, and it has led to judges having a strong proclivity to rely on policy considerations in their rulings. Moreover, not all constitutionalists welcome the idea that the Canadian Constitution should be interpreted in light of federalism.[46] Frank R. Scott often protested against attempts to apply a strict federalist interpretation to the constitutional text. According to him, the traditions, historical context, and practical necessities that confronted the founding fathers do not justify sacrificing the various centralizing elements found in the *Constitution Act*, 1867, on the altar of an abstract vision of federalism.[47] The Supreme Court's decision in the Quebec Secession Reference handed down in 1998, which asserted federalism as an implicit constitutional principle grounding the whole Canadian Constitution, has probably diminished the relevance of Monahan's and Scott's views on federalism as an overarching principle of constitutional law. Nevertheless, this decision has attracted relatively few comments in the juridical literature.[48] While stating in 2000 that the "analysis of Canadian constitutional law and jurisprudence based on systematic reflections concerning the relationship between constitutional adjudication and democratic politics has been, for the most part, sorely lacking," Sujit Choudhry and Robert Howse, in their analysis of the Quebec Secession Reference, offer few thoughts on federalism.[49] In an article published in the same year, Donna Greschner bemoans the paucity of legal scholarship on federalism during the 1990s.[50] The focus that legal academics have placed on the *Charter* has created an imbalance that was partially corrected in 2002 by John Saywell's huge historico-empirical study of more than 130 years of judicial interpretations of the *Constitution Act, 1867*.[51] This study, however, avoids theoretical definitions of federalism, preferring to applaud the work done by the Supreme Court over the last twenty years to rebalance the division of powers by expanding federal jurisdictions. In doing this, the Court departed progressively from the decisions of the British Judicial Committee of the Privy Council, whose jurisprudence, which was decentralizing and legally unsound, was the product, according to Saywell, of the influence of some extravagant Scottish Law Lords.

Like their anglophone colleagues, francophone constitutionalists begin their study of federalism with K.C. Wheare's analysis of the quasi-federal character of Canada in 1867. However, they do not follow the same path as do their English-speaking colleagues with respect to the evolution of the constitutional system. As a matter of method, many francophone constitutionalists define their concepts beforehand, often on the basis of a doctrinal corpus drawn largely from French literature. Many of them directly draw on the famous "laws" of George Scelle, a French law professor who made his mark by authoring a treatise on public international law. In this work, Scelle enunciates a set of "laws" that are characteristic of all federations – laws of superposition, participation, and autonomy.[52] In French literature on law and politics, these laws are still the starting point for defining regimes of federation.[53] For Guy Tremblay and Henri Brun, Canada is still a quasi-federation, although it has experienced some decentralization – a phenomenon that is due more to the magnanimity of the federal government than to a constitutional guarantee. In contemporary Canada, they argue, provincial autonomy still lacks a sufficient legal guarantee, with no mechanism provided for provincial input into the federal decision-making process and no equilibrium between legislative powers and fiscal resources.[54] Relying explicitly on Scelle's laws, André Tremblay came to the same conclusions.[55] Without going so far as to state that Canada is still a quasi-federation, Jacques-Yvan Morin, José Woerhling, Gérald Beaudoin, and Benoit Pelletier observe that its constitutional system has ensured that many unifying features are still in force.[56]

The newly published work of Eugénie Brouillet, *La négation de la nation*, is now viewed in Quebec as a major contribution to the study of Canadian federalism. It is a landmark contribution that distinguishes itself from the doctrinal literature normally written by French-speaking constitutional lawyers.[57] In order to provide a hermeneutical and comprehensive analysis of the genesis and evolution of Canadian federalism and how it relates to culture, Brouillet goes beyond the formalistic approach to law to provide a broad interpretation that is based in political science, philosophy, history, and sociology as well as law. Her thesis is that, contrary to the majority view that the 1867 Dominion of Canada constituted a highly centralized quasi-federation, it was a genuine federal system that was designed to accommodate Quebec's cultural specificity and national aspirations. The federal spirit that imbued the Constitution, thanks to the jurisprudence of the British Judicial Committee of the Privy Council, lasted until the Second World War; afterwards, the Supreme Court consistently gave precedence to building a Canadian national project rather than to accommodating the federalism inherited from the founding fathers. According to her definition of a federation, what she refers to as the "juridical definition of the federal state," the autonomy of member states is ensured by a rigid constitution that divides powers and that is interpreted by an independent tribunal. Surprisingly, she attributes little importance to the participation of member states in the federal decision-making process. This even though the European literature heralds the principle of participation as an essential feature of federal states. Brouillet's definition of a federation as being strictly tied to autonomy confirms what François Rocher observed of francophone literature on federalism: it is reluctant to contemplate dimensions of federalism that do not entail a strictly unfettered autonomy. Among constitutional lawyers in Quebec, analysis normally derives from case law on the distribution of powers produced by the Supreme Court. And the quasi-unanimous view is that the Court has, as a matter of judicial policy, managed to centralize the division of powers for the sake of a functionalist conception of efficiency by unscrupulously altering the bulk of rulings bequeathed by the British Judicial Committee of the Privy Council.[58]

The Federal Dynamic since 1982

To understand the federal dynamic in Canada, it is important to take into account how the constitutional reform of 1982 and the failure of the Meech Lake and Charlottetown accords affected Canada's political system. The fact that these events have diminished the importance attached to federalism is well acknowledged in the literature. Moreover, they have also led to the emergence of new social and political actors whose claims and strategies challenge executive federalism's dominance of the political agenda.

Since 1982, Canadian society has been fraught with contradictory tendencies, some favouring the federalization of the country, others favouring defederalization. It has become commonplace in Canada to view the independence movement in Quebec as the main seat of resistance to federalism. But social pluralism does not always buttress a federal system; it can also induce a logic of action and a discourse that are foreign, if not hostile, to the territoriality attached to federalism. Indeed, social pluralism and political pluralism do not necessarily go hand in hand, and this can be seen in the transformations of political culture that Canada has experienced since the entrenchment of the *Canadian Charter of Rights and Freedoms* in 1982. The *Charter*'s architects believed that it would foster national unity, which would henceforth be defined by individual entitlement to a common set of rights rather than by belonging to a particular territory, language, or culture. They counted on a reinforced national sentiment, crystallized by an expanded legal citizenship that would reduce the disparities created by the federal system and weaken the allegiance of Canadians (especially Quebeckers) to their provincial governments. According to Alan Cairns, the "constitutional refashioning of the community"[59] brought about by the 1982 reform has given rise to "constitutional minoritarianism"; that is, to the fragmentation of Canadian society into vocal social minorities whose identities are based on physical, social, or ethnic distinctions and whose status is enhanced by constitutional provisions.[60] According to Guy Laforest, the 1982 *Charter* "reinforces minoritarian identities that have no other territorial basis than the Canadian national community as a whole."[61] This mobilization of social and linguistic minorities around the Canadian *Charter* was made possible by a strategic alliance between these minorities and the federal government. This alliance has been in force since the end of the 1960s and, in the 1970s, resulted in the establishment of a federal program whose purpose was to finance the lawsuits put forth by these groups.[62]

However, one should be careful not to lump First Nations with these minorities or *Charter* groups. It is true that, since 1982, both these groups and First Nations have backed up their claims for recognition and better status by referring to the Constitution, and both have succeeded in entering the constitutional arena. Moreover, both First Nations and *Charter* groups have privileged lawsuits as a means of exerting influence over governments. However, although it may seem as though the Canadian *Charter* generated a unifying dynamic in Canada with respect to identity and citizenship, the Aboriginal challenge to the Canadian state, in the form of claims for self-government, is notably federalist in texture. Thanks to the constitutional entrenchment of Aboriginal peoples' rights in 1982, First Nations could expect to progressively free themselves from paternalistic tutelage and become, both as individuals and as peoples, real political subjects. One might have expected that the formal recognition of Aboriginal rights would proceed from the same foundations as did those related to individual liberties and official languages. However, the amendments made to section 35 of the *Constitution Act*, 1982, soon showed that Aboriginal claims were ultimately aimed at establishing autonomous governments with a constitutionally guaranteed territorial basis. To this can be added the attempts made by Aboriginal leaders to enter the Canadian government as legitimate representatives with mandates to deal with federal and provincial executives. In Canada, since 1982, an Aboriginal type of federalist regime has been emerging in juxtaposition with the existing dualistic federal system. This federal Aboriginal system is far from being symmetrical, which is hardly surprising, given that Aboriginal self-government has been created on an ad hoc basis and has developed in distinct patterns in various parts of the country. It would be easy to conclude that the rejection of the Charlottetown Accord in the 1992 referendum would have halted this process of federalization. However, it only halted the creation of a third order of Aboriginal governments; it did not keep First Nations from making claims for territorial autonomy, either through settlements negotiated with federal and provincial governments or through litigation.

Aboriginal autonomy, created by treaties and, in particular, by land claims agreements, has an ambiguous status. First Nations can no longer be seen as simple decentralized entities subject to the sovereign power of the Parliament. At the same time, they do not enjoy the prerogatives and the powers that are constitutionally guaranteed for provinces. Aboriginal governments have not yet obtained their share of the constituent power given by section 5 of the *Constitution Act*, 1982, but Aboriginal leaders have to be invited to constitutional conferences when Aboriginal rights are at stake. With the automatic entrenchment of treaties and land claims agreements, which freezes the distribution of powers negotiated by First Nations and governments, many labelled this process "treaty federalism." This form of federalism meets two requirements for making a federation: autonomy and separation. In that sense, Aboriginal autonomy amounts to a kind of sui generis quasi-federal system integrated into the existing Canadian constitutional framework. That Aboriginal claims have a federalist tinge is not something that is foreign to the culture of Aboriginal peoples, as is shown by several historical studies.[63]

Constitutional reforms attempted between 1987 and 1992 also reveal the unstable relationship between federalism and the federation. These constitutional rounds were the stage for two clashing demands: one contesting the pre-eminence given to federalism (and coming from groups seeking recognition of their non-territorial identities), the other expressing the willingness of governments to further federalize Canada. It may not be far-fetched to say that what was at stake in these constitutional rounds was the completion of an unfinished enterprise; that is, the total federalization of a constitutional system that was only partially conceived as federal at its inception in 1867. This goal, which is only slightly perceptible in the Meech Lake Accord, was made manifest in the Charlottetown Accord, albeit few actors and analysts at that time seemed aware of it.

The Charlottetown Accord wanted to do more than simply respond to Quebec's minimal demands for approving the 1982 reform: it wanted to satisfy demands arising from across Canada. It proposed recognizing federalism as a fundamental characteristic of the country, establishing mechanisms to improve intergovernmental relations, giving a reformed Senate a new federal dimension, clarifying the distribution of powers, and putting limits on the use of the declaratory power. The long-sought reform of the federal system finally seemed on the verge of finding a satisfactory form. The magnitude of the contemplated changes shows that, in the mind of the accord's crafters, Canada was not a true federation.

Another way in which the Charlottetown Accord contemplated the federalization of Canada was through the creation of an Aboriginal order of government. The settlement of Aboriginal claims would be solved by extending the federal system to First Nations, who would be vested with an inherent right to self-government enforceable by the judiciary. Through agreements concluded between governments and First Nations, a sort of asymmetrical and variable system for distributing powers was provided. As well, Aboriginal governments were given a share of constituent power.

Among the reasons given to explain the failure of the Meech Lake and Charlottetown accords, one of the most prominent involves the complexity of applying the 1982 amending formula. Another involves the difficulty of reaching consensus in pluralistic democracies – a difficulty that is evident in the unpredictable nature of formal constitutional reform in many federations (particularly Australia). These may be plausible explanations, and to them I would add the hypothesis that, since 1982, the relationship between federalism and federation in Canada has changed. It is clear that, after 1982, pluralism was not limited to the confines of territorial identities and, indeed, has become somewhat indifferent, if not hostile, to the federal paradigm. However, one should not exaggerate this. Federalism, particularly among English-speaking scholars during the postwar period, has never been seen as a stable and enduring principle in Canada. In the 1960s, John Porter and many others predicted that social class would displace federalism as the major source of political cleavages.[64] Federalism was seen as an obsolete principle forged by elite accommodation that stood in the way of modernization. Following the *Constitution Act, 1982*, it became commonplace to foretell a similar displacement, whereby the *Charter of Rights* would impose its unifying logic on Canadian society.[65]

In this sense, societies in Canada may be viewed as being torn by a double process of federalization and defederalization. On the one hand, we are witnessing a process of nationalization that shapes representations of the political community and results in claims for new national policies. Using the discourse of rights as expressed through judicial politics, this process of nationalization seems to disregard the constraints of the federal system. One may even argue that this process has been deeply rooted in Canada since before 1982. As Guy Laforest and Stéphane Kelly point out in their introduction to the French version of Canada's founding debates, it is striking to note that, apart from Quebec, not a single province found it appropriate to hold a legislative debate on the proposal tabled in 1981 to repatriate the Constitution. In contrast, between 1864 and 1867, all of the founding colonies fiercely debated the pros and cons of joining the union. On the other hand, so far, the reinforcement of cultural pluralism through multiculturalism and *Charter* politics has not resulted in the fading away of territorial politics. Provinces are still fairly strong with regard to their share of public expenses and their influence on the country's agenda. The quest for provincial autonomy is obviously fuelled by Quebec nationalism, but this is not exclusive to Quebec: decentralization is advocated throughout Canada, though on a lesser scale and for different reasons. Surprisingly, the most sophisticated critics of *Charter* politics are to be found in the Calgary school of political science rather than at Laval or at the University of Montreal.[66] One can say, with Alan Cairns, that federalism is able to channel the expression of all forms of cultural pluralism; however, it has proven to be strong enough to survive the clash of many nationalisms – the pan-Canadian, the Québécois, and now the Aboriginal – and to adapt itself to a postindustrial society.[67] Yet, the fact remains that federations are mortal: they disintegrate either by explosion or by an internal falling away of their constitutive principles. Many argue that federalism in Canada is a matter of unfinished business. And there is no doubt that the absence of a common language or theory with regard to federalism does not help.

Notes

1 See Richard Arès, *Dossier sur le pacte fédératif de 1867* (Montréal: Les éditions Bellarmin, 1967).
2 See Carl J. Friedrich, *Constitutional Government and Democracy* (Waltham: Blaisdell, 1968), 195-96.
3 Laurent Bouvet and Thierry Chopin, *Le Fédéraliste: La Démocratie apprivoisée* (Paris: Éditions Michalon, 1997), 106-19.
4 On the 1867 "mixed regime" as the epitome of Montesquieu's thought, see Philip Resnick, "Montesquieu Revisited, or the Mixed Constitution and the Separation of Powers in Canada," *Canadian Journal of Political Science* 26, 1 (1987): 97-129.
5 Will Kymlicka and Jean-Robert Raviot. "Vie commune: Aspects internationaux des fédéralismes," *Revue Études internationales* 28, 4 (1997): 786.
6 A.R.M. Lower, "Theories of Canadian Federalism: Yesterday and Today," in *Evolving Canadian Federalism*, ed. A.R.M. Lower and F.R. Scott, 5 (Durham: Duke University Press, 1958).
7 See David A. Stager, *Lawyers in Canada* (Toronto: University of Toronto Press, 1990); Rainer Knopff and Frederick L. Morton, *The Charter Revolution and the Court Party* (Peterborough: Broadview Press, 2000).
8 Kenneth C. Wheare, *Federal Government* (London: Oxford University Press, 1963).
9 See James R. Mallory, *The Structure of Canadian Government* (Toronto: Macmillan of Canada, 1971), 325-31; A.H. Birch, "Approaches to the Study of Federalism," *Political Studies* 14, 1 (1966): 15-33; Michael Stein, "Federal Political Systems and Federal Societies," in *Canadian Federalism: Myth and Reality*, ed. J. Peter Meekison, 37-48 (Toronto: Methuen, 1968); Ian Robinson and Richard Simeon, "The Dynamics of Canadian Federalism," in *Canadian Politics*, ed. James P. Bickerton and Alain-G. Gagnon, 366-88 (Toronto: Broadview Press, 1994).
10 Peter H. Russell, "Overcoming Legal Formalism: The Treatment of the Constitution, the Courts and Judicial Behaviour in Canadian Political Science," *Canadian Journal Law and Society* 1 (1986): 5-33.
11 See Edwin R. Black and Alan C. Cairns, "A Different Perspective on Canadian Federalism," *Canadian Public Administration* 9, 1 (1966): 27-45. See also Ronald L. Watts, *Comparing Federal Systems in the 1990s* (Montreal/Kingston: McGill-Queen's University Press, 1996).
12 Thomas O. Hueglin, "Federalism in Comparative Perspective," in *Perspectives on Canadian Federalism,* ed. R.D. Olling and M.W. Westmacott, 16-31 (Scarborough: Prentice-Hall Canada, 1988).
13 Donald V. Smiley, *Canada in Question: Federalism in the Eighties* (Toronto: McGraw-Hill Ryerson, 1980); Ronald L. Watts, *Executive Federalism: A Comparative Analysis* (Kingston: Institute of Intergovernmental Relations, 1989).
14 Donald V. Smiley and Ronald L. Watts, *Intrastate Federalism in Canada* (study for the Royal Commission on the Economic Union and Development Prospects for Canada) (Ottawa: Supply and Services Canada, 1986).
15 Richard Simeon, *Federal-Provincial Diplomacy* (Toronto: University of Toronto Press, 1972 [re-edited in 2006]).
16 See Alan C. Cairns, "The Government and Societies of Canadian Federalism," *Canadian Journal of Political Science* 10, 4 (1977): 695-725. See also Donald Smiley, *The Federal Condition in Canada* (Toronto: McGraw-Hill Ryerson, 1987); Miriam Smith, "L'héritage institutionnaliste de la science politique au Canada anglais," *Politique et Sociétés* 21, 3 (2002): 113-38.
17 See Peter M. Leslie, *Federal State, National Economy* (Toronto: University of Toronto Press, 1987); Kenneth Norrie, Richard Simeon, and Mark Krasnick, *Federalism and Economic Union in Canada* (study for the Royal Commission and the Economic Union and Development Prospects for Canada) (Ottawa: Supply and Services Canada, 1986).

18 See Keith Banting, *The Welfare State and Canadian Federalism* (Montreal/Kingston: McGill-Queen's University Press, 1982); Antonia Maioni, *Parting at the Crossroads: The Emergence of Health Insurance in the US and Canada* (Princeton: Princeton University Press, 1998); Kenneth McRoberts, "Federal Structures and the Policy Process," in *Governing Canada: Institutions and Public Policy*, ed. Michael M. Atkinson, 149-78 (Toronto: Harcourt Brace, 1993).

19 See Philip Resnick, *The Masks of Proteus: Canadian Reflections on the State* (Montreal/Kingston: McGill-Queen's University Press, 1990).

20 See Janet Ajzenstat, Paul Romney, Ian Gentle, and William D. Gairdner, *Canada's Founding Debates* (Toronto: Stoddart, 1999). French edition by Stéphane Kelly and Guy Laforest, *Débats sur la fondation du Canada* (Québec: Presses de l'université Laval, 2004). See also Jennifer Smith, *Federalism* (Vancouver: UBC Press, 2004); and Marc Chevrier, "La genèse de l'idée fédérale chez les pères fondateurs américains et canadiens," in *Le fédéralisme canadien contemporain: Fondements, traditions, institutions*, ed. Alain-G. Gagnon, 19-61 (Montréal: Les Presses de l'université de Montréal, 2006).

21 Michael Burgess and Alain-G. Gagnon eds., *Comparative Federalism and Federation* (Toronto: University of Toronto Press, 1993).

22 See Marc Chevrier, "Le juge et la conservation du régime politique au Canada," *Politiques et Sociétés* 19, 2-3 (2000): 65-87.

23 See Watts, *Comparing Federal Systems*, 6-14.

24 See also Raoul Blinderbacher and Ronald L. Watts, "Federalism in a Changing World: A Conceptual Framework for the Conference," in *Federalism in a Changing World: Learning from Each Other*, ed. Raoul Blinderbacher and Arnold Koller, 7-25 (Montreal/Kingston: McGill-Queen's University Press, 2002).

25 See, for example, Cameron's description of the Canadian federal system, which he views as a genuine parliamentary federation that, in spite of a highly centralized constitution, experienced an ongoing process of decentralization. See David R. Cameron, *Canada: Guide des pays fédéraux*, ed. Ann L. Griffiths, 156-70 (Montreal/Kingston: McGill-Queen's University Press, 2005).

26 However, by insisting on the vital role played by second chambers with regard to the representation of regional interests in most federations, Watts implicitly admitted the unfinished federal character of Canada's central institutions. See Ronald L. Watts, "Le bicaméralisme dans les régimes parlementaires fédéraux," in *Protéger la démocratie canadienne: Le Sénat en vérité ...* , ed. Serge Joyal, 78 (Montreal/Kingston: McGill-Queen's University Press, 2003).

27 André Bernard, *La vie politique au Québec et au Canada* (Québec: Presses de l'université du Québec, 2000), 19-20. See also Guy Lachapelle, Gérald Bernier, Daniel Salée, and Luc Bernier, *The Quebec Democracy: Structures, Processes and Policies* (Toronto: McGraw-Hill Ryerson, 1993), 29-37; Réjean Pelletier, "Constitution et fédéralisme," in *Le parlementarisme canadien*, ed. Manon Tremblay, Réjean Pelletier, and Marcel R. Pelletier, 47-87 (Québec: Les Presses de l'Université Laval).

28 See Alain Noël, "Le principe fédéral, la solidarité et le partenariat," in *Sortir de l'impasse: Les voies de la réconciliation*, ed. Guy Laforest and Roger Gibbins, 263-95 (Montréal: Institute for Research on Public Policy, 1998).

29 This is less true since the publication of *Multinational Democracies*, in which Dimitrios Karmis, Alain-G. Gagnon, François Rocher, Christian Rouillard, Pierre Coulombe, and André Lecours compare Canada to many multinational federations or quasi-federations. See Alain-G. Gagnon and James Tully, ed. *Multinational Democracies* (Cambridge: Cambridge University Press, 2001).

30 Edmond Orban, *La dynamique de la centralisation dans l'État fédéral: Un processus irréversible?* (Montréal: Québec/Amérique, 1984); François Rocher, ed., *Bilan québécois du fédéralisme canadien* (Montréal: VLB Éditeur, 1992).

31 Herman Bakvis and Grance Skogstad, "Canadian Federalism: Performance, Effectiveness, and Legitimacy," in *Canadian Federalism, Performance, Effectiveness, and Legitimacy,* ed. Herman Bakvis and Grace Skogstad, 4-22 (Oxford: Oxford University Press, 2002); Watts, *Comparing Federal Systems*, 111.

32 Guy Laforest, *Pour la liberté d'une société distincte* (Québec: Les Presses de l'Université Laval, 2004), 141-62.

33 See François Rocher and Christian Rouillard, "Le processus d'intégration continentale: Une redéfinition des lieux de pouvoir au Canada," in *La capacité de choisir: Le Canada dans une nouvelle Amérique du Nord*, ed. George Hoberg, 243-76 (Montréal: Les Presses de l'université de Montréal, 2002).

34 Laforest, *Pour la liberté d'une société distincte*, 343.

35 François Rocher, Christian Rouillard, and André Lecours, "Recognition Claims, Partisan Politics and Institutional Constraints: Belgium, Spain and Canada in a Comparative Perspective," in Gagnon and Tully, *Multinational Democracies*, 195.

36 Richard Simeon, *Political Science and Federalism: Seven Decades of Scholarly Engagement* (Kingston: Institute of Intergovernmental Relations, 2000), 39-41.

37 Guy Laforest, "Préface," in Eugénie Brouillet, *La négation de la nation: L'identité culturelle québécoise et le fédéralisme canadien*, 11 (Sillery: Septention, 2005).

38 This is not to say that such an approach is absent in the English-language literature. See, for example, Thomas Hueglin, "Federalism at the Crossroads: Old Meanings, New Significance," *Canadian Journal of Political Science* 36, 3 (2003): 275-94; and the major contribution of Samuel LaSelva, *The Moral Foundations of Canadian Federalism: Paradoxes, Achievements, and Tragedies of Nationhood* (Montreal/Kingston: McGill-Queen's University Press, 1996).

39 Alain-G. Gagnon, "The Moral Foundations of Asymmetrical Federalism: A Normative Exploration of the Case of Quebec and Canada," in Gagnon and Tully, *Multinational Democracies*, 319-37.

40 Dimitrios Karmis and Wayne Norman, "The Revival of Federalism in Normative Political Theory," in *Theories of Federalism: A Reader*, ed. Dimitrios Karmis and Wayne Norman, 3-21 (New York: Palgrave Macmillan, 2005).

41 Dimitrios Karmis, "Les multiples voix de la tradition fédérale et la tourmente du fédéralisme canadien," in Gagnon, *Le fédéralisme canadien*, 63-86.

42 François Rocher, "La dynamique Québec-Canada ou le refus de l'idéal fédéral," in Gagnon, *Le fédéralisme canadien*, 93-146.

43 "Opening New Perspectives on Federalism," in *The States and Moods of Federalism: Governance, Identity and Methodology*, ed. Jean-François Gaudeault-Desbiens and Fabien Gélinas, 53 (Cowansville, QC: Éditions Yvon Blais, 2005).

44 See Christopher Edward Taucar, *Canadian Federalism and Quebec Sovereignty* (New York: Peter Lang, 2000), 135-58; Patrick J. Monahan, *Constitutional Law* (Toronto: Irwin Law, 2002), 100-4; Peter W. Hogg, *Constitutional Law of Canada* (Toronto: Carswell, 1999), 101-4.

45 Patrick J. Monahan, "At Doctrine's Twilight: The Structure of Canadian Federalism," *University of Toronto Law Journal* 34, (1984): 81-90.

46 W.R. Lederman's seminal article is known for having celebrated federalism as an ideal of moderation that should govern the interpretation of the distribution of powers. See W.R. Lederman, "Unity and Diversity in Canadian Federalism: Ideals and Methods of Moderation," *Canadian Bar Review* 53 (1975): 597-620.

47 Frank R. Scott, *Essays on the Constitution: Aspects of Canadian Law and Politics* (Toronto: University of Toronto Press, 1977), 251.

48 See, for example, Donna Greschner, "The Quebec Secession Reference: Goodbye to Part V?" *Constitutional Forum* 10, 1 (1998): 19-25; Donna Greschner, "The Supreme Court, Federalism, and the Metaphors of Moderation," *Canadian Bar Review* 79 (2000): 47-76. See also the special issue of the *National Journal of Constitutional Law* 11 (1999): 1-168.

49 Sujit Choudhry and Robert Howse, "Constitutional Theory and the Quebec Secession Reference," *Canadian Journal of Law and Jurisprudence* 13, 2 (2000): 144-45.

50 There were some exceptions. See Katherine Swinton, *The Supreme Court and Canadian Federalism: The Laskin-Dickson Years* (Toronto: Carswell, 1990); Bruce Ryder, "The Demise and Rise of the Classical Paradigm in Canadian Federalism: Promoting Autonomy for the Provinces and First Nations," *McGill Law Journal* 36 (1991): 308.

51 John T. Saywell, *The Lawmakers: Judicial Power and the Shaping of Canadian Federalism* (Toronto: University of Toronto Press, 2002).

52   George Scelle, *Précis de Droit des gens* (Paris: Sirey, 1934).

53   Maurice Croisat, *Le fédéralisme dans les démocraties contemporaines* (Paris: Montchrestien, 1995), 25; Réjean Pelletier referred implicitly to Scelle's laws.

54   Henri Brun and Guy Tremblay, *Droit constitutionnel* (Cowansville: Éditions Yvon Blais, 2001), 408-37.

55   André Tremblay, *Droit constitutionnel: Principles* (Montréal: Les éditions Thémis, 2000), 199-223.

56   Jacques-Yvan Morin and José Woehrling, *Les constitutions du Canada et du Québec du régime français à nos jours* (Montréal: Les éditions Thémis, 1992), 153-68; Benoît Pelletier "L'expérience fédérale canadienne," in *La réforme de l'État ... et après?* ed. Serge Jaumain, 55-74 (Bruxelles: Éditions de l'université de Bruxelles, 1997).

57   Eugénie Brouillet, *La négation de la nation: L'identité culturelle québécoise et le fédéralisme canadien* (Sillery: Septentrion, 2005).

58   See Jean Leclair, "The Supreme Court of Canada's Understanding of Federalism: Efficiency at the Expense of Diversity," in *The States and Moods of Federalism,* 383-414; Vilaysoun Loungnarath, "Le rôle du pouvoir judiciaire dans la structuration politico-juridique de la fédération canadienne," *Canadian Bar Review* 57 (1997): 1003; Ghislain Otis, "La justice constitutionnelle au Canada à l'approche de l'an 2000: Uniformisation ou construction plurielle du droit? *Revue de droit d'Ottawa* 27 (1995): 261; Micheline Patenaude, "L'interprétation du partage des compétences à l'heure du libre-échange," *Revue de droit de l'université de Sherbrooke* 21 (1990): 1.

59   Alan Cairns, *Charter versus Federalism: The Dilemmas of Constitutional Reform* (Montreal/ Kingston: McGill-Queen's University Press, 1992), 33-61.

60   Alain Cairns, "Constitutional Minoritarianism in Canada," in *Canada: The State of the Federation, 1990,* ed. Ronald Watts and Douglas Brown (Kingston: Institute of Intergovernmental Relations, 1990), 8ff.

61   Guy Laforest, *Trudeau et la fin d'un rêve canadien* (Sillery: Les éditions du Septentrion, 1992), 190.

62   Linda Cardinal, "Le pouvoir exécutif et la judiciarisation de la politique au Canada: Une étude du Programme de contestation judiciaire," *Politique and Sociétés* 18, 2-3 (2000): 43-64.

63   Thomas Hueglin, *Exploring Concepts of Treaty Federalism: A Comparative Perspective* (study for the Royal Commission on Aboriginal Peoples) (Ottawa: Supply and Services Canada, 1996).

64   See John Porter, *The Vertical Mosaic: An Analysis of Social Class and Power in Canada* (Toronto: University of Toronto Press, 1965).

65   For the opposite view, see Janet Hiebert, "The Charter and Federalism: Revisiting the Nation-Building Thesis," in *Canada: The State of the Federation,* ed. Douglas Brown and Janet Hiebert (Kingston: Institute for Intergovernmental Affairs, 1994), 153 and esp. 156.

66   See Knopff and Morton, *Charter Revolution,* 2000.

67   Alan C. Cairns, "Constitutional Government and the Two Faces of Ethnicity: Federalism Is Not Enough," in *Rethinking Federalism: Citizens, Markets, and Governments in a Changing World,* ed. Karen Knop, Sylvia Ostry, Richard Simeon, and Katherine Swinton, 15-39 (Vancouver: UBC Press, 1995).

Part 2:
The Management of Pluralism in Canada through Constitutional Law and Policy

6

Repositioning the Canadian State and Minority Languages: Accountability and the *Action Plan for Official Languages*

Daniel Bourgeois and Andrew F. Johnson

A decade ago, discourse on the end of the nation-state was a growth industry as one treatise after another was published on the subject.[1] External and internal forces – namely, globalization and substate nationalism – were alleged to be weakening the authority of the nation-state.[2] Canada was supposedly a prototypical case.

Nineteen-ninety-five apparently foreshadowed the end. The forces of globalization seemingly shaped the 1995 budget, which reduced federal spending by billions of dollars. Reduced spending on health, education, and welfare – policies that are said to be the "glue" that binds Canada together – was to result in a dismantling of the state.[3] With a sovereigntist near miss in the 1995 referendum, speculation began on various constitutional "scenarios."[4]

However, over a decade has passed and federal spending has not abated. It continues to grow, as do concomitant revenues; spending has simply been restructured. Sovereigntist sentiment remains significant, but it is not the same menace to the Canadian federal state that it was a decade ago. Put otherwise, external and internal forces have not significantly eroded the authority of the Canadian state. Canada has repositioned itself to face threats from globalization and nationalism that, ten years ago, seemed like insurmountable challenges. And the 2003 *Action Plan for Official Languages* (hereafter *Action Plan*) is one of several major policy initiatives designed to strengthen the authority of the Canadian state against centripetal exogenous and endogenous forces. At least, that is the overall theme of this chapter.[5]

More specifically, our purpose is twofold: first, to explain the *Action Plan* as a policy intended to reposition the federal state within the context of challenges posed by globalization and nationalism; second, to assess accountability issues, which pertain to federalism and moral choice, stemming from the *Action Plan* as a policy designed to reposition the state. The concept of "accountability" is divided into its objective and subjective aspects.[6] Its objective aspect refers to issues of control, or "answerabilty," and involves analyzing the implications of the *Action Plan* for federalism and federal political institutions. Its subjective aspect refers to moral choice and involves assessing the potential risks for wrongdoing that may result from the *Action Plan*.

This chapter is divided into four sections. The first analyzes the role of the *Action Plan* as a prop to protect and reinforce the state in the face of the corrosive forces of globalization and nationalism; the second identifies issues of accountability as they relate to the implications of the *Action Plan* for federalism and for federal political institutions; and the third assesses the *Action Plan* in terms of accountability as it pertains to moral choice, a subject that is of particular concern to Canadians and to the federal government in the wake of accountability scandals that plagued the Canadian state a few years ago. Finally, there is a section that draws conclusions about globalization, national integration, and accountability as they relate to federalism and the *Action Plan*.

Globalization, Nationalism, the Canadian State, and the *Action Plan*

If language policy can build nations by nurturing a common means of communication and a common culture, it seems probable that language policy can also neutralize the fissiparous tendencies of globalization vis-à-vis the state – a notion that Maureen Covell does not appear to accept. Covell points out that there are three approaches to language policy: the modernization or nation-building approach, the human rights approach, and the ecological approach.[7] While citing Marshall and Gonzalez, Covell infers that the ecological approach is as much normative as it is empirical: "The authors argue for the preservation of a diversity of languages as a way of preserving the unique point of view they see as enshrined in each language and avoiding the dangers of 'monoculism' (the ability to see things from only one point of view)."[8] The human rights approach is strictly normative inasmuch as it posits that it is simply a human right to be able to function in one's mother tongue. The modernization, or nation-building, approach argues that minority language rights are obstacles to the emergence and existence of the nation-state. Whatever the empirical merits, the nation-building approach misses the obvious: attempts at assimilation may tear some nations apart whereas endeavours to advance minority language rights may enhance the authority of the nation-state qua nation-state.

Covell argues that one or another of the above approaches has been employed at different times in Canada's history.[9] However, it also seems that an approach that enhances minority language rights as a primary means of enhancing the state has been used by the federal government since the Royal Commission on Bilingualism and Biculturalism (B&B Commission) reported that there was a language "crisis" in Canada.[10] And now the *Action Plan* is being used not only as a policy to further national integration by enhancing access to federal government services for minority language groups from each of the two official languages communities but also to enhance Canada's competitive position in the global economy – at least according to a former prime minister and a former minister of intergovernmental affairs, who believe that language skills are a key ingredient in nurturing a competitive workforce.[11]

The *Action Plan for Official Languages* advances linguistic dualism in order to revitalize the federal *Official Languages Act*, 1969, and its amended version, the *Official Languages Act*, 1988. Despite considerable progress in establishing language rights and in promoting the practice of bilingualism in Canada's population and in federal institutions, the *Action Plan* has been considered as a way to redress the "noticeable erosion" of the Official Languages program since the early 1990s.[12] The *Action Plan* basically invigorates and integrates existing efforts under the aforementioned Acts. Thus, it places new and existing efforts within a framework that includes four goals, twenty-five objectives, and sixty-four means – plus $751 million in additional funds to be assumed by eight key federal institutions: Canadian Heritage, Treasury Board Secretariat, Health Canada, Human Resources Development Canada, Industry Canada, Justice Canada, Citizenship and Immigration Canada, and the Privy Council Office. In addition, it innovates by way of providing a new accountability framework. But more on that later.

The point is that the *Action Plan* is primarily an initiative to promote linguistic and cultural dualism. However, the former minister perceived it also as endorsing "linguistic pluralism," which he referred to as a "new value," a value that could be viewed as an "asset" in the context of globalization.[13] Moreover, it is important to note that the new Conservative government officially endorsed the *Action Plan* and accepted the amendment of section 41 of the *Official Languages Act*, thereby forcing federal institutions to take positive measures to contribute to the vitality of minority language communities. However, the Conservatives have not related any of this to globalization, as did the originators of the *Action Plan*. But then this raises the question, "What is meant by globalization?"

Globalization has been given all sorts of captivating meanings, but perhaps Thomas L. Friedman best articulates the definition that is standard in the serious literature:

> [Globalization refers to] the inexorable integration of markets, nation-states, and technologies to a degree never witnessed before – in a way that is enabling individuals, corporations and nation-states to reach around the world farther, faster, deeper and cheaper than ever before ... [it is] the spread of free-market capitalism to virtually every country in the world.[14]

Hence, globalization primarily refers to free trade and a concomitant legitimizing free market ideology. Thus, in concrete terms and in the Canadian case, globalization refers to the General Agreement on Tariffs and Trade (GATT), the Bretton Woods/World Trade Organization (WTO) regime, as well as to the North American Free Trade Agreement (NAFTA) – the "supra-constitution," as Clarkson puts it[15] – along with ideological support (neo-liberalism and neoconservatism are interchangeable in this regard) for free market forces worldwide. However, in the literature economic forces are associated with cultural (and other) significant consequences, one of which is cultural homogenization.[16]

The *Action Plan* can be interpreted as a means of shoring up linguistic and cultural dualism against the forces of globalization and the latter's supposed concomitant cultural homogenization as well as a means of bolstering (language) skills that will enable Canada to effectively compete in a global context. However, globalization, as an independent variable, tends to explain so much that it ends up explaining very little. More often than not, it neglects human agency, which is the intervening variable between itself and the *Action Plan*, and which requires us to place the latter in its historical and economic context. This, in turn, requires two general observations.

First, Canada is and always has been a trading nation.[17] Accordingly, all Canadian policies are influenced by this status, and it is inconceivable that they would not be influenced by the institutional structures of globalization, the WTO, and NAFTA. Second, Canada, since its inception, has been a borrowing nation-state and, as such, must attend to the requirements of international financial markets, a principle agent of globalization. In the mid-1990s, it was feared that international creditors might negatively assess Canada's mounting deficit and debt liability, with serious consequences. As a result, the federal government's main objective became deficit elimination and debt reduction, all of which has been chronicled elsewhere.[18] Suffice it to say, the federal government successfully met these objectives, which were initiated in the 1995 budget. But it did not stop spending. Spending continues to rise, but it is directed towards a different objective – investment in human capital (of which language policy has been a major component).

Whereas federal government spending emphasized expenditure on social consumption, it is now directed towards investment in human capital. Consider the three new major spending initiatives of the Liberal government since 1995: innovation and related projects centred on the Canadian Foundation for Innovation (CFI), Millennium Scholarships, and the *Action Plan*.[19] Each is an endowment or, better still, a tribute to Paul Martin, Jean Chrétien, and Stéphane Dion, respectively. But, more important, each is a long-term investment project and each is perceived as a way of overcoming the forces of globalization, which may threaten the integrity of the

Canadian state. The policies are not designed to fight globalization; rather, they are intended to play the competitive globalization game by investing in human capital. Above all, they are intended to win the game. This is precisely where human agency enters and connects globalization to the *Action Plan*.

The former minister of intergovernmental affairs, Stéphane Dion, explains this in terms of personalities, but then personalities give life to ideas that materialize in current events.[20] Dion read a policy proposal on job skills for the future, which was developed by two of his cabinet colleagues, one of whom was Jane Stewart, the Human Resources and Development Canada (HRDC) minister. The draft document catalogued a long list of skills, but there was no mention of language skills. Dion considered language skills to be essential if Canadians were to compete in a global economy. He raised the issue in cabinet. Cabinet was receptive (due to reasons identified below), and the Dion Plan was approved. Subsequent to extensive consultations with community groups, Dion ended up writing most, or at least the core of, the *Action Plan* on his own.[21]

At any rate, the *Action Plan* was presented as a way of giving Canadians, especially young Canadians, an advantage in competing for jobs in the global economy.[22] It was also sold as a way of staving off the otherwise destructive ramifications of globalization by having the state invest and compete in the world economy. Dion gave over half a dozen speeches on the benefits of the *Action Plan* as a way for Canada to triumph within the context of globalization, and his assertions were endorsed by the official languages commissioner and, notably, by Prime Minister Chrétien, who wrote a prefatory message for the plan, claiming that "our linguistic duality means better access to markets and more jobs and greater mobility for workers [and,] in that spirit, the Action Plan strives to maximize these advantages for all Canadians."[23] All Canadians may eventually benefit because the *Action Plan*, in promoting "English- and French-language instruction ... often serves as a spring board for learning a third or fourth language."[24]

As a bonus, there was a widespread perception that bilingualism would be an asset with regard to gaining access to labour markets and to providing labour mobility, especially in the global economy. This was the belief of Canadian parents, at least according to polls that were conducted prior to the tabling of the *Action Plan*. At that time, a CRIC poll indicated that 87 percent of francophones agreed that, "in today's global economy people with an ability to speak more than one language will be more successful," as did about the same proportion of anglophones.[25] (The questionnaire did not ask specifically about English or French, but this was implicit because it dealt with Canada's official languages policy.) More important – in a strictly economic sense – employers also seemed to believe this, at least according to a COMPAS Inc. poll conducted late in 2003.[26]

More than half of Canadian business leaders, surveyed towards the end of November 2003, believed that people who spoke more than one language would have an easier time finding employment than would those who did not. Moreover, business leaders considered second language skills – especially second language skills in French – to be an asset. Only 16 percent of those polled claimed that bilingualism in French and English was not an asset in a prospective worker, while all others assigned varying levels of importance to the skill.

As much as business leaders value bilingualism, the private sector has been negligent in providing language training. Only 37 percent of businesses do so – a figure that does not reveal anything about the quality of language instruction provided. Thus, there is reasonable justification – endorsed by the *Action Plan* – for the government to step in to fill the gap left by the private sector with regard to satisfying language training needs.

But the *Action Plan* is more than just a means of addressing the challenge of globalization: it is also a means of addressing the ongoing problem of national integration – a problem that became a state crisis in the mid 1990s. It was the "carrot" of an official "carrot-and-stick" policy that Dion used to forge national integration, the "stick" being the Clarity Bill. However, once again, the former minister of intergovernmental affairs connected the genesis of broad events to human initiative inspired by civic duty.

Dion explains it this way: spending on bilingualism had declined beginning in 1995, as might be expected, given the intent of the 1995 budget.[27] Accordingly – and it was not just a matter of funding – the momentum for advocating bilingualism slowed. This was made apparent in 2000 in the *Report of the Commissioner of Official Languages*. But the weakening of Canada's bilingual policy only came to the fore when former prime minister Trudeau died in 2001. Apparently, Prime Minister Chrétien's chief of staff and long-time Trudeau stalwart, Jean Pelletier, raised the issue when he indicated that the original *Official Languages Act* had been a monument to Trudeau as well as Trudeau's primary reason for entering the Canadian political arena. Pelletier's lament for the status of bilingualism struck a cord with Chrétien, and Dion was charged with resuscitating the original *Official Languages Act*.

The *Action Plan* was brought into being by a diligent minister (Dion) from a central agency in collusion with at least one other minister (Stewart), as well as with the prime minister and his chief of staff. They were responding to the long and dark shadow that the 1995 referendum cast in Quebec, and, at least rhetorically, they were also responding to the exigencies of globalization. In fact, they were using these apparent exigencies as primary justifications for the *Action Plan*.

At the mid-term of the *Action Plan*'s implementation, rhetoric on globalization was absent. The accommodation of both official languages as a means of advancing national integration appears to be the main preoccupation with regard to maintaining continuity with the past. According to the mid-term report, the $123.4 million (of the originally allocated $751.3 million) already spent, created a "momentum" from which "intergovernmental collaboration in official languages ... derived new strength."[28] But the document is also revealing for what it neglects to address: the lack of consultation and accountability in several sectors, most notably with regard to education. Perhaps this explains why minority language groups are lamenting the lack of an agreement in the educational sector, in which "negotiations have been dragging until very recently," and in which funds from the *Action Plan* are alleged to have been allocated on a "piecemeal basis."[29]

The *Action Plan* must be implemented cautiously if it is to succeed, especially given that it has come very close to intruding on provincial legislative prerogatives, particularly in the education and health sectors. However, the *Action Plan*, as a means of forging national integration and as a means of strengthening Canada linguistically so as to make it an effective global competitor, can be construed as both weakening and strengthening the Canadian state in terms of accountability. It is to this subject that we now turn.

Accountability, Federalism, Political Institutions, and the *Action Plan*
Accountability is at the core of the Canadian state. Indeed, the 1979 Royal Commission on Financial Management and Accountability claims that it is "the essence of our democratic form of government" and explains that "it is the liability assumed by all those who exercise authority to account for the manner in which they have fulfilled responsibilities entrusted to them."[30] However, the claim is not as apparent as it was one-quarter of a century ago. It may be that globalization supersedes democracy and blurs the legislative responsibilities allocated to each level of government in Canada's federal system.

Garth Stevenson states the obvious: that "status quo" federalism is very much a myth.[31] Of course, we have long been accustomed to the changing faces of federalism in Canada. But Stevenson's remarks are most engaging because he explains that the status quo, as it were, will be influenced for the foreseeable future by three circumstances: NAFTA, the neoliberalism concomitant with NAFTA, and the apparent ongoing desire for an independent Quebec. The three are interrelated. NAFTA and neoliberalism are alleged to have required the state to shed its interventionist role. And, as the costs of regional development and social policy expenditure decline, the risk of Quebec declaring itself to be a sovereign state will increase because there will be little in the way of policy expenditures to tie that province to Canada. This may or may not be the case, but we can deduce from Stevenson that globalization is a prime mover in shaping Canadian federalism, largely because it sets a new policy agenda that may well be detrimental to the system that currently exists: a coalition of provinces in consort with the federal government, with Quebec constantly threatening to withdraw. Accordingly, because it is set by supranational forces – namely, globalization – control over the policy agenda is not compatible with democracy.

Others would disagree, claiming that globalization, in the form of "glocalization,"[32] accommodates itself to local circumstances and/or generates decentralizing tendencies.[33] But McBride is not in this camp. He claims that the ratification of international trade agreements – globalization – constitutes a component of a process that may be referred to as "quiet constitutionalism."[34] The process refers to "fundamental changes that have occurred affecting Canadian sovereignty and the degree to which democracy matters."[35] McBride identifies a variety of such changes, including changes in the decision-making process and changes to the division of federal-provincial legislative powers. Basically, the changes resulting from globalization to which McBride refers are institutional and federal. In both instances, centralization is the norm. Put otherwise, decentralization may well be the norm in other policy areas, but it does not appear to be the norm with regard to a policy issue that has long been understood as quintessential to the integration of the federal state – namely, language policy.

Thus, the deficiencies in objective accountability – the "democratic deficit," which includes "transparency" and "openness," to use the popular lexicon – resulting from globalization and efforts to forge national integration, are ostensibly threefold: first, globalization eclipses the domestic policy agenda and sets its own; second, it centralizes decision-making processes within the federal government; and, finally, it facilitates the ability of the federal government to usurp provincial legislative powers specifically to serve the forces of globalization. In other words, the "quiet federalism" to which McBride refers amounts to a creeping centralization brought on by the federal government's endeavours to comply with the exigencies of globalization and, we suggest, national integration.

The *Action Plan* may, for the most part, serve as an example of "quiet federalism." In our perspective, globalization, on its own and without human agency, cannot set the agenda. But federal politicians can act to redress globalization and to promote national integration by encouraging centralization and by progressively appropriating provincial powers, which is what has been happening within the context of the *Action Plan*.

The *Action Plan*'s goals fall under eleven priority sectors: education, health, economic development, justice, early childhood, immigration, federal-provincial partnerships, community life, an exemplary public service, the language industries, and an accountability and coordination framework. Most of the eleven sectors require direct provincial involvement, but, historically, the two following sectors – education and health – have been among the policy areas that the provinces have sought to protect from federal incursions wrought by its spending power.

Education Sector

The education sector, among the most likely to generate disputes related to objective accountability, is, in fact, the "the cornerstone of the official languages policy,"[36] and the funding certainly demonstrates as much. More to the point, the *Action Plan* adds $381.5 million – over half of its disbursement – over five years to an existing $929 million for minority language and second language education "fully respecting constitutional jurisdictions,"[37] although its six goals are bound to overlap with provincial responsibilities.[38] Atypically, the spending and the goals, most of which fall clearly within the exclusive provincial domain of education, simply have not stirred the same degree of acrimony between the two levels of government that they would have in the past. This is because the *Action Plan* is largely – but not entirely – related to enhancing the French language in the predominantly English-speaking provinces.

Over one-third of a century has passed since the B&B Commission tabled its recommendations, and, at best, the provinces have only agreed to federal assistance in providing French-language instruction where minorities exist. They have steadfastly resisted federal involvement in establishing minority language schools. As a matter of fact, it took thirteen years of bilateral constitutional negotiations for the provinces to finally agree to include section 23 in the 1982 *Charter of Rights and Freedoms*. Section 23 provides distinct French-language schools "where numbers warrant," with francophone parents' managing these schools through their elected school boards. However, the full implementation of these minority education rights is still incomplete a full generation after their adoption, despite a plethora of Supreme Court judgments favouring the positions taken by francophone parents and backed by the federal government to counter the inaction of numerous provincial governments.[39]

Other federal initiatives to promote minority language education also show that the provinces have stood ready to defend, even surreptitiously, their constitutional prerogatives in education. The federal Official Languages in Education Program (OLEP) was established in 1971 to help provinces offset higher costs associated with minority-language education. Bilateral multi-year agreements are signed by the federal Canadian heritage minister and provincial ministers of education to fund first-language (mother tongue) and second-language (immersion) education, either in English in Quebec or in French elsewhere. But francophone groups have been concerned because the agreements were arrived at in camera; they have also been troubled because the funds seem to disappear into provincial coffers, where they are used for other purposes. In a scathing 1996 report, one group asked, "Where did all the billions go?"[40] lambasting the federal government and, more especially, provincial governments for apparently not spending the money on the designated object – French-language (mother tongue) education.

The federal Official Languages Program (OLP), established in 1995, encourages provincial governments to improve their public services and to promote the recognition and use of both official languages. British Columbia has thus far refused to partake in such bilateral agreements on bilingual public services, and the other provinces have been slow to implement the OLP, as might be expected given the federal government's own laxity in this regard over the last decade. Yet, the *Action Plan* seeks to double the federal government's investment – from $12.1 million to $26.7 million in five years – and there are no visible signs that the provinces will resist cooperating in this.

There is still light at the end of what has been, if not a dark, then at least a pretty dim tunnel. In September 1999, the premiers and the prime minister signed a declaration on early childhood development that, among other things, ensures adequate consideration of the child's mother tongue. Both levels of government sponsor early childhood care, although the provinces are more directly involved through health and social services, while federal support usually focuses on information and research. The light, as it were, also includes well over one-third of a billion dollars, to which the provinces have not raised their customary jurisdictional concerns.[41]

Health Sector

Health care continues to be a source of conflict, but this is certainly not due to minority language provisions past, present, or future. The main source of controversy between the federal and provincial governments is that the former does not transfer sufficient funds through the Canada Health and Social Transfer (CHST) – a block fund initiated in 1995 that led to a substantial curtailment of funds for health and social services to the provinces – and through equalization transfers, which have also diminished since 1995. The provinces still deem the $2.5 billion infusion of funds from the federal government in the 2004 budget to be insufficient to enable them to revitalize their flagging health care delivery systems.

In April 2000, the federal Department of Health established the Advisory Committee on Francophone Minority Communities, which is co-chaired by one of the associate deputy ministers and a member of a francophone community group. This was followed, in October 2001, by the creation of the Advisory Committee on (Quebec's) Anglophone Minority Communities. The mandate of these committees is to advise the federal minister on ways the Department of Health could contribute to the vitality and development of the official languages communities. They did this in a report that ultimately became a $119 million (over five years) component of the *Action Plan*.[42]

Dion, who was then the minister of intergovernmental affairs, describes the process of creating a health component in collaboration with committees, community groups, and his provincial counterparts who were responsible for francophone affairs as "a story of exemplary cooperation."[43] But then, the story begins and proceeds with minority language groups, largely bypassing the provincial government in the first instance and applying pressure on them in the second, aided and abetted by the federal government. But then, how could any province resist, even if it wanted to, with the former federal minister of intergovernmental affairs proclaiming a new health right: "Everyone has a right to die in his own language,"[44] a right which has yet to be fully realized.

Thus, the obvious question is: "why have the provinces been complacent in their response to the initiatives of the *Action Plan*, which seem to infringe on their legislative responsibilities?" The federal government appears to be setting the legislative agenda. However, the Canadian state is not in fact less interventionist than it was prior to 1995; it is repositioning itself in the context of globalization. Repositioning entails "quiet federalism," a discrete centralizing tendency. It also requires a certain complacency or flexibility on the part of the provinces – provinces that are normally very sensitive to and protective of their legislative responsibilities – to accede to long-term investments in human capital. These investments will benefit them as provincial governments, responsible for prosperity or the lack thereof, in the future.

The complexity of contemporary public policies is such that any major spending initiative on the part of the federal government, especially any initiative designed to address a general phenomenon such as the effects of globalization, is bound to touch on a variety of its own policy domains as well as those of provincial legislatures. This is precisely why federal policy making has a centralizing bias, as noted by McBride:[45] spending initiatives tend to originate from the centre of government. The *Action Plan* is no exception, with the Department of Intergovernmental Affairs, in conjunction with the Treasury Board, having taken the initiative. But the centralizing bias has long been recognized by academics.[46] More to the point, the effectiveness of central agencies in serving to coordinate overall policy goals is not lost on the provinces. The provinces recently established a (provincial) council of the federation to centralize and coordinate their efforts to get what they think they deserve from the federal government, particularly in relation to transfers.

Finally, the centralizing tendency with regard to achieving policy goals may also be found in the federal government's continuously consulting with civil society groups, thereby circumventing and lessening provincial input into the formulation of federal policies. For example, according to one senior official,[47] the minister and Privy Council Office (intergovernmental affairs) officials met with 350 civil society groups (as well as with provincial ministers responsible for francophone affairs) to prepare the *Action Plan*. It is little wonder that the provinces have not reacted strongly to federal incursions into provincial legislative responsibilities. Civil society organizations, to which the provinces must also pay attention, have a lot to gain by cooperating with federal authorities.

In the end, accountability may be the Achilles' heel of federal endeavours to reposition the state in order to counter certain effects of globalization. According to pollsters, perceived deficiencies in subjective accountability (i.e., accountability as moral choice) appeared to turn public opinion, and probably voters, against the former federal Liberal government during the 2004 election.[48] The significance of the issue had declined prior to the 2006 election. However, an Environics Poll, taken just prior to the 2006 election, indicated that 94 percent of a sample of Canadians, polled in November 2005, said that "honesty and integrity in government are either somewhat or very important in determining how they plan to vote."[49] Canadians overwhelmingly want honesty (i.e., subjective accountability) in government. Of course, public opinion polls are temporary, but people could easily become disenchanted with the federal government if it is not fully able to enforce its own norms of accountability.

Accountability as Moral Choice and the *Action Plan*

The federal government under Paul Martin, has, in fact, modified subjective accountability norms and rules, and the new Conservative government continues to strengthen them. However, institutionally, the government may find itself in a quandary when it comes to choosing between the standard hierarchical norms of subjective accountability and the individualistic, decentralized, and business-oriented norms of the New Public Management (NPM) perspective. Free market principles, which are concomitant with globalization, govern the NPM. More important, the NPM is firmly embedded in the *Action Plan*'s "accountability and coordination framework."

Briefly, traditional approaches advocate the centralization of authority and hierarchical lines of responsibility governed by impersonal and written rules. In short, Weberian-inspired accountability espouses hierarchical control and the procedures that ensure that control. By contrast, NPM models of accountability are results-based rather than rules-based. Managerial initiatives and innovation are advocated to ensure that "clients" – namely, citizens – receive the best possible services and value from their tax dollars. In the end, there is a trade-off between procedure and results.

However, NPM results do not appear to be as effective as had originally been anticipated. The Association of Public Service Financial Accountants reported that, over the last twenty years, management reforms have led to "breakdowns in financial controls," which indicate that "the pendulum has swung too far."[50] The association, representing the government's three thousand accountants and financial officers, has called on the government to "re-establish order" by bringing back many of the practices shelved over the past decade; that is, by restoring traditional accountability.

The *Action Plan* framework is in accord with traditional approaches to accountability inasmuch as the Treasury Board (TB) is primarily responsible for implementing it, while Canadian Heritage is responsible for coordinating its activities. Justice is given additional responsibilities – and funds – to evaluate the legal implications of new initiatives and programs designed to promote the objectives of the *Action Plan*. TB and Canadian Heritage are also given additional responsibilities. However, new responsibilities are assigned to portfolios that were supposed to implement the old *Official Languages Act*. The government, by its own admission, failed to fully live up to its obligations under the *Official Languages Act* and concedes that these agencies, in turn, failed to meet their obligations under the *Act*. Was the failure a consequence of deficient organizational structures and responsibilities? If so, there is no reason to repeat them.

From a traditional hierarchical perspective on accountability, new structural changes and obligations raise other important issues. An obvious question, given the new responsibilities of TB, is *qui custodiet custodies*? The TB minister announced $800,000 to subsidize eighteen "innovative" projects, selected from proposals submitted by federal ministries and organizations as well as by regional councils that promote linguistic duality in their respective organizations. Some $14 million will be disbursed for innovative projects – and innovation is at the core of NPM – from the same fund over a five-year period.

However, TB is also responsible for program evaluation. Thus, the spender is its own evaluator, at least in part. And other central agencies – the Privy Council Office, for one – have also been granted funds under the *Action Plan*. These may just be administrative funds, but still, TB's responsibility sets a new precedent in which the spender gets to evaluate its own spending. In any event, although the situation is not usual from a traditional accountability perspective, it may be warranted in terms of results.

There are other features of the *Action Plan* that abandon traditional norms of accountability. All federal institutions analyze the impact of proposals set out in the memoranda to cabinet on the language rights of the public and of federal public servants. Above all, consider the additional requirements that departments and agencies are bound to discharge under article 17 of the accountability framework. The five new requirements – from determining the impacts of policies and programs on linguistic duality to providing for longer-term results mechanisms – translate into huge and additional administrative responsibilities.

In all fairness, new monies are provided to cover new administrative costs. But then the accountability framework is more than just "an ongoing reminder to ministers and public servants of their responsibility to making bilingualism a priority."[51] And it is more than just a clarification of the responsibilities of federal departments and agencies with respect to Canada's official languages.[52] There are detailed responsibilities under section 17, which amount to a crushing administrative burden on top of the normally assigned responsibilities for the delivery of program services.

This brings us to another core element of the NPM approach: culture change. Culture change is etched into the *Action Plan*. Managers are expected to change the "culture" of the public service. But from what culture to what culture? Has the public service heretofore been remiss in its "culture" of accountability with regard to bilingualism? More to the point, it is not clear how the broad impact of culture change is to be uniformly measured by the twenty-seven departments and institutions required to submit action plans on bilingualism.

In one significant instance – the Sponsorship Program (or the $100 million "Adscam," as it unfortunately came to be known) – certain federal officials made questionable moral choices to counter forces that supposedly threatened the Canadian state. The imperative of foiling sovereigntists by deliberately not keeping files on the Sponsorship Program was not in line with normal accountability procedures. But even if one were to have kept files, consider the accountability risks involved in spending money through second and, particularly, third parties.

First, spending money through the cash-strapped provinces always entails risk. In the context of the *Action Plan*, the federal Canadian Heritage Department will hold provincial and territorial departments of education accountable for spending federal funds in efforts related to the stated goals for language education. Additionally, the Department of Intergovernmental Affairs will hold provinces and territories accountable for spending federal funds in efforts to improve the allocation of public services and to promote and recognize the use of both official languages. Thus far, the federal government has relied on bilateral agreements, but without audits and measurable results.

Second, the *Action Plan* requires public officials to interact with private groups, communities, and the language industry by way of funding. Of course, funds are expected to enable the government to collaborate with communities on mutually agreed upon projects whose aim is to promote bilingualism. Moreover, the public financial assistance given to community groups is expected to empower communities. However, the $19 million allocated to minority communities only represents 2.5 percent of the *Action Plan*'s total expenditures. Many groups have complained that the policy invests more in government than in the communities and that the policy has become "bureaucratized."[53] Of course, it is not clear whether or not their complaints bode well for accountability because sometimes non-governmental groups adhere to different norms of accountability than do those associated with the government.

Moreover, there may be an optimal mix of policy tools – tax expenditures, tax credits, loan guarantees, and so on – besides direct grants (and/or in addition to direct grants). And these could be more effective than they were in the past in ensuring proactive compliance with government accountability norms while still empowering community and private groups. However, the effectiveness of the different combinations of tools is exceedingly difficult to measure under current accountability procedures, especially given the number of groups involved. Accordingly, taxpayers may not be receiving the best value for their tax dollars in relation to *Action Plan* expenditure.

Be that as it may, it is essential that Canadians get the best value for their tax dollars. Moreover, it is in the interest of the Canadian state to provide open and respectable accountability in governance as it repositions itself in an effort to advance national integration and to strengthen Canada's skills in the context of global competition while maintaining the confidence of Canadians.

Conclusion: Whither the Canadian State?

The confidence of Canadians in government has been eroding over the long term, as is well-documented elsewhere.[54] The waning confidence of Canadians, much of which relates to accountability, is a major part of the "democratic deficit," one of four crises of legitimacy challenging the Canadian state, according to Bakvis and Skogstad.[55] The three others crises are: (1) the failure to adequately integrate linguistic minorities, (2) the failure to recognize the specificity of Quebec, and (3) the failure to adequately resolve issues pertaining to Aboriginal claims and rights.

The *Action Plan* can certainly help to redress the democratic deficit by virtue of its inclusiveness, and it can help to integrate linguistic minorities. It can help to build a bridge to Quebec by fully integrating francophone linguistic minorities into the Canadian state, although it is difficult to determine how it can help to resolve Aboriginal issues, despite rhetoric that implies otherwise. If it can help to redress three out of four supposed "crises of legitimacy," then the *Action Plan* can serve as a powerful force in generating confidence and, thus, in fostering national integration and, concomitantly, strengthening the state within the context of globalization.

Globalization is not among the "crises of legitimacy" identified by Bakvis and Skogstad – and rightly so. The alleged disintegrative forces of globalization have been redressed by the Canadian state, which has shifted its resources from policies oriented to human consumption to policies oriented to human capital. It has made long-term investments to generate sustained economic activity in the knowledge sector and, thus, to spawn new high-value and high-paying jobs in that sector and, as a spin-off, to spawn low-value and low-paying jobs in what remains of the old economy.

The Canadian state has begun to effectively reposition itself, starting with national integration via the *Action Plan*, and to take on the challenges posed by globalization. But all this may come to naught if accountability were to emerge as a crisis of legitimacy.

Notes

1 See Andrew F. Johnson and Andrew Stritch, eds., *Canadian Public Policy: Globalization and Political Parties* (Toronto: Copp Clark Ltd., 1997), 9-12, for an overview of these theories.
2 Mathew Horsman and Andrew Marshall, *After the Nation State: Citizens, Tribalism and the New World Order* (London: Harper Collins, 1994), 85.
3 Stephen McBride and John Shields, *Dismantling a Nation: The Transition to Corporate Rule in Canada*, 2nd ed. (Halifax: Fernwood Press, 1997).
4 Robert Young, *The Struggle for Quebec: From Referendum to Referendum?* (Montreal/Kingston: McGill-Queen's University Press, 1999).
5 Privy Council Office (PCO), *The Next Act: New Momentum for Canada's Linguistic Duality* (Ottawa: Minister of Supply and Services, 2003). (Hereafter cited as PCO, *Action Plan for Official Languages*.)
6 Robert Gregory, "Accountability in Modern Government," in *Handbook of Public Administration*, ed. B. Guy Peters and Jon Pierre, 559-60 (Thousand Oaks, CA: Sage, 2002).
7 Maureen Covell, "Minority Language Policy in Canada and Europe: Does Federalism Make a Difference?" in *Canadian Federalism: Performance, Effectiveness, and Legitimacy*, ed. Herman Bakvis and Grace Skogstad, 240-41 (Don Mills, ON: Oxford, 2002).
8 Ibid., 241; and, in reference to David F. Marshall and Roseann D. Gonzalez "Why We Should Be Concerned about Language Rights: Language Rights as Human Rights from an Ecological Perspective," in *Language and the State: The Law and Politics of Identity*, ed. D. Schneiderman (Cowansville, QC: Y. Blais, 1991), 290.
9 Ibid., 241.
10 Canada, *Royal Commission on Bilingualism and Biculturalism* (Ottawa: Minister of Supply and Services, 1970).
11 PCO, *Action Plan for Official Languages* (Message from the prime minister of Canada and interview with the Honourable Stéphane Dion, March 26, 2004.)
12 Michael Wernick, "French to Follow? Revitalizing Official Languages in the Workplace," presentation to the Canadian Centre for Management Development University Seminar, May 15, 2003.
13 The Honourable Stéphane Dion, "The Action Plan for Official Languages Needs Research to Be a Success," address delivered to the Canadian Institute for Research on Linguistic Minorities, Ottawa, Ontario, December 5, 2003, p. 1.
14 Thomas L. Friedman, *The Lexus and the Olive Tree: Understanding Globalization* (New York: Farrar, Straus, Giroux, 1999), 11.
15 Stephen Clarkson, *Uncle Sam and Us: Globalization, Neoconservatism, and the Canadian State* (Toronto: University of Toronto Press), 49.
16 See Kari Levitt, *Silent Surrender: The American Economic Empire in Canada* (New York: St. Martin's Press, 1970), 71-89; and Benjamin R. Barber, *Jihad vs McWorld* (New York: Random House Inc., 2005), 3-32.
17 Michael Hart, *A Trading Nation: Canadian Trade Policy from Colonialism to Globalization* (Vancouver: UBC Press, 2002).
18 David Johnson, *Thinking Government: Public Sector Management in Canada* (Peterborough, ON: Broadview, 2002), 341-85.

19 The CFI was provided with a $3.15 billion endowment in 1997 to enhance the capabilities of universities, colleges, research hospitals, and other not-for-profit institutions. The Millennium Scholarship Fund was provided with a $2.5 billion endowment primarily to help students in need as well as to reward academic merit. The *Action Plan*, 2003, provides for $751.3 million in additional spending over five years.

20 Interview with the Honourable Stéphane Dion, March 26, 2004.

21 Ibid.

22 PCO, *Action Plan for Official Languages*, vii.

23 Ibid.

24 Ibid., 2. In addition, the *Action Plan*, "in the spirit of openness and pluralism," is promoted as a way to "help Canada's Aboriginal peoples preserve their own languages."

25 Andrew Parkin and André Turcotte, *Bilingualism: Part of Our Past or Part of Our Future?* (Montreal: Centre for Research and Information on Canada, 2004).

26 *National Post*, December 1, 2003.

27 Interview with the Honourable Stéphane Dion, March 26, 2004.

28 Privy Council Office, Government of Canada, *Update on the Action Plan for Official Languages* (Ottawa: Minister of Supply and Services, October 2005), 31. Although the *Action Plan* has not been given much attention by the national media, minority language groups are well-acquainted with it. Indeed the federal minister responsible for official languages consults the national sectoral federations every year, and officials from several federal departments hold an annual meeting with these groups. Also, both the Fédération des communautés francophones et acadienne and the Quebec Community Groups Network participated in the mid-term review of the *Action Plan*.

29 Ibid., 11.

30 Canada, *Royal Commission on Financial Management and Accountability* (Ottawa: Minister of Supply and Services, 1979), 21.

31 Garth Stevenson, "Canadian Federalism: The Myth of the Status Quo," in *Reinventing Canada: Politics of the 21st Century*, ed. Janine Brodie and Linda Trimble (Toronto: Pearson Education Inc., 2003), 207-8.

32 T. Courchene, "Globalization and the Regional International Interface," *Canadian Journal of Regional Science* 18, 1 (1995): 1-20.

33 See, for example, Trevor C. Salmon and Michael Keating, eds., *The Dynamics of Decentralization: Canadian Federalism and British Devolution* (Montreal: McGill-Queen's University Press, 2001).

34 Stephen McBride, "Quiet Constitutionalism in Canada: The International Political Economy of Domestic Institutional Change," *Canadian Journal of Political Science* 36, 2 (2003): 253.

35 Ibid., 253-54.

36 PCO, *Action Plan for Official Languages*, 17.

37 Ibid., 26.

38 The *Action Plan* identifies six educational goals to be attained over the next decade: first, to increase the number of eligible students enrolled in francophone schools outside Quebec; second, to support French-language instruction for anglophones and to expand options available to students outside Montreal; third, to double the proportion of secondary school graduates with a functional knowledge of their second official language; fourth, to improve access to postsecondary education; fifth, to improve bursary and monitor programs; and, sixth, to help promote research.

39 Michael D. Behiels, *Canada's Francophone Communities: Constitutional Renewal and the Winning of School Governance* (Montreal/Kingston: McGill-Queen's University Press, 2005).

40 Commission nationale des parents francophones, "Où sont passés les milliards?" *Étude sommaire sur la répartition des subventiones du Programme des langues officielles en enseignement, 1970-71 à 1995-96* (Ottawa, October 1996).

41 The provinces that continue to depict themselves as cash-strapped in the educational sector are hard pressed to object to federal infusions of cash. In Quebec, anglophone minority rights in the educational sector are already well protected, at least relative to those in the other provinces.

42 In its health component, the *Action Plan* identifies three "priorities" for funding: (1) training, recruitment, and retention of health professionals; (2) networking (e.g., organizing symposiums and research-oriented conferences); and (3) primary health care. Significantly, the $119 million disbursement makes health care the second biggest budgetary item, after education, in the *Action Plan*.

43 The Honourable Stéphane Dion, President of the Privy Council and Minister of Intergovernmental Affairs, "The Health Component of the *Action Plan for Official Languages*: A Story of Exemplary Cooperation," speech delivered at the Symposium for the Creation of a French-Language Health Network for Nova Scotia, Halifax, May 23, 2003.

44 Interview with the Honourable Stéphane Dion, March 26, 2004.

45 McBride, "Quiet Constitutionalism," 258. See also R. Daniel Kelemen, *The Rules of Federalism: Institutions and Regulatory Politics in the EU and Beyond* (Cambridge: Harvard University press, 2002), 3.

46 See, for example, Thomas A. Hockin, *Apex of Power: The Prime Minister and Political Leadership in Canada* (Scarborough, ON: Prentice-Hall Inc., 1971); and Donald J. Savoie, *Governing from the Centre: The Concentration of Political Power in Canada* (Toronto: University of Toronto Press, 1999).

47 Interview with Privy Council Office official, April 2004.

48 See http://www.Canada.com/national/national post/news/storyhtml?id=e1ofe1c4-b12e-4a8d-83e9-F29cbca2c88, which indicates that the Adscam scandal became a prominent issue in the 2004 election.

49 See http://www.cbc.ca/Canadavotes/analysiscommntary/poll.html.

50 The Association of Public Service Financial Administrators (APSFA), *Checks and Balances: Rebalancing the Service and Control Features of the Government of Canada (GOC) Financial Control Framework* (Ottawa: APSFA, December 2003), 1.

51 The Honourable Marlene Jennings, "Canada's Linguistic Duality, *Issues*, April 2, 2003, http://www.marlenejennings.parl.gc.ca/issue_details.asp?lang=en&IssueID=128.

52 Canadian Heritage, *Formative Evaluation of the "Interdepartmental Partnership with Official Language Communities" (IPOLC) Component of the Promotion of Official Languages Program*, http://www.canadianheritage.gc.ca/progs/em-cr/eval/1004/2004_03/6_e.cfm.

53 Interviews with minority language group leaders, October 2005.

54 See Andrew F. Johnson, "Democracy, Prosperity, Citizens and the State," *Canadian Foreign Policy* 10, 1 (2002): 23-40; and Neil Nevitte, ed., *Value Change and Governance in Canada* (Toronto: University of Toronto Press, 2002).

55 Herman Bakvis and Grace Skogstad, "Canadian Federalism: Performance, Effectiveness, and Legitimacy," in Bakvis and Skogstag, *Canadian Federalism*, 17-21.

7
Making International Agreements and Making Them Work within a Multicultural Federal State: The Experience of Canada
Hugh Kindred

The multicultural nature of Canadian society, while subject to much introspection, also deserves consideration from an outward-looking perspective. Such a view takes account of how Canada developed by means of massive immigration and how, as a consequence, Canadians have connections to many cultures and societies beyond its borders. In short, it invites inquiry into the ability of the Canadian constitutional process to cope with the many transnational relations of a culturally diverse society. One technique of accommodation, the subject of this chapter, involves adjustment by international agreements. Indeed, the high degree of interdependence of peoples and countries in modern society necessitates making international agreements to coordinate and manage human affairs.

International agreements, also commonly called treaties, are binding legal instruments under international law between the states that conclude them. Traditionally, treaties regulated the diplomatic relations between states. Normalizing foreign relations was the chief purpose for their conclusion. Peace treaties, defence pacts, settlements of interstate claims, and the exchange of various diplomatic agents were common. Not so today. Treaty practice has greatly changed in subject matter, volume, and domestic impact. In addition to continuing to regulate diplomatic relations, the bulk of modern international agreements now greatly affect the daily lives of individual members of the public regarding such matters as citizenship, family relations, health, education, property, work, and communications.

These changes in treaty practices are particularly significant for an immigrant society made up of many cultural traditions, such as Canada, whose residents engage in numerous transnational transactions with their former "home" territories. Indeed, maintenance of the Canadian cultural mosaic is supported by the relative ease and freedom of international communications as well as by the recognition and respect for transnational human rights, responsibilities, and status that the network of modern treaties provides. Consequently, the process of making treaties internationally and then implementing them domestically is crucial to the provision and protection of people's rights.

Unfortunately, within Canada, constitutional principles create complex problems. However, judicial views about the constitutional impact of treaties have recently become more open and inclusive. In particular, fresh approaches to the interpretation of statutes allow for greater, if indirect, domestic influence of internationally binding but nationally unincorporated treaties. This opening of the constitutional process to greater interaction with international agreements allows Canadian courts to pass on the benefits of modern treaties to Canada's multicultural citizenry in ways that it is the purpose of this chapter to explore.

Constitutional Complexity of International Agreements

Making agreements internationally is a different and separate activity from implementing them nationally. In Canada, following the constitutional model of the United Kingdom, the power to conclude treaties internationally lies with the government (executive) as a matter of royal, or Crown, prerogative. But the power to give effect to the contents of a treaty thus concluded frequently rests with the relevant legislature(s). The constitutional principle of supremacy of parliament requires that any changes to domestic law mandated by treaty obligations must be effected by legislation. In 1937, in the judgment of the Judicial Committee of the Privy Council in the *Labour Conventions Case*, a well-known case in Canadian constitutional law, Lord Atkin affirmed the operative principle in these words: "Within the British Empire there is a well-established rule that the making of a treaty is an executive act, while the performance of its obligations, if they entail alteration of existing domestic law, requires legislative action."[1]

Thus the process of concluding a treaty in international law and the mechanism for implementing it in national law involve different bodies with separate powers. In Canada, this process is further subdivided as a result of the country's federal system. According to the Canadian Constitution, as expressed by the Imperial Parliament in the *British North America Act*, 1867, now renamed the *Constitution Act*, 1867,[2] plenary authority is allocated either to the federal government or to the provinces. For example, federal authority extends to national defence, shipping and navigation, fisheries, criminal law, patents and copyrights, currency, banking, and taxation and bankruptcy, while provincial powers cover companies, business and professional licensing, and property and civil rights,[3] which include education, health, and social services.

In regard to foreign affairs, the federal government exercises the prerogative power to engage Canada in international agreements, but it cannot change the law within Canada to accord with the treaties it makes. That power lies with the federal or provincial legislatures, according to the division of responsibilities under the Canadian Constitution. As Lord Atkin also said in the *Labour Conventions Case*:

> [I]n a federal state where legislative authority is limited by a constitutional document, or is divided up between different Legislatures in accordance with the classes of subject-matter submitted for legislation, the problem is complex. The obligations imposed by a treaty may have to be performed, if at all, by several Legislatures: and the executive have the task of obtaining the legislative assent not of the one Parliament to whom they may be responsible, but possibly of several Parliaments to whom they stand in no direct relation ...
>
> For the purposes of ... the distribution of legislative powers between the Dominion [of Canada] and the Provinces, there is no such thing as treaty legislation as such. The distribution is based on classes of subjects; and as a treaty deals with a particular class of subjects so will the legislative power of performing it be ascertained.[4]

Thus, in Canada, to the separation of powers between executive and legislature must be added the division of powers between federal and provincial authorities. The result for the application of international treaties within Canada is a somewhat dysfunctional constitutional process. If the subject matter of a treaty falls within the plenary jurisdiction of the provinces, any one of them may thwart the federal government's intentions to conclude or adhere to it by refusing, or simply failing, to pass implementing legislation. Alternatively, the federal government may adhere to the treaty at the risk that provincial legislatures will not implement it and, thus, potentially place Canada in breach of its international obligations. Furthermore, it is clear under international law that a deficiency in a country's internal legal system is no defence for the violation of an international agreement.[5]

This is not a happy state of constitutional affairs. It arose in Canada as a result of the United Kingdom's gradual devolution of sovereignty to its former colony and dominion. In 1867, when Canada was founded, the *Constitution Act* created it with a federal system of internal self-government and "a constitution similar in principle to that of the United Kingdom."[6] Nothing was said about foreign relations powers since Her Majesty's government at Westminster continued to exercise the royal prerogative for Canada. The only reference to treaties was to the power granted to the federal Parliament for "performing the Obligations of Canada or of any Province thereof as part of the British Empire toward Foreign Countries, arising under Treaties between the Empire and such Foreign Countries."[7] When Canada ultimately achieved full sovereignty, the remaining prerogative powers devolved to the federal government, which, by implication, took over the former role of the British government for foreign relations, including the power to make treaties for Canada generally.[8] Shortly thereafter, as noted above,[9] the *Labour Conventions Case* determined that making Canada's treaties internally operative is solely a matter for the legislature responsible for the subject matter of the treaty.

Importance of International Agreements in a Multicultural Society

The complexity of the Canadian constitutional process with regard to concluding and applying treaties would matter little if their subject matter had remained the same as it was in the mid-1800s, when Canada was born, or even since 1928, when the Canada Treaty Series, a record of Canada's independent treaty practice, was initiated.[10] In the Canada Treaty Series' first fifty years (from 1928 to 1978), the *Canadian Treaty Calendar*, prepared by Christian Wiktor, reports that 1,417 treaties were published,[11] of which thirty were made by Great Britain on behalf of Canada prior to 1928.[12] Of the eighty categories of subject matter, the ten most common in order of frequency were commerce, defence, aviation, taxation, telecommunications, finance, fisheries, atomic energy, economic and technical cooperation, and scientific cooperation.[13] Most of these subjects exclusively concern the administration of foreign affairs, and, therefore, the federal government may execute them without seeking any further authority. They do not affect internal laws, so they do not require legislation in order to be implemented. Further, all but (possibly) commerce are subjects that come within federal authority, and, therefore, the government of Canada, having concluded a treaty with regard to them, may introduce in the federal Parliament any implementing legislation that might be necessary.

By contrast, in the past twenty-five years, 1,038 treaties were recorded in the Canada Treaty Series,[14] which amounts to almost a 50 percent increase in Canada's rate of treaty making. More significantly, the range of subject matter dramatically increased from 80 to 130 categories, of which the leading seven were aviation, taxation, trade and commerce, criminal matters, cultural affairs, social security, and atomic energy.[15] Noticeably, topics purely about foreign relations, such as defence, economic and technical cooperation, and scientific cooperation, disappeared from the list of leading subjects and were replaced by topics that reflected the varied human interests of individual Canadians. Significantly, such human-centred concerns, as opposed to the state-centred concerns connected to foreign relations, generally fall within the subject matter of local property and civil rights, over which the provinces have constitutional authority.[16] Hence, much more often than in the past, treaties require affirmative legislation to be brought into operation, and such legislation has to be enacted by each of the ten provincial legislatures.

The change in volume and variety of international agreements reflects the evolution of Canadian society. Two features of that evolution have particular significance for the making and applying of treaties. Modern technology, especially in the field of communications, has made human interactions across former natural boundaries and state frontiers so much easier, faster, and convenient. As a result, millions of people have discovered they can move about much more freely than ever before and are, in fact, migrating in ever larger numbers. This phenomenon of mass migration is contributing to the development of multicultural societies in a great many countries. It has had a spectacular effect on the human composition of Canada, which has become an extraordinarily plural society composed of immigrant peoples. Today almost a quarter of the population over fifteen years of age is comprised of new Canadians[17] (i.e., first-generation immigrants).[18]

Not surprisingly, there is a vast range of continuing human contacts between new and not so new Canadians and their former home countries.[19] These associations are expressed through family, cultural, religious, commercial, and financial connections, commitments, and transactions as well as, regrettably, through criminal ones. En masse, these individual actions heavily affect international relations, both for the good and for the bad. Inevitably, the Canadian government has variously to assist, mediate, defend, and assert the claims of Canadians on the international plane. It does this, apart from supporting individual cases, by concluding ever more administratively detailed intergovernmental treaties. Harmonization of national laws, reciprocal recognition of family relations, immigration protocols, cultural and educational exchanges, admission of foreign investors and investment, and mutual legal assistance in criminal justice are a few examples of the subjects of bilateral and multilateral treaties that the Canadian government concludes in its efforts to deal with the multicultural diversity of Canadian society. All of these kinds of treaties, it should be noted, are about human concerns regarding daily living and must, therefore, be translated into Canadian law by appropriate legislation through the requisite legislatures.

Coping with the Multicultural Consequences of International Agreements

What may be done to surmount the increasing problems of adopting and applying international agreements within the multicultural Canadian constitutional process? Constitutional reform would be a good idea, but it is politically impossible, for the time being at least. The two previous attempts in the last quarter century included discussions about treaty-making matters but failed with regard to much larger issues;[20] instead, the Canadian courts have increasingly been called upon to resolve problems at the point of applying the law. The courts, of course, cannot alter constitutional principles – indeed, they are bound to uphold them. But through their powers of interpretation with regard to both statutes and treaties, the courts may be able to moderate the effects of Canada's dilemma concerning its constitutional discontinuity.[21]

The way treaty problems frequently present themselves in specific cases before the courts is as a claim of right, status, or privilege that is expressed in an international agreement but that has not been incorporated into Canadian law through appropriate legislation. In the past, many courts simply ignored unincorporated treaties. Relying upon the affirmation in the *Labour Conventions Case*,[22] which held that international agreements that affect domestic law require legislative implementation in order to take effect domestically, courts refused to consider the provisions of a ratified treaty whose subject matter seemed relevant to the instant case if that treaty had not been implemented.[23] In recent times, this judicial attitude was most prevalent during Bora Laskin's tenure as chief justice of Canada. In this, as in all judicial matters, the Supreme Court of Canada is looked to for leadership. Chief Justice Laskin was a brilliant constitutional scholar who held a firm and narrow attitude towards the impact of international law on the Court. In *MacDonald v. Vapor Canada Ltd.*,[24] Laskin C.J.C. discussed the constitutional process and the need for certainty with regard to the legislative implementation of a treaty, without any comment on the relevance of the unimplemented treaty put before him. In *Capital Cities Communications Inc. v. Canadian Radio-Television Commission*,[25] the Supreme Court was invited to interpret the powers of the CRTC under the *Broadcasting Act* in light of the *Inter-American Radio Communications Convention*. Laskin C.J.C. refused, saying: "There would be no domestic, internal consequences unless they arose from implementing legislation giving the Convention a legal effect within Canada."[26]

Chief Justice Laskin's views were shared by other members of the Supreme Court,[27] but not without some resistance. Laskin C.J.C. drew a very rigid line in holding that an unimplemented treaty could have "no domestic, internal consequences" at all. Pigeon J., in the same case, expressed strong dissent:

> I cannot agree that the Commission may properly issue authorizations in violation of Canada's treaty obligations. Its duty is to implement the policy established by Parliament. While this policy makes no reference to Canada's treaty obligations, it is an integral part of the national structure that external affairs are the responsibility of the federal Government. It is an over-simplification to say that treaties are of no legal effect unless implemented by legislation.[28]

But since Chief Justice Laskin's leadership of the Supreme Court in the 1970s, judicial attitudes have changed. The shift in perspective was partly due to a change of personalities on the Court, but mostly it resulted from the impact of the new *Canadian Charter of Rights and Freedoms,* which was established as an entrenched set of human rights within the Canadian Constitution in the process of the latter's patriation from the United Kingdom in 1982.[29]

The *Canadian Charter* grants an extensive list of civil and political rights to all residents of Canada.[30] They are expressed very broadly indeed: for example, "Everyone has ... freedom of thought, belief, opinion and expression"; and "Everyone has the right to life, liberty and security of the person."[31] The *Charter* gives to the courts the task of determining the specific meaning and scope of the application of these rights.[32] Their authority includes the power to strike down federal and provincial enactments that violate *Charter* rights,[33] or to sustain statutory provisions that apparently contravene the *Charter,* when, in the saving words of section 1, they represent "such reasonable limits prescribed by law as can be demonstrably justified in a free and democratic society."[34] Thus, the courts gained enormous power to influence the social and economic fabric of Canada through their surveillance of the application of the rights expressed in the *Charter.*

Yet the acquisition of such generous discretionary power also brought new judicial problems. How were the courts supposed to interpret and apply the rights so generally expressed in the *Charter*? Little guidance was given to them, except for the admonition to interpret the *Charter* "in a manner consistent with the preservation and enhancement of the multicultural heritage of Canada."[35] The courts might have been narrow-minded and followed past precedents of similar rights still respected in common law. This would have been an entirely natural way for Canadian common law courts (i.e., courts outside of Quebec) to proceed;[36] instead, the Supreme Court chose to lead the way with a much broader and more inclusive approach to the task.[37] It sought to give a meaning to the rights in the *Charter* within the context of Canadian society today. The important aspect of this approach with regard to treaty application is that the Supreme Court determined that its contextual perspective of the *Canadian Charter of Rights and Freedoms* had to include advertence to international laws and conventions on human rights.

In *Slaight Communications Inc. v. Davidson,*[38] Chief Justice Dickson (who followed Chief Justice Laskin in that office but took a decidedly more open approach to international legal sources) reiterated in his majority judgment what he had said in dissent in the earlier case of *Ref. re Public Service Employee Relations Act:*[39]

The content of Canada's international human rights obligations is ... an important indicia of the meaning of the "full benefit of the *Charter's* protection." I believe that the *Charter* should generally be presumed to provide protection at least as great as that afforded by similar provisions in international human rights documents which Canada has ratified.[40]

Deploying this general statement, Dickson C.J.C. then enlarged on the particular relationship between international law and the *Canadian Charter*:

> Canada's international human rights obligations should inform not only the interpretation of the content of the rights guaranteed by the *Charter* but also the interpretation of what can constitute pressing and substantial section 1 objectives which may justify restrictions upon those rights. Furthermore, for purposes of this stage of the proportionality inquiry, the fact that a value has the status of an international human right, either in customary international law or under a treaty to which Canada is a party, should generally be indicative of a high degree of importance attached to that objective.[41]

The Supreme Court thus established that Canada's international human rights obligations should inform and nourish the interpretation of Canada's domestic *Charter of Rights and Freedoms*. Further, this position was achieved even though the *Charter* makes no reference to international human rights or the treaties that protect them.

The attention given by the Supreme Court to international human rights in the context of interpreting the *Canadian Charter* was surely appropriate, if unpredictable in light of the Court's past attitudes towards international sources of law. In noting the resort to international human rights laws, it is also important to observe a distinction in those sources that the courts seem to have ignored. Chief Justice Dickson was careful in the cases just quoted to refer to customary international law and to treaties to which Canada is a party, inferentially excluding other sources, including other treaties, which are not binding on Canada. But among the treaties binding on Canada, he did not distinguish between those that have been incorporated within Canadian law by implementing legislation and those that have not. In point of fact, virtually no international human rights conventions to which Canada is a party have been specifically implemented by provincial or federal legislation.[42] But, in respect to the law of the *Canadian Charter* at least, lack of domestic implementation does not matter; indeed, it is beside the point because the Supreme Court has been pleased to consider as part of the context of its interpretation all human rights treaties to which Canada is a party.

Human rights are a very important part of social life and are especially significant with regard to the diversity of life in a multicultural society like Canada, but they are not all of the legal rules affecting individuals in a personal way. So it has been of great interest to observe whether and to what extent the Supreme Court's changed attitude towards international treaties appertaining to human rights in the *Canadian Charter* has spilled over to other areas of Canadian law.[43]

It may now confidently be said of the Supreme Court that the interpretation of any legislation must be made in context, which includes all relevant national and international legal sources. This is a large assertion, and it leaves plenty of room for interpretive manoeuvres. It has also been subjected to objection, even in the Supreme Court. Remember that, though the federal government may make a treaty, it may not make law: that is the task of the appropriate legislature. Consequently, it has been argued that a court should not consider a treaty concluded by the government and binding on Canada, but that has not been incorporated within Canadian law, as an aid to the interpretation of any given statute since it would then be letting through the back door what it may not admit through the front door.[44] There is enough truth in this observation that the Supreme Court justices, in the majority, have, in fact, been quite circumspect in the way they have exercised their new-found readiness to invoke international legal sources. "Applying" statutorily unimplemented treaties would be entirely too strong an appellation to apply to their usage. Respecting the values to be found in the treaties to which Canada is a party as part of the social fabric of Canadian society and, therefore, as part of the legislative context of the statute under interpretation, might be a more appropriate description of the Supreme Court's current approach. The case of Ms. Baker may clarify the generality of this very important idea.

In *Baker v. Canada (Minister of Citizenship and Immigration)*,[45] a Jamaican citizen named Ms. Baker entered Canada in 1981 and bore four children here before she was ordered to be deported in 1992. Ms Baker then applied for permanent residency based on humanitarian and compassionate (H&C) grounds, pursuant to the Canadian *Immigration Act*.[46] Her application having been denied, she appealed on several grounds, including that the discretion of the immigration officer under the *Act* had been exercised improperly because inadequate account had been taken of the interests of her four Canadian children.

In allowing the appeal, the majority opinion of the Supreme Court delivered by Justice L'Heureux-Dubé contained an important argument.[47] She started from the premise that the *Immigration Act* required the immigration officer to exercise the discretionary power based upon humanitarian and compassionate considerations in a reasonable manner. She then noted that, to determine whether the approach used by the officer was within the boundaries of the discretionary power granted by the *Act*, one was required to use a contextual interpretation of that statute. As a result, in her opinion, a reasonable exercise of that power demanded close attention to the interests of Ms. Baker's children because children's rights are "central humanitarian and compassionate values in Canadian society."[48] Evidence for these contextual values was to be found, she held, in the purposes of the *Act*, in international instruments, and in departmental guidelines on making H&C decisions.

When Justice L'Heureux-Dubé examined the evidence of international instruments, she cited the *United Nations Convention on the Rights of the Child* as a relevant treaty.[49] She noted that it had been ratified by Canada and was, therefore, binding, but she reaffirmed that it could not be part of Canadian law unless it had been implemented by legislation,[50] which it had not. Yet, significantly, she continued: "Nevertheless, the values reflected in international human rights law may help inform the contextual approach to statutory interpretation and judicial review."[51] Finding that the values and principles of the *Convention* place importance on being attentive to the best interests of children when decisions are made that affect their future, Justice L'Hereux-Dubé determined that the immigration officer's decision, because it had minimized the interests of Ms. Baker's children, was in conflict with the H&C values of the *Immigration Act*. She therefore held the decision was unreasonable and so could not stand.

This judgment of the Supreme Court constitutes a full-scale demonstration of reference, even deference, to binding but unimplemented international agreements as a positive aid to statutory interpretation. It demands that courts make affirmative use of international law, and, particularly, of ratified treaties, in the interpretation and application of domestic legislation. Such attention to unincorporated international agreements gives them a more significant role in the national legal system.

The judicial change in approach is especially appropriate in the multicultural society of Canada today. It allows residents to test their international rights to the extent that, even when a treaty is unimplemented, they may at least rely on the values underlying its specific provisions. They have gained the means to realize domestically their expectations of the range of modern treaties pertaining to family relations and human rights. New and would-be Canadians are particularly likely to benefit, as the case of *Suresh v. Canada (Minister of Citizenship and Immigration)* demonstrates.[52]

Suresh was a Sri Lankan who came to Canada as a refugee. He was also determined by the Canadian government to be a member of a terrorist organization, the Tamil Tigers, and therefore was ordered to be deported. The order was made under the *Immigration Act*,[53] which implements the provisions of the *Convention on the Status of Refugees*,[54] which protects refugees

and forbids returning them ("refoulement") to their country of origin except when there are reasonable grounds for regarding them as dangerous to
the security of the receiving state. Suresh appealed the order against him,
claiming that he would be at risk of being tortured if he were returned to Sri
Lanka. He argued that two international human rights treaties, the *International Covenant for Civil and Political Rights*[55] and the *Convention against Tor-
ture*,[56] forbade his deportation to a country in which he would be tortured.
The Supreme Court of Canada, in accepting this argument, adopted the
approach of *Baker* towards internationally binding but domestically unincorporated treaties. Through the lens of the *Canadian Charter of Rights and
Freedoms*,[57] the Court employed these two human rights treaties to reinterpret the section of the *Immigration Act* that implemented the *Refugee Convention* by limiting the exception to "non-refoulement." Thus, the human
rights treaties radically influenced the decision about Suresh's right to stay
in Canada and, more generally, advanced respect for the multicultural make-
up of Canadian society.

In *Baker*, Justice L'Heureux-Dubé reached her seminal decision via a contextual approach to statutory interpretation. Such a perspective on statutory
interpretation is, nowadays, the guiding principle for this judicial task. This
was not always the case. Courts asserted that they applied clearly worded
statutes without recourse to any extrinsic aids to interpretation.[58] Inevitably,
then, binding but unincorporated treaties would never even be considered.[59]
But, as explained above, the introduction of the *Canadian Charter of Rights
and Freedoms* ushered in a whole new judicial attitude towards the courts'
societal functions. With it followed a series of cases expounding an inclusive
approach to statutory interpretation generally, which, in turn, demanded a
search for the meaning of legislative words within their whole context.[60]

Yet such an approach raises the question of what is meant by "context."
For instance, if the statute subject to interpretation refers to a treaty but does
not incorporate it, may the terms of the treaty be called in aid? If so, might
the court go further and review the international preparatory work on the
treaty or the interpretation and application of the treaty in foreign courts or
other fora? The Supreme Court settled this issue in a line of cases that provided the most expansive solution. Once it was admitted that the plain-
meaning approach was inadequate and that a contextualized-meaning
approach should be taken towards legislative language, the judges accepted
references to all sorts of international resources as extrinsic aids to their
interpretive task. Thus, the Supreme Court has used the treaty itself, related
international agreements, preparatory documents, general principles of international law, relevant UN resolutions, and other UN documents (such as
guidelines for practice under the treaty), foreign governments' and foreign
courts' applications of the treaty, and scholarly commentaries about the
treaty and related international law.[61]

The current legal position is that unimplemented treaties, whether binding on Canada or not, as well as their associated documentary sources must not be ignored; rather, they must be employed to inform the application, including statutory operation, of Canadian law. In some respects, this new-found role for international agreements within the Canadian legal system hearkens back to two much more venerable principles of judicial responsibility. The first is the oft-reiterated idea that judges are bound to try to interpret statutes consistently with international law. In 1968, Pigeon J. spoke in the Supreme Court of a "rule of construction that Parliament is not presumed to legislate in breach of a treaty or in any manner inconsistent with the comity of nations and the established rules of international law."[62] In *National Corn Growers Association v. Canada (Import Tribunal)*, Gonthier J., writing for the majority of the Supreme Court, observed: "where the text of the domestic law lends itself to it, one should also strive to expound an interpretation which is consonant with the relevant international obligations."[63] In the case of *Baker*, L'Heureux-Dubé J. quoted approvingly from Driedger on the Construction of Statutes (itself a respected study of Canadian court practice):

> [T]he legislature is presumed to respect the values and principles contained in international law ... These constitute a part of the legal context in which legislation is enacted and read. *In so far as possible, therefore, interpretations that reflect these values and principles are preferred.*[64]

The rationale for this principle of interpretation is not hard to appreciate. It profoundly supports the legality of the actions of the legislatures and the courts. A different presumption would defeat the rule of law, which judges are sworn to uphold. In addition, states are bound by international law to fulfill their treaty obligations and may not invoke their domestic law as justification for their failure to do so.[65] If they can avoid doing so, the courts should not deliberately place Canada in breach of its international law obligations.

The second principle of judicial regard for international law is somewhat more ambivalent. As early as 1764, Lord Mansfield reported that Lord Talbot had declared a clear opinion "that the law of nations in its full extent was part of the law of England."[66] In more recent times, Lord Atkin, speaking for the Judicial Committee of the Privy Council when it was still the highest court of appeal for Canada, in *Chung Chi Cheung v. The King*, expounded the principle in greater detail:

> It must always be remembered that ... international law has no validity save in so far as its principles are accepted and adopted by our own domestic law. There is no external power that imposes its rules upon our own

code of substantive law or procedure. The Courts acknowledge the existence of a body of rules which nations accept amongst themselves. On any judicial issue they seek to ascertain what the relevant rule is, and, having found it, they will treat it as incorporated into domestic law, so far as it is not inconsistent with rules enacted by statutes or finally declared by their tribunals.[67]

This is a deeply ambiguous statement about the relationship of international and national law, which has been "cited with approval time and again"[68] by Canadian courts, including the Supreme Court.[69] Such frequent quotation may give judges the comfort of the superficial authority of the leading precedent, but it does nothing to explicate the meaning of that precedent. Lord Atkin probably knew precisely what he meant by this statement, but those after him have proved capable of reading his words in a variety of different ways.

The first two sentences seem to express the ordinary constitutional position of domestic law and the courts that administer it. Judges hold their position by virtue of the Constitution, and they must be consistent with it in exercising their judicial authority, including determining and applying the law. So the critical issue is to what extent the constitutional process admits international law as part of the law of the land. Lord Atkin's third sentence indicates that the courts recognise the body of international law, which, by his fourth sentence, they treat as incorporated into domestic law. Most of the confusion has arisen over the proviso at the end of Lord Atkin's statement. A relevant rule of international law will be applied "so far as it is not inconsistent with rules enacted by statutes or finally declared by ... [domestic] tribunals." In the context of the status and effect of binding but legislatively unimplemented treaties, it is the exception for inconsistency with statutes that poses the principle problem with this precedent.

At different times, courts have felt free to deny any domestic legal effect to binding treaties that appear to them to be inconsistent with a relevant statute. They have not stopped to consider how the treaty may be read with the statute so as to avoid any prima facie inconsistency.[70] Thus, the Supreme Court under Chief Justice Laskin, as explained above,[71] essentially promoted the exception into the rule and displaced all relevant international agreements that were not clearly and deliberately enacted into Canadian law. Fortunately, this attitude has now been eclipsed. The Supreme Court's present contextual approach to statutory interpretation ensures that respect for binding international law is the rule and that this rule will only be subject to genuine exception when a piece of legislation is insurmountably in conflict with it.

Happily, therefore, the application of international law in general, and unimplemented treaties in particular, has been reinforced in contemporary judicial practice by the conjunction of these three principles: (1) contextualized interpretation of domestic law, which includes (2) affirmative use of binding international agreements to discover a statutory meaning consistent with international obligations, unless (3) the statutory wording in question is irremediably conflicting.

Conclusions

The expectations of Canada's multicultural society impel the Canadian government to make many international agreements that fall to the provincial governments to decide upon with regard to internal implementation. This division of powers creates a discontinuity between governing authority and the execution of external and internal affairs, which is obviously not conducive to the smooth functioning of Canada's foreign relations or its multicultural federalism. It is ironic that the constitutional system of federalism, which was deliberately established to allow for a certain cultural and regional diversity in governance,[72] should have unwittingly become an obstacle to the ready conduct of the transnational relationships of Canadians.

The Supreme Court of Canada has recently moved into the constitutional gap, handing down some constructive decisions. The *Baker* case is one example of an ongoing story.[73] The Supreme Court is still addressing the constitutional tension between legal recognition of the supremacy of Parliament and the legislatures, on the one hand, and the impelling force of binding international treaty obligations, on the other. It also continues to struggle over the appropriate limits of its own judicial powers with regard to interstitial constitutional change. Even so, a few features of the larger story are becoming clear.

1 The making of binding international agreements is the prerogative of the federal government, but the domestic operation of these agreements depends, in the first place, on the transformative action of the appropriate federal or provincial legislatures. In the absence of treaty implementing legislation, or in the face of discordant local legislation, the task of making international agreements operate falls to the courts.

2 The Supreme Court has accepted, if at times uncomfortably, that it (and consequently all the courts below it as well) now has a significantly enhanced social role in Canadian society. Brought to notice through litigation concerning the interpretation and application of the *Canadian Charter of Rights and Freedoms*, its decisions, and hence its composition and processes, are increasingly the subject of media commentary as well as public and personal discussion.

3 This social duty is a very sensitive public function in a multicultural society like Canada because the role of the Supreme Court, which is at the apex of a hierarchy of courts from fourteen different federal, provincial,

and territorial jurisdictions, is to induce an acceptable unity from among the diversity of claims and rulings from all regions of the country.

4 One consequence has been judicial recognition that the determination of the correct application of law, particularly statutory law, now requires an interpretation in context, which includes any relevant international laws binding on Canada.

5 Thus, international law informs the interpretation and application of Canadian law. In the absence of implementing legislation by the appropriate federal or provincial legislatures, binding international agreements that may alter Canadian law may not be applied directly within that law. But neither may they be ignored since they are part of the transnational reality of Canada's multicultural society, which the law is bound to take into account (along with all the usual national legal sources) if it is going to successfully serve that society. Even if the legislatures do not incorporate international agreements, the courts have a constitutional duty to pay attention to their values and principles in the process of determining the legal rights and duties of Canadians, in all their social and cultural diversity.

Undoubtedly, this constitutional predicament is not a satisfactory or enduring position, but it does show that the Canadian Constitution is a living process, not a static set of documents and rules, and that it is capable of being moulded by the courts and legislatures to meet the challenges that a multicultural society poses for the making and applying of international agreements.

Acknowledgments
I am grateful to Research Services of Dalhousie University and the SSHRCC for financial support in preparing this chapter.

Notes

1 *A.-G. Canada v. A.-G. Ontario (Labour Conventions Case)*, [1937] A.C. 326 at 347.
2 (U.K.) 30-31 Vic. c. 3, R.S.C. 1985 Appendix II, no. 5.
3 Ibid., ss. 91 and 92.
4 *Supra* note 1 at 351.
5 *Vienna Convention on the Law of Treaties*, 1155 U.N.T.S. 331, Can. T.S. 1980 No. 37, (1969) 8 I.L.M. 679 arts. 26 and 27. This principle was recognized by the Supreme Court in *Zingre v. The Queen*, [1981] 2 S.C.R. 392 at 410.
6 Preamble to the *Constitution Act*, 1867, *supra* note 2.
7 *Constitution Act*, 1867, *supra* note 2, s. 132.
8 See Canada, Department of External Affairs, *Federalism and International Relations* (Ottawa, 1968), 11-33.
9 At note 4.
10 Prior to 1928, Great Britain generally made treaties on behalf of Canada. For the record of how this gradually changed over time, see C.L. Wiktor, *Canadian Treaty Calendar, 1928-1978*, 2 vols. (London/Rome/New York: Oceana Publications, 1982), xii.
11 Ibid., xiii.

12 Ibid., xliv.
13 Ibid., li.
14 C.L. Wiktor, *Index to Canadian Treaties, 1979-2003* (Halifax, NS: Dalhousie Law School, 2003), viii. The *Index* is a supplement to C.L. Wiktor's *Canadian Treaty Calendar, supra* note 10.
15 Ibid., viii.
16 See the discussion *supra* at note 2.
17 Excluding the Aboriginal population.
18 Statistics Canada, *Ethnic Diversity Survey: Portrait of a Multicultural Society* (Govt. of Canada, Catalogue no. 89-593-XIE, Sept. 2003), 5.
19 Ibid., 10.
20 The so-called Meech Lake Accord and the Charlottetown Agreement.
21 See G. van Ert, *Using International Law in Canadian Courts* (The Hague/London/New York: Kluwer Law, 2002); K. Knop, "Here and There: International Law in Domestic Courts," *NYU School of Law – Journal of International Law and Politics* 32 (2000): 501; J. Brunnée and S. J. Toope, "A Hesitant Embrace: The Application of International Law by Canadian Courts," *Canadian Yearbook of International Law* 40 (2002): 3.
22 *Supra* note 1.
23 See, for example, *Francis v. The Queen,* [1956] S.C.R. 618, *R. v. Canada Labour Relations Board* (1964), 44 D.L.R. (2d) 440 (Man. Q.B.). But compare the judgments in the even earlier case of *Re Arrow River and Tributaries Slide and Boom Co. Ltd.,* [1932] 2 D.L.R. 250 (S.C.C.).
24 [1977] 2 S.C.R. 134. For a fuller account of Chief Justice Laskin's influence, see Hugh Kindred, "The Use of Unimplemented Treaties in Canada: Practice and Prospects in the Supreme Court," in *Trilateral Perspectives on International Legal Issues: Conflict and Coherence,* ed. C. Carmody, Y. Iwasawa, and S. Rhodes, 19-20 (Washington, DC: American Society of International Law, 2003).
25 [1978] 2 S.C.R. 141.
26 Ibid., 173.
27 See, for example, the judgment of Estey J. in *Schavernoch v. Foreign Claims Commission,* [1982] 1 S.C.R. 1092.
28 *Supra* note 25 at 188.
29 Contained in Schedule B of the *Canada Act, 1982,* (U.K.) 1982, c.11, R.S.C. 1985, Appendix II, no. 44.
30 In addition to the pre-existing rights at common law.
31 *Supra* note 29, ss. 2(b) and 7, respectively.
32 Ibid., s. 24.
33 Unless the legislation is re-enacted expressly notwithstanding its contravention of the *Charter*. See ibid., s. 33.
34 Ibid., s. 1.
35 Ibid., s. 27.
36 As they did with the forerunner to the *Canadian Charter,* the unentrenched *Canadian Bill of Rights,* which was enacted in 1960, S.C. 1960, c. 44.
37 See, for example, the early decision on the *Charter* in *R. v. Oakes,* [1986] 1 S.C.R. 103.
38 [1989] 1 S.C.R. 1038.
39 [1987] 1 S.C.R. 313.
40 *Supra* note 38 at 1056.
41 Ibid. at 1056-57. For commentary, see Brunnée and Toope, *supra* note 21, esp. at 33-35. See also *R. v. Keegstra,* [1990] 3 S.C.R. 697 at 749-55.
42 However, strong arguments have been made that the implied intention of the *Canadian Charter* was, in part, to implement many of Canada's international human rights treaty obligations. See A.F. Bayefsky, *International Human Rights Law: Use in Canadian Charter of Rights and Freedoms Litigation* (Toronto: Butterworths, 1992); and W.A. Schabas, *International Human Rights Law and the Canadian Charter,* 2nd ed. (Scarborough, ON: Carswell, 1996).
43 See W. A. Schabas, "Twenty-Five Years of Public International Law at the Supreme Court of Canada," *Canadian Bar Review* 74 (2000): 174 at 183.

44 See the dissenting judgment of Iacobucci J. in *Baker v. Canada (Minister of Citizenship and Immigration)*, [1999] 2 S.C.R. 817 at 865-66. A similar objection was voiced in the House of Lords in *R. v. Home Secretary ex p. Briand*, [1991] 1 A.C. 696 at 762.

45 *Ibid*. The next three paragraphs present my commentary on this case in the article cited *supra* note 24 at 22-23. See also *114957 Canada Ltée (Spraytech, Société d'arrosage) v. Hudson (Town)*, [2001] 2 S.C.R. 241; *Suresh v. Canada (Minister of Citizenship and Immigration)*, [2002] 1 S.C.R. 3; *Ahani v. Canada (Minister of Citizenship and Immigration)*, [2002] 1 S.C.R. 72.

46 R.S.C. 1985, c.I-2, s. 114(2) now replaced by the *Immigration and Refugee Protection Act*, S.C. 2001, c.27.

47 On behalf of five justices with two dissenters.

48 *Supra* note 44 at 860.

49 Can. T.S. 1992 No. 3, (1989) 28 I.L.M. 1448.

50 Citing for authority *Francis v. The Queen*, *supra* note 23; and *Capital Cities*, *supra* note 25.

51 *Supra* note 44 at 861.

52 [2002] 1 S.C.R. 3. See also *Ahani v. Canada*, *supra* note 45.

53 *Supra* note 46.

54 Can. T.S. 1969 No. 6.

55 Can. T.S. 1976 No. 47.

56 Can. T.S. 1987 No. 36.

57 *Supra* note 29.

58 For example, *Capital Cites*, *supra* note 25; *Schavernoch*, *supra* note 27; Wilson J.'s dissent in *National Corn Growers Association v. Canada (Import Tribunal)*, [1990] 2 S.C.R. 1324.

59 *Ibid*. And see *Francis v. The Queen*, *supra* note 23; *R. v. Canada Labour Relations Board*, *supra* note 23; *Gordon v. R. in Right of Canada*, [1980] 5 W.W.R. 668 (B.C.S.C.) aff'd [1980] 6 W.W.R. 519 (B.C.C.A.).

60 See *Verdun v. Toronto-Dominion Bank*, [1996] 3 S.C.R. 550l; *Royal Bank of Canada v. Sparrow Electric Corp.*, [1997] 1 S.C.R. 27 411; *R. v. Hydro-Quebec*, [1997] 3 S.C.R. 213; *Re Rizzo & Rizzo Shoes Ltd.*, [1983] 1 S.C.R. 27; and *R. v. Gladue*, [1999] 1 S.C.R. 688.

61 See, for example, *R. v. Parisien*, [1988] 1 S.C.R. 950 at 958; *National Corn Growers Association v. Canada (Import Tribunal)*, *supra* note 58; *Canada (Attorney General) v. Ward*, [1993] 2 S.C.R. 689; *Thomson v. Thomson*, [1994] 3 S.C.R. 551 at 578; and *Baker*, *supra* note 44. For a fuller account of this line of cases, see my work cited *supra* note 24 at 15-16.

62 *Daniels v. White and The Queen*, [1968] S.C.R. 517 at 541. This paragraph draws on my article, cited *supra* note 24 at 12-13.

63 *Supra* note 58 at 1371.

64 *Baker*, *supra* note 44 at 861 (emphasis added by L'Heureux-Dubé J.).

65 *Supra* note 5.

66 *Triquet v. Bath* (1763), 3 Burr 1478 (K.B.).

67 [1939] A.C. 160 at 168.

68 *Gordon v. R. in Right of Canada*, *supra* note 59.

69 *Ref. re Foreign Legations*, [1943] S.C.R. 208.

70 As they should, were they to recall the previous principle of statutory interpretation that courts should, where possible, expound an interpretation of a statute that is consistent with international law. See the discussion *supra* at notes 57-60.

71 See the discussion *supra* at notes 23-27.

72 Namely, the French and English colonists and, to some extent, the First Nations peoples.

73 See also the cases in note 45.

8

New Constitutions and Vulnerable Groups: Brian Dickson's Strategies in Interpreting the 1982 *Charter*

Jameson W. Doig

> Language is more than a mere means of communication, it is part
> and parcel of the identity and culture of the people speaking it ...
> The vitality of the language is a necessary condition for the
> complete preservation of a culture.
>
> – Brian Dickson, *Mahe v. Alberta*

> The many, many Canadians who belong to identifiable groups
> surely gain a great deal of comfort from the knowledge that the
> hate-monger is criminally prosecuted ... Equally, the community
> as a whole is reminded of the importance of diversity and multi-
> culturalism in Canada, the value of equality and the worth and
> dignity of each human person.
>
> – Brian Dickson, *Regina v. Keegstra*

This chapter explores the strategies used by Brian Dickson, Chief Justice of
Canada when the *Charter of Rights and Freedoms* came into effect, as he led
the effort to advance the rights of Aboriginal peoples, members of distinctive religious and ethnic groups, and other "vulnerable groups" in Canada.
Dickson wrote many of the Supreme Court's most important judgments,
and his opinions often framed the issues before the Court in large ways and
rendered decisions with extensive sweep. The two quotations above capture important facets of the Dicksonian vision.

Dickson's strategies in interpreting the *Charter* to protect minority rights,
and his critical approach to *Charter* powers that could override these rights,
shaped the Court's policies during his years as chief justice (1984-90), and
they have significantly influenced Canadian jurisprudence in the past fifteen years as well.

In undertaking the task of leading the Supreme Court in new directions during the first years of the *Charter* era, Dickson had to confront two important resisting forces. The first was the long tradition of parliamentary supremacy, with its corollary that courts must defer to clear legislative pronouncements. The second was an important tradition, influenced by American law and policy, that placed a high premium on individual liberty and, in particular, on freedom of speech. Both perspectives were used in challenging specific decisions by the Dickson Court and in a broader effort to undermine the Court's power during his years as chief justice and beyond.

In the pages below, I first describe the tradition of parliamentary sovereignty and note some of the developments leading to the creation of the *Charter* and to the selection of Brian Dickson as chief justice. I also refer to Dickson's earlier judicial opinions, which provide hints of the approach he might take when issues of cultural diversity appeared before the Supreme Court in the *Charter* era.

In the longest section of the chapter, I note several dimensions of "cultural pluralism" that have engaged Dickson and the Court, discuss some important challenges that Dickson and his colleagues faced during his years as chief justice, and analyze how Dickson responded to those challenges. Then I offer preliminary observations on the long-term impact of Dickson's leadership.

Finally, I turn to the more general point suggested by this specific history – the importance of the choice of high-court leadership, especially in a new or renewed constitutional system. The individual selected to lead the Court will be especially likely to have an enduring influence if he or she develops a systematic strategy to use in interpreting the new Constitution. In these circumstances, the Supreme Court can be expected to have a powerful impact on the long-term shape of individual rights and cultural vitality, particularly in a society that is diverse in language, religion, and ethnicity.[1]

A New Role for Canada's Judiciary

Until 1982, Canada had no counterpart to the First Amendment or other provisions in the American Bill of Rights – that is, it had no statement of individual rights enshrined in its Constitution, and it had no judiciary that could declare legislative actions null and void as violations of those Constitutional rights. Canadians relied on their elected officials to protect their liberties; following the doctrine of legislative supremacy, the federal Parliament and provincial legislatures could, in most areas, overturn any court decision.[2]

All that changed in 1982. With the creation of the *Charter of Rights and Freedoms* in April of that year, the Canadian Constitution was provided with an extensive list of individual rights and, adding a complexity not found in the American system, an array of "group rights" as well. The Supreme Court in Ottawa now had the role that its American counterpart had successfully asserted in the first years of the nineteenth century under Chief Justice John Marshall – the power to declare null and void any government action that the Court found to be inconsistent with the *Charter*. Within a few years, the Canadian judiciary would exercise this power, and those who preferred to rely on legislative majorities would be unhappy.

Prime Minister Pierre Trudeau took a leading role in pressing for an entrenched bill of rights. He encountered resistance from officials of the ten provinces, whose political power might be constrained by a newly invigorated Supreme Court, and the final draft of the *Charter* included two provisions intended to address these concerns. The first is section 1:

> The *Canadian Charter of Rights and Freedoms* guarantees the rights and freedoms set out in it subject only to such reasonable limits prescribed by law as can be demonstrably justified in a free and democratic society.

The "reasonable limits" clause offered the Court a rationale for finding laws and administrative actions to be constitutional *even if* the justices conclude that such actions violate freedom of religion or speech or other provisions of the *Charter*. How section 1 would limit guaranteed rights would depend on the actions of the Canadian Supreme Court.

In the view of the provincial premiers, section 1 did not adequately protect legislative power, and they pressed successfully for an added provision that could be used to restore legislative supremacy to its traditional, central place. Section 33 reads:

> Parliament or the legislature of a province may expressly declare in an Act of Parliament or of the legislature ... that the Act or a provision thereof shall operate *notwithstanding* a provision included in section 2 or sections 7 to 15 of this Charter (emphasis added).

Section 2 of the *Charter* provides for freedom of conscience, religion, opinion, and the press as well as freedom of assembly and association. Sections 7-15, inter alia, prohibit unreasonable search as well as arbitrary arrest and imprisonment, and provide for equal protection of the law. Under the *Charter*, the provinces and the federal government could use the "notwithstanding" clause to suspend any of these rights for up to five years. And the suspension could then be renewed indefinitely.[3]

Whether the new *Charter* would fulfill Trudeau's hopes would depend in part on whether the legislatures used section 33 with restraint – and in part (a very large part, as it turned out) on the behaviour of the Supreme Court.

The New Chief Justice

Bora Laskin, chief justice when the *Charter* was approved in 1982, died in 1984, just as the first *Charter* cases reached the Court. Trudeau then appointed Brian Dickson, who had been a member of the Supreme Court since 1973, as Laskin's successor. From the viewpoint of those who supported the values embedded in the *Charter*, Dickson's record was somewhat mixed. For example, he had shown little visible concern for the difficulties facing women – an important "vulnerable group" that had fought for expanded rights.[4]

Dickson did, however, have several evident advantages. Tradition favoured appointing the chief justice from within the Court, and Dickson was the most senior, other than Roland Ritchie, who was in poor health. Also, Dickson had emerged during a decade on the high court as highly influential in shaping Court decisions, and he was known to be a strong supporter of a bilingual and multicultural Canada – a crucial concern for Trudeau.[5] Most significantly, in relation to the theme of this chapter, Dickson had demonstrated – through twenty years of judicial experience – a sensitivity to the traditions and values of distinct cultural groups and an uncommon ability to sort out complex issues when the rights of vulnerable minorities were involved.

Notable from his years as a trial judge in Manitoba (1963-67) was his opinion in *Hofer v. Hofer*, which involved a conflict between the tenets of the Hutterian Brethren Church and "liberal individualism." Those who join the Hutterian Church agree to give up individual ownership of all their worldly goods: "all property" is owned by the colony "for common use."[6] In the early 1960s, several members of the Church embraced religious practices that were in conflict with Hutterian principles, and they were expelled. The dissenters then sought to claim ownership of portions of the land and other assets of the Church, and the case came before Dickson in 1966. Their argument was, in effect, that the Church had a religious element but that it was also a business partnership (since the colony members raised pigs and other products for sale); they pointed to the statutory Bill of Rights, which protects "the right of the individual to life, liberty ... and enjoyment of property" and "freedom of religion," in support of their claim.[7]

After a "hotly contested trial," Dickson rejected the view that Hutterian religious practices could be separated from their farming activities. "The totality of religion permeates all life" in the colony, Dickson wrote, "and uniform doctrinal belief is essential to survival." The Bill of Rights could not be used as a club to break the colony, and the dissenters' expulsion from the colony was warranted.[8]

The Manitoba Court of Appeal upheld Dickson's judgment, and the Supreme Court of Canada agreed. As Dickson's biographers, Robert Sharpe and Kent Roach, point out, his analysis in *Hofer* suggested that Dickson "had a profound respect for religious diversity and for distinctive communal arrangements. He was quite prepared to deny individual rights that were incompatible with the continued survival of a distinctive community." They also note that the justices on the Supreme Court were "impressed by his work on this difficult case" and marked him as a possible future appointee to the high court.[9]

Dickson served as a trial-court judge for four years, and in 1967, he was appointed to the Manitoba Court of Appeal, where he served until named to the Supreme Court in 1973. Perhaps his most notable Manitoba appeals-court opinion concerning vulnerable groups was *Canard v. Attorney-General of Canada*,[10] in which he confronted the issue of racism embedded in the *Indian Act* of 1970. The case involved the accidental death of Alexander Canard and the effort of his widow to administer her husband's estate. Under the *Indian Act* she was denied that right, as the act assigned all power over the estates of deceased Indians to a federal official. Dickson wrote for a unanimous court in rejecting that portion of the federal law. He noted that Mrs. Canard was being denied "a civil right which other Canadians, not of her race, enjoy," argued that this violated the equality provision of the 1960 Bill of Rights, and granted her the right to administer her husband's estate.[11]

In 1973, Trudeau appointed Dickson to the Supreme Court. His inclination to use the Bill of Rights actively (as in *Canard*), and his stance in favour of bilingualism may have tilted Trudeau towards appointing him to the high court.[12] In his early years on the Court, however, Dickson was inclined to interpret Aboriginal rights and the rights of labour narrowly. Yet, by the end of the decade, he became "increasingly willing" to defend the rights of "disadvantaged groups – prisoners, religious and linguistic minorities, workers, and aboriginal people."[13] Notable were his dissent in *Jack v. The Queen*, in which he argued that ambiguities in the law should be resolved in favour of a broader interpretation of Aboriginal rights, and his defence of Aboriginal rights in *The Queen v. Sutherland*.[14] The fact that the 1982 *Charter* was a part of the Constitution of Canada – not a "mere law" like the 1960 Bill of Rights – appears to have had an immediate and significant impact on the judges of the Court, and that impact was perhaps greatest on Dickson, who assumed the leadership position at a critical moment. Some years later, Dickson recalled:

> When the *Charter* came along, I think everybody recognized that this was a complete change and that we were facing something of extreme importance for Canada and for the court. So we were all of the view that this was something that we had to take very seriously, and give it a generous interpretation.[15]

Dickson Searches for Standards to Discipline Court Action

If the new chief justice was to give the rights under the *Charter* a "generous interpretation," he would need to develop standards that the Supreme Court could use to control its use of the new power, else the judges would be in danger of behaving as an unelected mini-legislature; and the elected legislatures could be expected to wield the "notwithstanding clause" scimitar with vigour, cutting off new Supreme Court protections right and left. In the paragraphs below, I first discuss Dickson's strategy in articulating standards that the court could use in tackling cases under the *Charter*. Then I explore the use of these standards in three areas in which the tension between legislative action and *Charter* rights was evident during the Dickson era: Aboriginal issues, the field of "language rights, and the issue of "hate speech."

We begin with *Hunter v. Southam*, Dickson's first opinion interpreting the *Charter*. "The task of expounding a constitution is crucially different," Dickson argued, "from that of construing a statute. A statute defines present rights and obligations. It is easily enacted and easily repealed. A constitution, by contrast, is drafted with an eye to the future." Therefore, a "broad, purposive analysis, which interprets specific provisions of a constitutional document in the light of its larger objects" was essential. The Court would no longer ask, "What goals did the legislature hope to achieve in enacting this statute?" (a key question under the doctrine of legislative supremacy); instead, the judges would ask, "Does this statute (or behaviour) conflict with the language and *underlying purposes* of the Charter?" In embracing this wide-ranging and "purposive" approach to *Charter* cases, which drew on American constitutional experience, Dickson was able to win the endorsement of his colleagues on the Court without dissent.[16]

The important role of section 1 – and a distinctive difference between the *Charter* freedoms and the American Bill of Rights – was demonstrated a few months later in *Queen v. Oakes*. Applying the usual standard, "beyond a reasonable doubt," an Ontario court had found David Oakes guilty of unlawful possession of hashish. However, under section 8 of the federal *Narcotic Control Act*, a lower standard of proof was then used by the court to find Oakes guilty of the more serious offence of possession "for the purpose of trafficking" in the drug.[17] Oakes challenged the conviction as a violation of the *Charter*, section 11(d): "Any person charged with an offence has the right ... (d) to be presumed innocent until proven guilty according to law." For a unanimous Supreme Court, Dickson agreed that, under the *Narcotic Control Act*, Oakes was "denied his right to be presumed innocent and subjected to the potential penalty of life imprisonment unless he can rebut the presumption" (120, 134).

In American jurisprudence, the case would have ended there. But the government argued that, even if section 8 of the *Act* violated section 11(d) of the *Charter*, it should be upheld under section 1 as a "reasonable limit."

Now Dickson and the Court were faced with the need to construct a set of conditions under which *Charter* rights could be *overridden* by the government. In consultation with his colleagues, Dickson fashioned a systematic response to this challenge. In order to justify setting aside a *Charter* right, Dickson argued, the government must show that the goal is important and that the means chosen by the government are rationally linked to this goal (139). Moreover, the means chosen should "impair 'as little as possible' the right or freedom in question." And the severity of the impact on individuals or groups would need special scrutiny: "the more severe" the impact of the law, "the more important" must be the goal of the law that is to be upheld under section 1 (139-40).

Applying these tests to David Oakes' violation, Dickson concluded that the goal of reducing drug trafficking was "substantial and pressing." However, section 8 of the narcotics law failed the "rational connection test"; it would, he argued, "be irrational" to infer that "a person had an intent to traffic" simply based on possession of "a very small quantity of narcotics." Thus, section 8 was declared unconstitutional under the *Charter*, and Oakes was guilty only of possession (142). Dickson's colleagues endorsed his analysis and findings unanimously.

Dickson's opinion was, in the view of legal scholar Peter Hogg, "brilliant." The "stringent requirements of justification imposed in that judgment," Hogg argued, have strengthened the *Charter*, and *Oakes* "remains the keystone of judicial review under the *Charter*." Others were more critical. Pierre Blache objected to the *Oakes* hurdle that required the government to prove that the law under attack was not more severe than necessary to achieve the goal. This "least drastic means" test was almost impossible to meet, he argued, since there would always be some slightly less severe law or rule that might well achieve the same objective. More broadly, Blache noted the criticism levelled against the *Oakes* test by champions of the "majoritarian conception of democracy": in this view, the legislature has already "balanced the pros and cons of limiting a right" and its decision "deserves great respect" – not the heavy burden of proof required under Dickson's approach.[18]

Despite the divided opinion among scholars and other observers, the Supreme Court was united on the best way to grapple with the crucial issue of section 1. In the paragraphs below, we see how Dickson and his colleagues then used a "broad, purposive analysis" (Dickson in *Hunter v. Southam*, 1984) together with the approach set forth in *Oakes* in considering the rights of Aboriginal groups and other issues raised in the early *Charter* years.

Interpreting the *Charter* and Section 35

During his six years as chief justice, Brian Dickson applied the principles set forth above in a wide variety of fields. I begin with Aboriginal rights and then turn to two other areas associated with the theme of "cultural pluralism" – language rights and protections against "hate propaganda" directed at vulnerable groups.[19]

Expanding Aboriginal Rights

In contrast with the American Bill of Rights, the Canadian *Charter* includes several provisions that are intended to protect the rights of groups of people. For example, section 25 offers some protection for First Nations peoples and other Aboriginal groups:

> 25. The guarantee in this Charter of certain rights and freedoms shall not be construed so as to abrogate or derogate from any aboriginal, treaty or other rights or freedoms that pertain to the aboriginal peoples of Canada.

Further protection is provided by section 35, added in 1982. Section 35(1) states:

> The existing aboriginal and treaty rights of the aboriginal peoples of Canada are hereby recognized and affirmed. (S. 35 is not part of the *Charter*, but it is included, together with the *Charter*, in the *Constitution Act*, 1982.)

Finally, section 27 potentially provides an additional route to assist Aboriginal peoples and other distinct cultural groups:

> 27. This Charter shall be interpreted in a manner consistent with the preservation and enhancement of the multicultural heritage of Canadians.

Because of Dickson's distinctive contributions to the legal rights of First Nations and other Aboriginal peoples, his work in this field has been the subject of several essays.[20] His 1990 opinion in *R. v. Sparrow* is viewed as "truly seminal," and it is the focus of discussion here.[21]

In 1984, Ronald Edward Sparrow, a member of the Musqueam Indian Band, was charged with fishing with a drift net longer than that permitted under the band's licence, which had been issued under the federal *Fisheries Act* of 1970. Found guilty, Sparrow appealed, arguing that he was exercising "an existing aboriginal right to fish" and that any net restriction was, therefore, invalid under section 35(1) of the 1982 *Constitution Act* (*Sparrow* at 1083).

In examining this case, the Supreme Court was required for the first time to explore the scope of section 35. The initial challenge was to define "existing aboriginal and treaty rights." The Court would also face a further challenge. It was widely acknowledged that some of these rights could be limited by government action (e.g., to meet conservation goals, essential to ensuring that treaty rights regarding fishing would be protected in the long run).

However, section 35 had been added to the 1982 Constitution separately from the *Charter*, and it was not subject to section 1; therefore, the systematic *Oakes* test could not be used in deciding what government restrictions could be placed on these rights.

The chief justice had already written several important opinions concerned with Aboriginal rights (e.g., *Nowegijick*,[22] *Guerin*,[23] and *Simon*[24]), and he agreed to tackle this one. The opinion was drafted by Dickson and Judge La Forest and was delivered by Dickson. It had the unanimous support of the Court.

The Crown had argued that "existing ... rights" in this case meant simply the rights under the licence provided to Sparrow's band. However, Sparrow had been fishing in the Fraser River, where ninety-two tribes had fishing rights, often with licences that set different requirements on line length and other matters. To accept the Crown's argument, Dickson and La Forest argued, would be to incorporate into the Constitution a "patchwork quilt" of regulations. Rejecting that view, they sought a broader framework, consistent with their view that "existing aboriginal rights" must be "interpreted flexibly so as to permit their evolution over time" (1093).

They then reviewed the evolution of Canada's relations with Aboriginal peoples, a history they found replete with neglect and at times marked by deception (1102-8). They concluded that section 35(1) "represents the culmination of a long and difficult struggle" and that it must be viewed in relation to its underlying purpose – "the affirmation of aboriginal rights." Thus, a "generous, liberal interpretation" would be required (1105-6). Notably, they argued, section 35(1) implies that there must be a "strong check on legislative power." Hence the government would "bear the burden of justifying any legislation that has some negative effect on *any aboriginal right* protected under s. 35(1)" (1110; emphasis added).

The analysis in *Sparrow* proceeded in the systematic fashion we have seen in Dickson's *Oakes* opinion. In examining the validity of any federal or provincial legislation challenged under section 35(1), the courts must first determine whether the law or regulation interferes with an existing Aboriginal right; and "rights" are to be understood according to the traditions of Aboriginal peoples (1111). "Interference" is defined essentially as a government action that imposes "undue hardship" on an Aboriginal group.[25]

If interference is shown, then the courts must examine whether that infringement of section 35(1) is justified. In view of the government's "special trust relationship" with Aboriginals, its officials would face a substantial hurdle in arguing for regulations that infringe. Methods aimed at conservation – for the long-term benefit of Aboriginal peoples and the larger society – would generally qualify; but benefits to "sport fishing and commercial fishing" would yield to the right of Aboriginal groups to fish (1113-16).[26] Moreover, the courts would need to ensure that there has been "as little infringement as possible" in order to achieve the government's goal, *and* they should probe whether the Aboriginal group affected "has been consulted" in developing the law or regulation. Endorsed by the entire Court, these concerns formed the *Sparrow* test, which would henceforth shape the Supreme Court's approach in weighing the power of Parliament and provincial lawmakers to legislate in areas affecting Aboriginal rights.[27]

Protecting Language and Culture

In the early years of the *Charter*, Dickson showed more sensitivity to the problem of language rights than some of his colleagues. A notable instance is the 1986 case, *Societe des Acadiens v. Association of Parents*. Section 19 of the *Charter* gives every person the right to use "either English or French" in "any pleading" in a federal or New Brunswick court. When the *Societe des Acadiens* protested that a judge in one case was not able to understand the defendant's language (French), the Supreme Court majority responded that the right to speak in either French or English did not include any guarantee "that the speaker will be heard or understood" by the judge! Dickson registered a sharp dissent: "What good is a right to use one's language if those to whom one speaks cannot understand? ... It is fundamental, therefore, to any effective and coherent guarantee of language rights in the courtroom that the judge or judges understand ... the language chosen by the individual coming before the court." Reflecting more broadly, Dickson argued that "linguistic duality has been a longstanding concern in our nation ... We must take special care to be faithful to the spirit and purpose of the guarantee of language rights enshrined in the Charter."[28]

Four years later, Dickson won a significant victory for his broad interpretation of language rights – and thereby added fuel to the ire of those who preferred to rely on legislatures to decide important public policies. The case arose in Edmonton, Alberta, when Jean-Claude Mahe and other francophones argued that they should have the right (under section 23 of the *Charter*) to their own public school, with instruction only in French, and administered by their own school board. They noted that the Edmonton schools included more than three thousand students whose first language was French – a large enough number, in their view, to justify the creation of a separate school. School officials in Edmonton rejected their proposal, and they appealed to the courts.[29]

Writing for a unanimous Supreme Court, Dickson framed the issue broadly: "Language is more than a mere means of communication, it is part and parcel of the identity of the people speaking it." The purpose of section 23, therefore, was to "preserve and promote" the two cultures as well as the two languages. Moreover, this general purpose was in part designed to "remedy an existing problem": the difficulties in various provinces of maintaining two vibrant linguistic and social communities (*Mahe*, 362-64). Dickson noted that section 23 provided "a novel form of legal right" – a right for a group, but on a "sliding scale." In other words, it provides the right to separate educational facilities, but only "where the number of children" is large enough to justify such separation (365-66). Dickson concluded that, when the number of children is too few to justify a separate school and school board, francophones (or anglophones, if in the minority) should have guaranteed representation on a "shared school board" and "exclusive control over all of the aspects of minority education which pertain to linguistic and cultural concerns" (375-76).

Applying these general guidelines to Edmonton, Dickson said he thought that a separate francophone school was a "reasonable requirement"; however, a separate school board was not required, though guaranteed francophone representation on existing boards was essential (388-89). He then placed the issue back in the hands of Alberta and Edmonton: "the government should have the widest possible discretion in selecting" the means for carrying out its duties; "the courts should be loath to interfere and impose ... procrustean standards" (393).

This apparent deference to elected officials did not win the support of the Supreme Court's critics. In his analysis of judicial power, Christopher Manfredi points out that Dickson's approach permits the francophone parents, once Alberta has taken steps to meet his guidelines, to appeal to the courts again, immersing the judiciary further in the "management of education policy." Thus *Mahe* illustrates, to Manfredi, the "expansion of judicial supremacy" and the consequent undermining of liberal democracy.[30]

Hate Propaganda and the Power of Section 1

One of Dickson's last opinions was, if evaluated from the perspective of cultural pluralism, one of his most important. In this 1990 case, *Regina v. Keegstra*, Dickson embraced section 1, and its defence of legislative power, against a strong dissent by Justice McLachlin.[31]

James Keegstra was a school teacher in Alberta, where he was convicted of unlawfully promoting hatred, in violation of section 319 of the Criminal Code. In the classroom, he had regularly denigrated Jews as "sadistic," "money-loving," and "power hungry," and he expected his students to "reproduce his teachings in class and on exams" if they expected good grades (36). Keegstra appealed his conviction, arguing that section 319 was unconstitutional as it violated the *Charter*, which protects "freedom of thought, belief, opinion and expression."[32] The Court agreed unanimously that section 319 did violate the Charter (63); but Dickson then used the case to develop an important argument in defence of the right of the government to override that *Charter* provision.

Dickson first commented on the *Oakes* test, drawing attention to aspects of the test that (as he viewed the issue) may not have been fully recognized by the legal community. His analysis deserves attention not only with regard to Canada but also because the values captured in section 1 resonate for other societies. In a sense, Dickson used this opinion to *reinterpret* his opinion in *R. v. Oakes*, described above as restricting government power, so that, under some conditions, it becomes a standard that essentially *requires* the government to act.

Dickson drew attention to the final words of section 1 (emphasized here): "The Canadian Charter of Rights and Freedoms guarantees the rights and freedoms set out in it subject only to such reasonable limits prescribed by law as can be demonstrably justified in a *free and democratic society*." Therefore, "the court must be guided," Dickson argued, "by the values and principles essential to a free and democratic society," and these include "commitment to social justice and equality, accommodation of a wide variety of beliefs, respect for cultural and group identity" and other underlying values. Dickson drew attention in particular to those provisions in the *Charter* that provide protection to these values.[33] Any limit on freedom of speech or other *Charter* rights can be justified only if the limitation protects these basic values (73-74).

He then reviewed American cases, which in recent decades have tended to use "freedom of speech" doctrine to "protect offensive, public invective" of the kind displayed by James Keegstra (78). But the United States has no section 1, Dickson pointed out, and section 1 accentuates "a uniquely Canadian vision of a free and democratic society" – a vision that gives a "special role" to "equality and multiculturalism in the Canadian Constitution" (85-86).

Dickson now employed the standards of the *Oakes* test to emphasize this unique vision. Was the goal of section 319 focused on concerns that are "pressing and substantial"? Government studies convinced Dickson that the answer was clear: "There has been a recent upsurge in hate propaganda ... Not only is it anti-Semitic and anti-Black, as in the 1960s, but it is also now anti-Roman Catholic, anti-East Indian, anti-Aboriginal people and anti-French." Moreover, hate propaganda caused emotional damage to those targeted and might lead them to respond by isolating themselves from non-group members or by trying to "blend in" with the majority population. "Such consequences," Dickson argued, "bear heavily in a nation that prides itself on tolerance and the fostering of human dignity" in part through "respect for the many racial, religious and cultural groups in our society." And those "prejudiced messages" may "gain some credence" among the majority, perhaps leading to discrimination and even violence against minority groups in Canada (87-93). These and other conditions led Dickson to conclude that the "first part of the [Oakes] test" under section 1 was "easily satisfied" (112).

The second branch of the *Oakes* test focuses on the question: is the limitation on free speech proportionate to the problem or too severe? Dickson concluded that hate propaganda was "expression largely removed from the heart of free expression," and the benefits of penalizing that form of speech outweighed the modest harm to free-speech principles.[34] In a notable passage, he argued that

> the many, many Canadians who belong to identifiable groups surely gain a great deal of comfort from the knowledge that the hate-monger is criminally prosecuted and his or her ideas rejected. Equally, the community as a whole is reminded of the importance of diversity and multiculturalism in Canada, the value of equality and the worth and dignity of each human person. (130).

In conclusion, Dickson upheld Keegstra's conviction and endorsed section 319 of the *Criminal Code* as "a reasonable limit prescribed by law in a free and democratic society" (161). His position was supported by only three other members of the Court, however, with the dissenters arguing, in effect, that hate propaganda deserved *Charter* protection.[35]

Dickson's Values and His Influence on the Evolution of Canadian Jurisprudence

The opinions discussed above capture, in my view, the most important arguments concerning vulnerable groups developed by Brian Dickson during his six years as chief justice of Canada. These arguments are also set forth in a number of other cases involving "cultural pluralism," in which he wrote insightfully.[36]

What seems clear from his wide array of opinions is that Dickson had an uncommon capacity to understand the problems that face religious, ethnic, and linguistic minorities; and his sustained focus, in creating the *Oakes* and *Sparrow* tests, and in probing cases affecting these groups, was to use the *Charter of Rights and Freedoms* as shield and sword to protect their interests. He was motivated in part, evidently, by empathy for the difficulties they faced and for their need for judicial protection. Equally or more important, as his views in *Keegstra* suggest, Dickson believed that the vitality of Canadian democracy would depend, in the long run, on whether these vulnerable individuals were treated as – and felt themselves to be – equally valued citizens of the larger community. And in achieving these goals, the courts would have a crucial role.

Dickson's approach to interpreting the 1982 Constitution was not shared by all members of the Supreme Court during his years as chief justice. Notably, Justice William McIntyre, who served on the Court from 1979 until 1989, often argued in favour of greater deference to decisions made by elected officials. Beyond the Court, Christopher Manfredi, F.L. Morton, and several other scholars criticized what they viewed as too much "judicial activism" during the early *Charter* years, and their criticisms have continued in the post-Dickson era.

My own view is that the text of the *Charter* and section 35, and the debates surrounding their enactment, support Brian Dickson's interpretation as found, for example, in his statements quoted in the epigraphs at the beginning of this chapter and in the text at note 16. Many of the critics, in contrast, appear to view the *Charter* as an unfortunate document. McIntyre was frank in his critical assessment. As his sympathetic biographer reports, McIntyre observed (after he retired) that "courts must not usurp the power of Parliament. The Charter should be used sparingly ... He feels it was not necessary to entrench the Charter." That basic issue was resolved, however, in 1982, leaving Dickson and the Court to interpret a document filled with phrasing that signalled an aspiration for equality, defence of minority rights, and other values that Dickson and his colleagues have had to use as "measuring rods" in deciding specific cases. Dickson's "generous interpretation" seems to me consistent with the text and history of the *Charter*, while the dissents of McIntyre capture a sentiment of regret that the era of legislative supremacy exists no more in Canada.[37]

The main outlines of Dickson's approach to the *Charter*, and to Aboriginal rights under section 35, have remained central to the Court's decision making since his retirement in 1990. The Court has used a "broad, purposive analysis" (*Southam*), and it has generally employed the *Oakes* test in addressing the issue of whether government action that infringes on *Charter* rights is justified. When exploring Aboriginal rights, *Sparrow*'s systematic approach is usually applied, and the substantive finding of the case – "that aboriginal rights do exist at common law, and that they are enforceable" when Aboriginal peoples sue – has been maintained.[38]

As the Canadian courts have moved into new and controversial domains, the perspective that Dickson brought to the *Charter* is also evident. In the 1998 case, *Vriend v. Alberta*, for example, the Supreme Court majority emphasized that the *Charter* was "part of a redefinition of our democracy," providing since 1982 new and independent powers to the judiciary. They then quoted Dickson's opinion in *Oakes*, emphasizing the importance of the "accommodation of a wide variety of beliefs, [and] respect for cultural and group identity," and they cited his opinion in *Keegstra* as well.[39] Employing these standards, they concluded that the government of Alberta had violated the *Charter*'s equality provisions by excluding sexual orientation from a 1990 provincial law that provided protection against discrimination based on race, religion, and other grounds. As Justice Iacobucci concluded, "the exclusion of sexual orientation from the [Alberta law] does not meet the requirements of the Oakes test and accordingly, it cannot be saved under s. 1 of the Charter" (112).

Three years later, provincial courts grappled with the question of same-sex marriage, and Dickson's way of analyzing the issue shaped the judges' analysis. In Ontario, for example, Judge LaForme concluded that the issue must be approached by "applying a progressive approach" to the *Charter*, as "judiciously noted in *Hunter v. Southam*."[40] He then determined that any denial of civil marriage to same-sex couples would violate the equality pro-visions of the *Charter*. But was a violation of *Charter* rights justifiable under section 1? Here LaForme quoted the lines from *Oakes* that Dickson himself had stressed in framing his *Keegstra* analysis: "The Court must be guided" by such values as "commitment to social justice and equality, accommoda-tion of a wide variety of beliefs, respect for cultural and group identity." Given this perspective, it is not surprising that LaForme concluded, after reviewing the attorney-general's arguments for excluding same-sex couples from civil marriage: "the infringement of the Applicants' Charter rights can-not be justified under section 1 of the Charter" (paras. 237, 265). In 2004, in a related case, the Supreme Court embraced Dicksonian breadth: "our Con-stitution is a living tree, which, by way of progressive interpretation, ac-commodates and addresses the realities of modern life."[41]

Wider Lessons from the Dickson era

This review of Brian Dickson's work suggests several general points that are applicable beyond Canada. First, if those who frame a new constitution – or modifications to an existing constitution – wish to provide protections for those of diverse cultural and religious orientations, the text of the docu-ment should capture some of the crucial themes. Perhaps this point seems obvious; but, as the US Constitution illustrates, it is possible for a nation to aspire to be culturally diverse without embedding protective elements in the constitutional document. However, American and Canadian experience in recent decades suggests the benefit of including some protective clauses. In the *Charter of Rights and Freedoms*, these include section 15 (especially subsection 2, protecting "affirmative action" laws and programs), sections 16-23 (on language rights), section 25 (Aboriginal rights), section 27 (on the "multicultural heritage of Canada"), and section 29 (on religious schools), as well as section 35 (Aboriginal rights) outside the *Charter*. Also relevant is section 28, which protects the rights of women in the event that the cul-tural traditions of any group deny equality to women.

Equally or perhaps more important, those chosen to serve on the nation's highest court – and the chief justice, in particular – should have demon-strated sensitivity to key elements of cultural diversity. Prior to his appoint-ment to the Supreme Court, Brian Dickson met that standard, notably in his opinions in *Hofer* and *Canard*, and, during his early years on the Court, his opinion in *Sutherland* provided further evidence. It is also desirable to select as chief justice someone who is inclined to interpret the new Constitution broadly in relation to the values of protecting cultural diversity, and again, Dickson's earlier opinions suggest this inclination.[42]

Notable as well is a capacity to use early cases in which the new document is applied in order to clarify key elements that have been phrased in general terms. Dickson's opinions in *Oakes* and *Sparrow* demonstrate that capacity at a high level. From these building blocks come his other important opinions in the field of Aboriginal and language rights, as well as his creative approach in *Keegstra*. As suggested at the start of this chapter, a court able to employ these tools of analysis will have a crucial influence on the cultural diversity of a nation whose citizens have many contending traditions.

Notes

1 For their advice in analyzing the views of Brian Dickson, I thank Robert J. Sharpe, DeLloyd J. Guth, and Dickson's son, Brian Dickson. And, for their comments on a draft of this chapter, my thanks to Stanley Katz, Ian Peach, Walter F. Murphy, Stephen Tierney, and two anonymous reviewers.

2 An important exception was the allocation of powers between the central government and provincial legislatures. Under the *British North America Act*, 1867, some powers were allotted only to the Canadian provinces (e.g., education), others exclusively to the federal government (e.g., banking), while still others were shared (e.g., agriculture). The Canadian courts could and did at times declare a provincial or federal law unconstitutional, but, with one or two exceptions, only because the statute violated the "federal" division of responsibilities set forth in the *BNA Act* (later retitled the *Constitution Act*, 1867).

3 While the United States has no counterpart to s. 33, the "exceptions" clause of Article III of the US Constitution does offer the possibility that Congress can bar judicial review of some categories of statutes.

4 He had, for instance, joined the majority opinion in *Bliss v. A.G. of Canada*, [1979] 1 S.C.R. 183 (pregnant women denied benefits available to other workers), in which the Court concluded that discrimination based on pregnancy was not discrimination based on sex.

5 See Robert J. Sharpe and Kent Roach, *Brian Dickson: A Judge's Journey* (Toronto: University of Toronto Press, 2003), 285-86. This is the definitive study of Dickson's career.

6 *Hofer v. Hofer* (1967), 59 D.L.R. (2d), 723, 724. On this case, see Robert J. Sharpe, "Brian Dickson: Portrait of a Judge," *Advocates' Society Journal* 17 (1998): 3-38, at 14-15.

7 That Bill of Rights was enacted by Parliament in 1960. It had no clear constitutional standing, as the Parliament could override its provisions with a simple legislative act, and Canadian courts rarely used it to invalidate other laws or executive actions.

8 *Hofer v. Hofer*, 732.

9 Sharpe and Roach, *Brian Dickson*, 109.

10 [1972] 5 W.W.R. 678 (Man. C. A.).

11 The federal government appealed, however, and the Supreme Court, adhering to its reluctance to overrule Parliament, rejected Dickson's reasoning and upheld the *Indian Act's* provision.

12 Also, the justice he replaced was from a Western province, and, in the tradition of balancing provinces and regions, "it was Manitoba's turn." See Sharpe and Roach, *Brian Dickson*, 137.

13 Ibid., 159.

14 *Jack*, [1980] 1 S.C.R. 294, and *Sutherland*, [1980] 2 S.C.R. 451. See discussion of Dickson's evolution in Sharpe and Roach, *Brian Dickson*, chap. 8.

15 Brian Dickson, as quoted in Sharpe, "Brian Dickson," 31.

16   *Hunter v. Southam*, [1984] 2 S.C.R. 145. The final two quotations in the paragraph above are the characterizations of Don Stuart. See his chapter, "Chief Justice Dickson and Criminal Law," in *The Dickson Legacy*, ed. Roland Penner, 34-36 (Winnipeg: Legal Research Institute, University of Manitoba, 1992). Some of the interpretations below are drawn from my article, "Happenings Wondrous and Strange," *Textual Studies in Canada* 17 (2004): 1-29.

17   Once found guilty of possession, the accused was given the burden of proving "on a balance of probabilities" that he or she was not in possession for the purpose of trafficking. *R. v. Oakes*, [1986] 1 S.C.R. 103, 116.

18   See the chapter by Peter W. Hogg and Ronald Penner (quotations at 176, 178) and that by Pierre Blache (quotation at 189) in Penner, *The Dickson Legacy*.

19   For a valuable set of essays on the complex terrain of "cultural pluralism," see Will Kymlicka, ed., *The Rights of Minority Cultures* (New York: Oxford University Press, 1995). See also his *Multicultural Citizenship: A Liberal Theory of Minority Rights* (New York: Oxford University Press, 1995).

20   See M.B. Nepon, "The Dickson Court and Native Law," 158-71, and J. Rod McLeod, "Commentary on Aboriginal Rights," 172-74, both in Penner, *The Dickson Legacy*. See also Geoffrey S. Lester, "The Dickson Impact on Aboriginal Rights," in *Brian Dickson and the Supreme Court of Canada, 1973-1990*, ed. DeLloyd J. Guth, 161-73 (Winnipeg: Faculty of Law, University of Manitoba).

21   See Robert J. Sharpe, "The Constitutional Legacy of Chief Justice Brian Dickson," *Osgoode Hall Law Journal* 38 (2000): 211; *R. v. Sparrow*, [1990] 1 S.C.R. 1075.

22   *Nowegijick v. The Queen*, [1983] 1 S.C.R. 29.

23   *Guerin v. The Queen*, [1984] 2 S.C.R. 335.

24   *Simon v. The Queen*, [1985] 2 S.C.R. 387.

25   Here the authors caution: "Fishing rights are not traditional property rights. They are rights held by a collective and are in keeping with the culture and existence of that group. Courts must be careful, then, to avoid the application of traditional common law concepts of property" (1112). Note the similarity to Dickson's 1967 opinion in *Hofer*, discussed earlier.

26   Dickson and La Forest make the point sharply by illustration: "If, in a given year, conservation needs required a reduction in the number of fish to be caught such that the number equaled the number required for food by the Indians, then *all* the fish available after conservation would go to the Indians" (1116; emphasis added).

27   On the impact of *Sparrow* on later Court decisions, see Peter W. Hogg, *Constitutional Law of Canada* (Scarborough, ON: Thomson, 2005), ss. 27.5, 27.8.

28   *Societe des Acadiens v. Association of Parents* [1986], 1 S.C.R. 549, at 574-75, 566, 564.

29   *Mahe v. Alberta*, [1990] 1 S.C.R. 342. The appeal was mainly focused on s. 23(3), which, in part, provides that the French or English "linguistic minority" in a province has the right to education in "minority language educational facilities provided out of public funds" – "where the number of children so warrants."

30   Christopher P. Manfredi, *Judicial Power and the Charter* (Don Mills, ON: Oxford University Press, 2001), 167, 196. For a favourable interpretation of Dickson's analysis in this case and in other language-rights cases, see Sharpe, "Brian Dickson," 209-11. The frustration expressed by Manfredi and others was only partly due to the "activism" of Dickson and his colleagues on the Supreme Court. Another crucial factor was the failure of Parliament and the provinces, except in two instances, to use s. 33 of the *Charter*, which allows them to block judicial review of legislative action in a variety of fields. The reasons for that failure are described in Manfredi, 2001, 181-88, and in Hogg, *Constitutional Law*, s. 36.

31   *Regina v. Keegstra*, [1990] 3 S.C.R. 697.

32   Section 319(2) of the Criminal Code provides that "Everyone who ... willfully promotes hatred against any identifiable group is guilty of (a) an indictable offence and is liable to imprisonment for a term not exceeding two years." The accused could avoid conviction "if the statements were relevant to any subject of public interest, the discussion of which was for the public benefit, and if on reasonable grounds he believed them to be true."

33   He referred to s. 15(1): "Every individual ... has the right to the equal protection and equal benefit of the law without discrimination," and s. 27: "This Charter shall be interpreted in

a manner consistent with the preservation and enhancement of the multicultural heritage of Canadians" (106-10).

34 "Condoning a democracy's collective decision to protect itself from certain types of expression may lead to a slippery slope," he admitted, eventuating in censorship of speech more central to "s. 2(b) values." However, "hate propaganda contributes little to ... the quest for truth" or other important Canadian values (124-25).

35 "Statements promoting hatred are not akin to violence or threats of violence," Justice McLachlin wrote for the dissenters, and "the argument that they should ... be excluded from the protection of s. 2(b) of the Charter should be rejected" (235).

36 For example, *Guerin v. The Queen*, [1984] 2 S.C.R. 335, and *Simon v. The Queen*, [1985] 2 S.C.R. 387, both on Aboriginal rights.

37 W.H. McConnell, *William R. McIntyre: Paladin of the Common Law* (Montreal: McGill-Queen's University Press, 1999), 222-23. See also Christopher P. Manfredi, *Judicial Power and the Charter* (Don Mills, ON: Oxford University Press); and Robert J. Sharpe, K.E. Swinton, and K. Roach, *The Charter of Rights and Freedoms*, 2nd ed. (Toronto: Irwin Law, 2002), chap. 2. For a discussion of "judicial activism" and its opponents in the United States compared with Canada, see J. Doig, "What Role for the Judiciary in Aiding 'Vulnerable People'?" paper prepared for May 2007 conference at the University of Regina.

38 See Hogg, *Constitutional Law*, s. 27.8. For an example of *Sparrow* in action, see *R. v. Adams* [1996], but see possible modification of the *Sparrow* standard in *R. v. Gladstone* [1996].

39 *Vriend v. Alberta*, [1998] 1 S.C.R. 493.

40 He then quoted from Dickson's opinion in the case: the Charter must "be capable of growth and development over time to meet new social, political and historical realities often unimagined by its framers." See *Halpern v. Attorney-General of Canada* [2001], para. 117.

41 Reference regarding Same-Sex Marriage, [2004] 3 S.C.R. 698, at 699.

42 One reader of a draft of this chapter commented: "That justices should be selected on the basis of their support for diversity seems a bit unusual and out of step with their role as impartial arbiters of the law." The idea that judges are "impartial arbiters" has a long tradition as a rhetorical defence of judicial power and independence; but the reality is better captured by Murphy and Pritchett: "Where problems are most likely to arise – where public policies clash with putative rights – legal rules are usually at their most imprecise, leaving room for discretion ... In many of the more important controversies that come before them, judges must either choose among a wide variety of potentially pertinent rules, modify one or more of those rules, or create new ones." And in using their discretion, judges will inevitably draw upon their personal experience and political or policy values. Where the basic document emphasizes the value of diversity, as does the 1982 Constitution, the argument for selecting justices who share that basic value seems strong. See Walter F. Murphy and C. Herman Pritchett, *Courts, Judges, and Politics*, 4th ed. (New York: McGraw-Hill, 1986), 598, and chap. 14 generally.

9
Whose Reality? Culture and Context before Canadian Courts
Robert J. Currie

A fundamental requirement for equality in citizenship, and a key for social participation, is encapsulated in the notion of equality before and under the law. This equality is enshrined in the *Charter of Rights and Freedoms*,[1] and it acts as an essential informant to all kinds of state action, whether executive, legislative, or judicial. I would submit that the demands that equality places upon the law are highlighted most starkly in situations in which citizens are facing the courts for determination of rights and obligations. Equality and fairness, naturally enough, go hand-in-hand in litigation as easily as in other settings. The right to a fair trial is enshrined in Canadian law, both in criminal trials (contests between state and individual)[2] and civil trials (legal actions between private individuals).[3] Appellate courts bear an equally grave obligation, given that these are often the fora within which social policy decisions, as well as individual conflicts, fall to be resolved.

In turn, a fundamental requirement for rendering a trial or appeal decision that is "fair" in any meaningful sense is the ability of institutional decision makers to properly accommodate the myriad of interests before them and to formulate responses that adequately address the diverse needs of citizens. This is true of all government decision makers but is particularly the case for courts since they are charged with making some of the most complex, important, sometimes life-changing decisions for people and for society.

A major issue emerges: do Canadian courts and judges have the tools they need to make decisions that take into account complex social and cultural realities? After all, multiculturalism, too, is constitutionally enshrined. Section 27 of the *Charter* states: "This Charter shall be interpreted in a manner consistent with the preservation and enhancement of the multicultural heritage of Canadians."[4] In its landmark 1997 judgment in the case of *R. v. S. (R.D.)*,[5] the Supreme Court of Canada recognized that lack of awareness of social and cultural context was an impediment to judges and courts truly being able to accommodate diversity and multicultural-ism. However, in many ways the law has yet to catch up.

Using several of the rules of evidence as a lens, this chapter surveys some of the various "cultural" issues that have emerged before Canadian courts and examines the bases on which such evidence has been received, rejected, and utilized by judges and (to some extent) juries. The hope is that some inspection of what evidence is admitted, and how much and for what pur-poses, will: provide a preliminary guide as to the impact that culture is having on court-based decision making, highlight areas that might be open to examination for reform, and serve the object of providing "lessons," whether by way of example or cautionary tale.

Definitions of culture are, of course, elusive. Tracing the term to its an-thropological roots reveals a disquieting "emergence of a widely accepted approach to culture in anthropology that dismisses its value as a category of 'thing,' as a noun that can be identified, described, compared with others ... and by extension, decided upon in courts."[6] Nonetheless, as I explore here, the courts of the land have decided that acknowledgment of Canada's cul-tural pluralism is a matter of note, not just on a macro or policy level but, indeed, as a "thing" or "concept" that is relevant to individual disputes and upon which evidence can be adduced. Moreover, it is fairly clear that no-tions of "equality" and "fairness" will and must engage cultural concerns at some point, and their place and significance in society's dispute resolution mechanisms is highly worthy of study and informed debate.[7]

The case law and writing surveyed here encompass a fairly conventional notion of "culture" based mostly on ethnicity and race, though I am alive to the potential of including other kinds of "culture," such as level of ability/disability and sexual orientation.

Credibility Assessment: Perspectivism and Contextualism

In any trial, as the saying goes, the credibility of witnesses is always an issue. Practically, this principle manifests itself in two ways. First, as part of weighing the evidence at the end of the trial, the "trier of fact" (either judge or jury) must consider the evidence given by each witness and decide whether they believe it in whole, part, or not at all. In effect, the trier determines whether the witness was telling the truth or not and, if so, how much of her testimony was true and/or reliable enough to factor into decision making. Second, credibility is a "live issue" at trial, and lawyers on both sides of a case invariably end up leading evidence that either "impeaches" (or attacks) a witness's credibility or supports it.

As such, a lawyer might impeach a witness by suggesting or leading evi-dence to the effect that: they have previously told a different story than they are telling on the stand; they are biased in favour of the party for whom they are testifying; they are of bad character and should not be believed; or they have a "defect of capacity ... to observe, remember or recount the matters testified about."[8] The other lawyer might lead evidence to counter this.[9] Both lawyers, in their closing remarks at the end of the trial, might draw the trier's attention to any credibility problems a witness had and invite the trier to give that witness's testimony little weight. This applies not only to the witnesses (including the complainant in a criminal case) but also to the parties themselves (e.g., the accused in a criminal case or the plaintiff and defendant in a civil case).

How, then, is the trier to determine the weight to be given a particular witness and her testimony? For such a central aspect of the trial process, there is actually very little in the way of "law" for the trier to draw upon. In *RDS*, Justice Cory described credibility assessment as "more of 'an art than a science'" and cited earlier Supreme Court of Canada authority to the effect that "[t]he issue of credibility is one of fact and cannot be determined by following a set of rules."[10] The starting point is well summarized by Professors Paciocco and Stuesser:

> In general, the trier of fact is entitled simply to apply common sense and human experience in determining whether evidence is credible and in deciding what use, if any, to make of it in coming to its findings of fact.[11]

In the last few decades, however, courts have wrestled with the obvious reality that one person's "common sense" can be counter-intuitive to another: humans do not necessarily share "experience" in a way that can allow people to successfully ground their decisions about others in their own backgrounds. Appropriately judging how much weight should be given to a witness's testimony could require that the trier have an understanding of the various contextual factors, including cultural factors, that might have shaped how an event played out or how the witness recounts it. The problem is that these factors could be out of the "common sense and human experience" of judges or jurors.[12]

The idea of culture as context came squarely before the Supreme Court of Canada in *RDS*,[13] where a black teenager was arrested by a white police officer when he happened upon the latter arresting another black teen, his cousin. The teenager was charged for various aspects of a physical altercation that took place thereafter and was tried, inter alia, for assaulting a police officer and resisting arrest. RDS and the officer were the only witnesses called, and they gave conflicting evidence as to what had happened. This being the case, credibility was the central issue. The trial judge, Judge Sparks (who herself was African Nova Scotian), had to determine which witness was telling the truth. Her reasons for acquitting RDS appeared to implicate cultural evidence, specifically racial relations between the Halifax Police and the African-Nova Scotian community. She suggested that white police officers had a tendency to overreact, particularly when they were dealing with members of non-white groups.[14]

The Crown appealed Judge Sparks' decision on the basis that her remarks indicated a reasonable apprehension of bias. As Paciocco and Stuesser note, "[n]one [of the trial judge's contextual comments] were supported by proof. The trial judge was relying upon her own knowledge and experience in the community to pose these propositions."[15]

In its 1997 decision in the case, a majority of the Supreme Court of Canada found that Judge Sparks' remarks did not give rise to a reasonable apprehension of bias. However, the Court was badly split over how the judge's remarks could be assessed as well as over how any trier could appropriately take "social context" into account when assessing credibility. A detailed analysis of the four interweaving judgments that the Court delivered is beyond the scope of this chapter,[16] but, as Devlin and Pothier remark, "the majority judges, to different degrees, all accept that social context can be factored into the judge's decision [on the credibility of a witness] ... [T]he crucial point ... is the assumption that it may be relevant even in the absence of specific evidence about particular witnesses."[17]

As was clear from the trial judge's remarks that the "cultural" issue at play in *RDS* was interracial conflict within the relevant community and, specifically, how it factored into relations between police officers and black community members. The problem the Court faced was that Judge Sparks had clearly drawn on her own experiences and knowledge as an African Nova Scotian in the course of making her decision, though the Court ultimately split on whether she had actually relied upon those experiences and knowledge in reaching her finding that RDS's account of the events was to be believed over the officer's. That racism and racialized relations existed in the community was beyond contesting, but how was a trier of fact to properly utilize this knowledge without displaying bias?

Justices McLachlin and L'Heureux-Dubé provided the most challenging and broad view on how perspective and context could inform judicial decision making. The cornerstone of their judgment was their recognition of

the reality that while judges can never be neutral, in the sense of purely objective, they can and must strive for impartiality. It [is] therefore ... inevitable and appropriate that the differing experiences of judges assist them in their decision-making process and will be reflected in their judgments, so long as those experiences are relevant to the cases, are not based on inappropriate stereotypes, and do not prevent a fair and just determination of the cases based on the facts in evidence.[18]

These judges posed the proposition that impartial judging could exist apart from the fictions of "objectivity" and "neutrality"; indeed, judges should be permitted to effectively leap into contextual analysis and draw upon both their own experiences and "the factual, social and psychological context within which litigation arises ... [A] conscious, contextual inquiry has become an accepted step towards judicial impartiality."[19] The latter can be informed by expert witnesses and by academic studies properly placed before the Court.[20] Also, as Devlin points out, "two sets of constraints are indicated":[21] the "reasonable person"[22] would have to think that the judge's exercise of his/her own experience was appropriate;[23] and the experiences drawn upon by the judge must be "relevant ... not based on inappropriate stereotypes and ... not prevent a fair and just determination ... based on the facts in evidence."[24] Applying this approach, the judges found that, "in alerting herself to the racial dynamic in the case, [Judge Sparks] was simply engaging in the process of contextualized judging which, in our view, was entirely proper and conducive to a fair and just resolution to the case before her."[25]

In a concurring judgment for himself and Justice Iacobucci, Justice Cory was somewhat more cautious than his colleagues on the issue of utilizing social context as a means of evaluating credibility. While social context could clearly be relevant, the requirement of judicial neutrality dictated that "the judge must avoid judging the credibility of the witness on the basis of generalizations or upon matters that were not in evidence."[26] What would give rise to a suggestion of bias on the part of a judge is any suggestion "that the determination of credibility is based on generalizations rather than on specific demonstrations of truthfulness or untrustworthiness that have come from the particular witness during the trial."[27] In effect, even if a generalization about social context were a correct one, there should be evidence linking the witness to the generalization (i.e., that the witness's credibility could fairly be explained and evaluated by the social context evidence). Thus, social context was seen by Cory J. as a consultative tool rather than as a generalized framing device for evaluation of credibility.

Proceeding from this framework, Cory J. characterized Judge Sparks' remarks as "unfortunate,"[28] "troubling,"[29] "worrisome," and "very close to the line."[30] Nonetheless, he was satisfied that, "viewed in their context," a reasonable person reading her comments would not perceive "that she prejudged the issue of credibility on the basis of generalizations"[31] and would conclude that she had not been biased.

RDS is a very complex case and cannot be said to have set out the law on social context in credibility assessment, given the deep divisions on the Court.[32] However, it presents a range of approaches for the ability of a trier of fact to take social (including, of course, cultural) context into account when assessing credibility. The textured and nuanced approaches taken by the majority justices have much to recommend them Together, they make a compelling case that, while "adjudicative neutrality" is necessary for proper non-biased decision making (the Cory approach), "fact neutrality" should be avoided since it produces excessive formalism and an inability to properly take context into account (the McLachlin/L'Heureux-Dubé approach). To simply proceed from the starting point that everyone is "equal" and "neutral" until the facts prove otherwise (which is what the dissent suggests) is, in effect, a formal equality analysis: it renders one oblivious to the social forces that got the witness onto the stand in the first place.

Hearsay

The hearsay rule is one of the best known (at least colloquially) but least understood of the rules of evidence. Hearsay is conventionally defined as an out-of-court statement offered to prove the truth of its contents.[33] Where it meets this test the evidence is excluded (subject to exceptions) because of its inherent unreliability and the common law preference for live witness testimony. In particular, it is the lack of ability to cross-examine the out-of-court speaker in court that makes the evidence of questionable worth.[34]

In recent years, the Supreme Court of Canada has undertaken a profound revision of the law of hearsay, described by one commentator as a "revolution,"[35] usually explained as applying the "principled approach."[36] Under this approach, while the hearsay rule and its exceptions remain essentially valid, the Court has suggested that the exceptional admission of hearsay is premised on two notions: necessity and reliability. Thus, a relevant hearsay statement can be admitted if it is necessary (i.e., if evidence of similar worth cannot be obtained other than through the hearsay statement) and if it is reliable (i.e., if, in the circumstances, the statement has "indicia of reliability"). Even hearsay statements that do not meet the conditions of the common law hearsay exceptions can be admitted if they are sufficiently necessary and reliable, a test sometimes referred to as the "residual approach."[37]

The heart of the "residual approach" is the assessment of the reliability of the statement, which, generally speaking, involves assessing the circumstances surrounding the making of the statement and concluding whether or not those circumstances disclose sufficient reliability.[38] Taking culture into account in reliability testing will certainly give rise to concerns about the out-of-court statement. A great deal hinges on the in-court reporting witness's perception of the hearsay statement and out-of-court speaker since cultural barriers could certainly produce ambiguity or misinterpretation. To build on an example posed by Professor Ontiveros,[39] suppose the in-court witness reports that, when confronted with an accusation by an authority figure, a Latina responded, "If you say so, sir." There is clear ambiguity here: the speaker may be expressing agreement or may be manifesting a cultural preference for avoidance of conflict or disrespect. The in-court reporter, especially if he/she emerges from a different culture than the out-of-court speaker, can provide us with little explanation; his/her lack of cultural context in understanding what the out-of-court speaker intended to convey merely magnifies that of the trier of fact. This difficulty, where present, must play a role in the reliability analysis, though there has as yet been no authoritative effort to build it in.

One very interesting area that has seen culture affect the hearsay rule involves Aboriginal rights cases. As part of the increasing amount of litigation in the 1990s regarding treaty rights, Aboriginal rights, and Aboriginal title, the courts were faced with a kind of evidence with which they were (largely) unequipped to deal: the tradition of oral history in Canadian Native cultures. As First Nations cultures often have little in the way of recorded history or even written language, history and tradition have been preserved through oral accounts that are passed down through generations.[40] This particular version of history would inevitably play an important role since, as Boyle and MacCrimmon note, Canadian Aboriginal law jurisprudence has consistently held that "Aboriginal rights depend on factual questions about pre-contact practices of the Aboriginal peoples and placed the burden on them to establish these facts in each case."[41] Yet, the difficulties of dealing with this "new" kind of evidence were profound,[42] no less because oral tradition was clearly a prima facie violation of the hearsay rule.

In the 1997 case of *Delgamuukw v. British Columbia*,[43] the Supreme Court of Canada squarely addressed the fact that oral tradition and history "does not conform precisely with the evidentiary standards" of other cases.[44] The lower courts were instructed that the laws of evidence must be adapted so that due weight could be given to "the Aboriginal perspective on their practices, customs and traditions and on their relationship with the land."[45] Specifically, oral histories were established as being potentially relevant to the material issues of land and resource ownership, rights, and entitlement. Witnesses (usually Aboriginal elders) could testify as to the content of these traditions, and such testimony was to be placed "on an equal footing with the types of historical evidence courts are familiar with."[46] Failure to do so, said the Court, would effectively "render nugatory any rights they have," given the lack of conventional historical records among Aboriginal societies.[47]

Judicial Notice

Judicial notice is properly understood as a technique by which certain facts may be admitted into evidence without having to be proven by the parties. By "judicially noticing" a fact, a judge (as trier of fact and law) accepts it as being given and may then proceed to base the disposition of the case upon it in some manner. These facts are usually not taken under oath or tested on cross-examination.[48] Judicial notice usually deals with facts that are either so generally known within the community that they cannot be readily disputed or that are amenable to confirmation by reference to authorities whose accuracy cannot be questioned.[49] So, for example, the fact that the CN Tower is located in Toronto, if it was relevant to a material issue, could be judicially noticed without having to be proven by a party.[50]

The importance of judicial notice to the present inquiry occurs when it involves consideration of proof of what are sometimes called "social framework facts," which "refer to social science research that is used to construct a frame of reference or background context for deciding factual issues crucial to the resolution of a particular case."[51] In effect, this was what Judge Sparks was doing in *RDS* when she spoke to her knowledge of the racial tension that informed interaction between Nova Scotia's police and its black communities.

Judicial notice of social framework facts presents a unique way for a court to accommodate cultural context. Two appellate court decisions from the 1990s are instructive. In *R. v. Parks*,[52] the accused was a black man of Jamaican origin who was charged with having murdered a white man. Before the jury selection process began, the accused applied to be permitted to challenge individual jurors on the basis of their potential bias by asking them questions about whether they could be impartial given the racial overtones in the case. The trial judge refused to allow this questioning. The Ontario Court of Appeal noted that the legal issue was whether there was "a realistic potential for the existence of partiality" among the jurors since, if this was so, the challenge for cause could be permitted. In ruling that there was such potential, Justice Doherty took notice of a substantial number of social science reports of varying origins, all of which disclosed the presence of racism and racial discrimination in Canada and in Ontario and ruled that "there can be no doubt that there existed a realistic possibility that one or more potential jurors drawn from the Metropolitan Toronto community would, consciously or subconsciously, come to court possessed of negative stereotypical attitudes towards black persons."[53] In other words, the accused was entitled to challenge jurors for cause, not because of any racism attributable to any particular jury candidate, but because the social framework of the Toronto community disclosed pervasive racism, which, in turn, produced the "realistic potential" that one or more jurors would be biased.[54]

In 1998, in *R. v. Williams*,[55] the Supreme Court of Canada validated a similar exercise regarding Aboriginal people in British Columbia and took notice of several sources regarding this kind of racism. This has led to an increased use of this kind of judicial notice in the lower courts.[56] Also, as Stack notes, the *Report of the Royal Commission on Aboriginal Peoples* has had an impact on various aspects of Aboriginal interaction with, in particular, the criminal law.[57] This was especially apparent in *R. v. Gladue*,[58] where the

Supreme Court of Canada drew upon the report, as well as many other sources, to put flesh on the bones of a Criminal Code provision (718.2(e)) that directed courts to take the circumstances of Aboriginal offenders into account when sentencing.[59]

This approach to judicial notice is not without its critics.[60] Judge Williams (as he then was), among others, has argued that social science data and interpretation "are value-laden and, in the views of many, always disputable."[61] Concern has been expressed about the Supreme Court of Canada's reliance on its own research, carried out predominantly by law clerks, which has the potential for distortion or unclear coverage. Moreover, there are reliability concerns since there will often be division of opinion among social scientists and streams of thought, and changing developments can make one year's judicially noticed fact next year's pooh-poohed fad. Social science work regarding culture may have particularly pernicious problems in this regard as social context literature is no less vulnerable to the exclusion of minority opinion than is the literature from any other discipline; the court, by judicially noticing it, can perpetuate the exclusions[62] – and, what is worse, enshrine them in law.

The response, to the extent that there is one, is that this criticism may be losing sight of the nature of the common law, which has always attempted to reflect the dominant trends in society even as it shaped them. The law itself evolves along with the social framework and changes as it must to reflect new realities. The fact of inevitable change should not prevent the courts from undertaking best efforts to "stay up to date," as it were. Moreover, the courts do not have the luxury of awaiting consensus; as Binnie J. was moved to state in *R. v. Marshall*, the courts, unlike the social scientists, must ultimately make a decision.[63] Finally, in the recent decision of *R. v. Spence*,[64] the Supreme Court of Canada has cautioned that judicial notice of "social fact" must be approached more strictly as, in any given case, the matter noticed approaches more closely to determinative issues. This may give trial judges a better set of tools for safeguarding reliability while at the same time acknowledging cultural reality – though this is a fine balance, indeed.

Conclusion

It is undeniable that the Canadian law of evidence has been evolving in a manner that addresses some cultural concerns. The advent of the *Charter* is a temporal and probably substantive demarcation point since it is at least arguable that the constitutionalization of multiculturalism has (expressly and/or implicitly) informed the developments in evidence law canvassed here. One might even say that a "cultural discourse" is under way, if only sotto voce, between and among the courts, that has fairness and equity as its basis.

It is worthy of note, however, that while these developments have, on balance, made trials better, fairer, and more consistent with Canada's multicultural reality, it certainly has not made them easier – or shorter. Expansive notions of relevance and materiality manifest themselves on the ground in longer trials, more expense, and, to some extent, justice delayed. Resource depletion is particularly intense; experts are expensive, as is research; greater numbers of evidentiary motions mean more legal fees, more consumption of court resources, more time. There is inequity, too, as pointed out earlier. Often the cultural evidence is relevant to a defence, particularly a criminal defence, yet these are often the parties with the least resources with which to defend themselves.

I should not be heard to suggest that accommodation of cultural reality in the courtroom should take second place to a firm eye on the purse-strings. Yet it has always been accepted that trial fairness also encompasses efficiency, economy, and the "resolution" part of "dispute resolution." Trial management concerns must play a role in the development of evidence law's "response" to culture. To build on Lord Hewart's famous dictum,[65] justice should not only be done, and not only must it be seen to be done, but it must get done.

The most efficient response to this concern, I suggest, is to "front-end load" the litigation process with, at least the potential for, cultural sensitivity. This is hardly an original idea, as the Canadian Judicial Council has already embarked on implementing what has been termed "social context education," a series of continuing education programs for judges that "provide[s] information about the social backdrop against which and out of which particular issues and particular litigants come before the courts."[66] While the manner in which the term "social context" is being used encompasses far more than what have herein been called "cultural" matters, the effort dovetails nicely with the concerns I have raised. Awareness, of course, is everything when it comes to implementing fairness and an egalitarian agenda in a court-based dispute resolution.

However, perhaps even this worthy effort is not enough. The problem is that there is still an enormous number of cases before the courts in which the jury is the trier of fact, and even the most doughty "socially context-ualized" judge will sometimes have his or her hands tied when it comes to the always unpredictable (and ultimately unknowable) way that the jurors will contextualize the evidence for themselves. The goal of social context education, after all, is to sensitize judges to the need for openness to the complex and varying perspectives that exist and, thus, make them more receptive to "cultural evidence." This will presumably mean that, as triers of law, they will be able to find more relevance and materiality in this kind of evidence and place it in front of the jury. However, it will not equip jurors to the same extent when they are called upon to make their decisions, as the "cultural evidence" will necessarily compete with their own versions of "common sense," and simply hearing one expert may be not enough to forestall falling back on myths, stereotypes, and internalized assumptions.

As such, I propose that inquiry needs to be made into law reform that is geared towards shaping the role of the trier of fact in cases where culture is relevant and material. There may be a need for more specific jury instructions that encompass these issues; perhaps there will be some instances where it will be incumbent upon the judge, as a matter of law, to instruct the jury to ignore certain stereotypes or assumptions they may hold (demeanour evidence comes to mind). Ultimately, the pressing and constitutionally driven need for fairness and egalitarianism may militate in favour of excluding trial by jury in some cases in which the arguably more sophisticated decision-making abilities of a judge are required. That, however, is an argument for another day.

Acknowledgments
An expanded and reworked version of this chapter appeared as "The Contextualized Court: Litigating 'Culture' in Canada," *International Journal of Evidence and Proof* 9 (2005): 73.

Notes

1 *Canadian Charter of Rights and Freedoms*, Part I of the *Constitution Act*, 1982, being Schedule B to the *Canada Act*, 1982 (U.K.), 1982, c. 11 (hereafter the *Charter*), s. 15.
2 See s. 7 of the *Charter*.
3 *Société des Acadiens du Nouveau-Brunswick Inc. v. Assn. of Parents for Fairness in Education, Grand Falls District 50 Branch*, [1986] 1 S.C.R. 549.
4 See generally J. Jedwab, "To Preserve and Enhance: Canadian Multiculturalism before and after the Charter," *Supreme Court Law Review* (2d) 19 (2003): 309.
5 [1997] 3 S.C.R. 484 (hereafter *RDS*).
6 R. Niezen, "Culture and the Judiciary: The Meaning of the Culture Concept as a Source of Aboriginal Rights in Canada" *Canadian Journal of Law and Society* 18, 2 (2003): 1.
7 The Honourable Justice Michel Bastarache of the Supreme Court of Canada has argued that interpretation of the *Charter*, too, must encompass the cultural realities of the state. See M. Bastarache, "The Canadian Charter of Rights and Freedoms: Domestic Application of Universal Values," *Supreme Court Law Review* (2d) 19 (2003): 371, at 377-79.
8 C. McCormick, *Evidence* (2nd ed.), as cited in R. Delisle and D. Stuart, *Evidence: Principles and Problems*, 6th ed. (Toronto: Thomson Carswell, 2001), 404.
9 Generally known as "rehabilitating the credibility of the witness."
10 *RDS*, para. 128, citing *White v. The King*, [1947] S.C.R. 268 at 272.
11 David Paciocco and Lee Stuesser, *The Law of Evidence*, 3rd ed. (Toronto: Irwin Law, 2002), 423.
12 This problem is compounded when the trier of fact is called upon to evaluate a witness's credibility by way of assessing her "demeanour"; that is, the manner in which her behaviour and comportment on the stand indicates her veracity. Cultural signals in an individual's behaviour may affect the judge or jurors in a manner that produces inaccuracy. For example, a lying witness may be believed because he/she is able to make eye contact with the questioner, reflecting a common but inaccurate bias in Anglo-Saxon culture. By contrast, it has been suggested that some Aboriginal persons avert their gaze as a sign of respect for authority figures, though this may adversely affect their credibility. See R. Ross, *Dancing with a Ghost: Exploring Indian Reality* (Markham, ON: Octopus Publishing Group, 1992), 4. See also J. Blumenthal, "A Wipe of the Hands, A Lick of the Lips: The Validity of Demeanour Evidence in Assessing Witness Credibility," *Nebraska Law Review* 72 (1993): 1157; A.

Kapardis, *Psychology and Law: A Critical Introduction* (New York: Cambridge University Press, 1997), 208-15; M. Ontiveros, "Gender and Race in the Evidence Policy: Adoptive Admissions and the Meaning of Silence: Continuing the Inquiry into Evidence Law and Issues of Race, Class, Gender and Ethnicity," *Southwest University Law Review* 28 (1999): 337.

13 On the Supreme Court of Canada's "contextual" approach to adjudication, see Shalin Sugunasiri, "Contextualism: The Supreme Court's New Standard of Judicial Analysis and Accountability," *Dalhousie Law Journal* 22 (1999): 126.

14 *RDS* at para. 74.

15 Paciocco and Stuesser, *Law of Evidence*, 384.

16 But, for a detailed analysis, see Richard Devlin and Dianne Pothier, "Redressing the Imbalances: Rethinking the Judicial Role After *R. v. R.D.S.*," *Ottawa Law Review* 31 (1999-2000): 1. See also C. Aylward, "Take the Long Way Home: *R.D.S.* and Critical Race Theory," *UNB Law Journal* 47 (1998): 249; B.P. Archibald, "The Lessons of the Sphinx: Avoiding Apprehensions of Judicial Bias in a Multi-Racial, Multicultural Society" (1997) 10 C.R. (5th) 54; and R.J. Delisle, Annotation to *R. v. S. (R.D.)* (1997), 10 C.R. (5th) 7.

17 Ibid., para. 22.

18 *RDS*, para. 29.

19 Para. 42, citing J. Nedelsky, "Embodied Diversity and the Challenges to Law," *McGill Law Journal* 42 (1997): 91. They also note the SCC's judgment in *R. v. Bartle*, [1994] 3 S.C.R. 173, which dealt with the right to counsel: "The Court, placing itself in the position of the accused, asked how the accused would have experienced and responded to arrest and detention. Against this background, the Court went on to determine what was required to make the right to counsel truly meaningful. This inquiry provided the Court with a larger picture, which was in turn conducive to a more just determination of the case" (at para. 43).

20 Para. 44.

21 Devlin and Pothier, "Redressing the Imbalances," para. 67.

22 Or, as the court put it, the "reasonable, informed, practical and realistic person who considers the matter in some detail ... not a 'very sensitive or scrupulous' person, but rather a right-minded person familiar with the circumstances of the case ... an informed and right-minded member of the community, a community which, in Canada, supports the fundamental principles entrenched in the Constitution by the [*Charter*] ... [and] a member of the local communities in which the case at issue arose ... [and] must be taken to possess knowledge of the local population and its racial dynamics" (*RDS*, paras. 36, 46, and 47).

23 *RDS*, paras. 36, 46, and 47.

24 Para. 29.

25 Para. 59.

26 Para. 129; see also para. 134.

27 Para. 129.

28 Para. 147.

29 Para. 148.

30 Para. 152.

31 Para. 158. His Lordship suggested that the remarks were made in response to the Crown's suggestion that she should "automatically" believe the testimony of the officer "by virtue of his occupation" and that this supported finding a lack of bias; paras. 153 and 157.

32 I have not summarized the dissenting judgment of Justice Major, who would have found that Judge Sparks' comments did give rise to a reasonable apprehension of bias.

33 See *R. v. Evans* (1993), 25 C.R. (4th) 46 at 522 (S.C.C.), per Sopinka J. See also *R. v. O'Brien* (1977), 38 C.R.N.S. 325 (S.C.C.) at 327, per Dickson J.

34 See the definitive work by E. Morgan, "Hearsay Dangers and the Application of the Hearsay Concept," *Harvard Law Review* 62 (1948): 177.

35 See B.P. Archibald, "The Canadian Hearsay Revolution: Is Half a Loaf Better Than No Loaf at All?" *Queen's Law Journal* 25 (1999): 1.

36 See D.M. Tanovich, "*Starr*-Gazing: Looking into the Future of Hearsay in Canada," *Queen's Law Journal* 28 (2003): 371. See also D.A. "Rollie" Thompson, "The Supreme Court Goes Hunting and Nearly Catches a Hearsay Woozle" (1995), 37 C.R. (4th) 282.

37 See *R.* v. *Khan*, [1990] 2 S.C.R. 531; and *R.* v. *Smith*, [1992] 2 S.C.R. 915.

38 See *R.* v. *Starr*, [2000] 2 S.C.R. 144.

39 Ontiveros, "Gender and Race," 344.

40 This is a rough attempt at defining oral tradition. For an informative review, see J. Borrows, "Listening for a Change: The Courts and Oral Tradition," *Osgoode Hall Law Journal* 39 (2001): 1.

41 C. Boyle and M. MacCrimmon, "To Serve the Cause of Justice: Disciplining Fact Determination, *Windsor Yb. Access Just.* 20 (2001) 55 at 66.

42 For a general discussion, see B. Gover and M. Macaulay, "Snow Houses Leave No Ruins: Unique Evidence Issues in Aboriginal and Treaty Rights Cases," *Saskatchewan Law Review* 60 (1996): 47.

43 [1997] 3 S.C.R. 1010.

44 Ibid., 1065.

45 Ibid., 1067.

46 Ibid., 1069.

47 Ibid. For more on "adapting" the rules of evidence in this context; with an eye towards enhancing reliability, however, see *Mitchell v. M.N.R.*, [2001] 1 S.C.R. 911.

48 B. Morrison, "The Bounds of Judicially Noticeable Facts," *Advocates' Quarterly* 27 (2003): 304, n.1, though the law is reasonably clear that the parties are entitled to a chance to respond to any proposed judicial notice. See *R.* v. *Peter-Paul* (1998), 18 C.R. (5th) 360 (N.B.C.A.).

49 See Paciocco and Stuesser, *Law of Evidence*, 376.

50 Judicial notice is often taken of evidence that is given in the form of "expert opinion," in that experts in particular fields can assist the court by providing their expertise on a point at issue. Space does not permit exploration of the admissibility regime for expert opinion evidence and how it interacts with "cultural" evidence. See, however, Currie, "The Contextualized Court"; and Currie, "The Bounds of the Permissible: Using 'Cultural Evidence' in Civil Jury Cases," *Canadian Journal of Law and Society* 20, 1 (2005): 75.

51 Claire L'Heureux-Dubé, "Re-examining the Doctrine of Judicial Notice in the Family Law Context," *Ottawa Law Review* 26 (1994): 556.

52 (1993), 84 C.C.C. (3d) 353 (Ont. C.A.), leave to appeal dismissed 87 C.C.C. (3d) vi (S.C.C.).

53 Page 370. His Lordship also noticed social science research from the United States detailing the impact race and racial discrimination had on jury trials in that country.

54 For further developments with regard to the so-called *"Parks* question," as well as with regard to judicial notice of what the Supreme Court of Canada has now definitively labelled "social fact," see *R.* v. *Spence*, 2005 SCC 171. An interesting and recent series of cases focusing on the cultural realities of the African-Canadian experience is also worthy of note. See *R.* v. *Hamilton and Mason*, [2003] O.J. No. 532 (S.C.J.) (varied [2004] O.J. No. 3252 (Ont. C.A.)); *R.* v. *Spencer*, [2003] O.J. No. 1052 (S.C.J.) (reversed [2004] O.J. No. 3262 (Ont.C.A.)).

55 [1998] 1 S.C.R. 1128.

56 See, for example, *R.* v. *Fleury*, [1998] 3 C.N.L.R. 160 (Sask. Q.B.).

57 D. Stack, "The Impact of RCAP on the Judiciary: Bringing Aboriginal Perspectives into the Courtroom," *Saskatchewan Law Review* 62 (1999): 471.

58 (1999), 171 D.L.R. (4th) 385 (S.C.C.).

59 For more on sentencing in the Aboriginal context, see P. Stenning and J.V. Roberts, "Empty Promises: Parliament, the Supreme Court and the Sentencing of Aboriginal Offenders," *Saskatchewan Law Review* 64 (2001): 137.

60 See, for example, C. Baar, "Criminal Court Delay and the *Charter*: The Use and Mis-Use of Social Facts in Policy Making," *Canadian Bar Review* 72 (1993): 305.

61 Judge R. James Williams, "Grasping a Thorny Baton ... A Trial Judge Looks at Judicial Notice and Courts' Acquisition of Social Science," *Canadian Family Law Quarterly* 14 (1996): 179, as cited in Morrison, "Bounds of Judicially Noticeable Facts," 326.

62 Devlin and Pothier, "Redressing the Imbalances," para. 54.

63 [1999] 3 S.C.R. 456, para. 37.

64 See note 54.
65 *R.* v. *Sussex Justices, Ex Parte McCarthy*, [1924] 1 K.B. 256 at 259: "justice should not only be done, but should manifestly and undoubtedly be seen to be done."
66 R. Cairns-Way, "What Is Social Context Education?" *National Judicial Institute* 10, 3 (1997): 5.

10
Multiculturalism, Equality, and Canadian Constitutionalism: Cohesion and Difference
Joan Small

Canada's pluralism, in terms of both its diverse population and its guiding philosophy, represents an experiment with the concept of "multiculturalism," a term that has been given legal effect by statute and that has been translated into a principle of *Charter* interpretation. Its effect on *Charter* law, and in particular on equality law, remains largely unrealized. But while Canadian constitutionalism requires that the unique Canadian constitutional settlement be protected, it also demands that "multiculturalism" be given legal effect. The legal principle of multiculturalism challenges substantive equality law not only for individuals in association with groups but also for the collective protection of groups.

Multiculturalism: Ideology, Policy, and Law
In 1971, "multiculturalism" was adopted to represent the official policy of the federal government.[1] A policy of bilingualism and *bi*culturalism, initially proposed to ease the state of relations between the two founding peoples – English and French – was rejected in favour of multiculturalism within a bilingual framework.[2] The policy was, in part, a response to criticisms made by ethnic groups, other than the English and French, who observed that the terms of reference of the Royal Commission on Bilingualism and Biculturalism, 1963-69, ignored the contribution of diverse cultures to Canadian society.[3] This policy was eventually enshrined in the *Multiculturalism Act*, 1988,[4] which specified the ability of all to identify with the cultural heritage of their choice, yet retain "full and equitable participation ... in all aspects of Canadian society."

The Department of Canadian Heritage, charged with the implementation of multicultural policy, describes multiculturalism as follows:

> Canadian multiculturalism is fundamental to our belief that all citizens are equal. Multiculturalism ensures that all citizens can keep their identities, can take pride in their ancestry and have a sense of belonging. Acceptance

gives Canadians a feeling of security and self-confidence, making them more open to, and accepting of, diverse cultures. The Canadian experience has shown that multiculturalism encourages racial and ethnic harmony and cross-cultural understanding, and discourages ghettoization, hatred, discrimination and violence.[5]

While, by the official account, multiculturalism is a general good, expressly founded on the concept of equality for all Canadian citizens, the policy of multiculturalism – as it has been put into practice – has been subject to criticism.

The policy has been primarily attacked for emphasizing difference among Canadians, at the expense of supporting any concept of a Canadian identity.[6] The policy, Bissoondath has argued, has led immigrants to adopt a "psychology of separation" from the mainstream culture, which has encouraged the isolation of ethno-racial groups and has pitted one group against another in the competition for power and resources.[7] Hutcheon has observed that, historically, although multiculturalism was originally proposed in the form of an enhancement of biculturalism as a means of unifying Canada, it rapidly became a movement proposing a contrasting vision of the country, an alternative to biculturalism rather than a complementary political objective. She sums up the evolution of multiculturalism as a political ideology as "the transformation of an idea for social reform based on the premise of equality of *opportunity* for *individuals* regardless of biological inheritance or ancestral history into its precise opposite: the idea of equality of *results* for ethnic groups, at the price of sacrificing hard-won individual rights."[8] The various critiques of multiculturalism construct a view of multiculturalism that is effectively ethnically essentialist and ultimately rooted in ideologies of cultural relativism.[9] Kymlicka, on the other hand, has defended Canadian multiculturalism as being closer to what Hollinger has termed the current American "cosmopolitan" model of multiculturalism,[10] which accepts "shifting group boundaries, multiple affiliations and hybrid identities and which is based on individual rights."[11]

Alternative conceptions of multiculturalism policy raise questions concerning opposing objectives for the development of Canadian society. Objectives such as social cohesion, integrating immigrants into Canadian society, combating discrimination, and equality seemingly run counter to notions of distinct cultures within Canada, which should arguably be accorded public assistance in order to maintain their diverse cultural attributes. In fact, policy discourse has mainly emphasized cohesion, and initiatives have been aimed at ethnic participation in employment and combating racism, and they have been driven – at least since the adoption of the *Charter* – by equality concerns.[12] And, despite the debate concerning the deleterious effects of policy on an evolving Canadian identity, the concept of multiculturalism now seems to have been embraced by the Canadian population.[13]

"Multiculturalism" has been translated into legal principle by section 27 of the *Canadian Charter of Rights and Freedoms*, which reads:

> This Charter shall be interpreted in a manner consistent with the preservation and enhancement of the multicultural heritage of Canadians.

Section 27 is an interpretative rule that is riddled with difficulty. The drafting history offers little help, except to confirm that there was "no clear consensus on the meaning of the term [multiculturalism] during the critical years 1980-82 when the *Charter* was being drafted."[14] The "multicultural heritage of Canadians" has been dismissed by Peter Hogg as "more of a rhetorical flourish than an operative provision."[15] Hudson has lamented that it is either "a barrier to discrimination that may be redundant in light of section 15 (the equality provision), or a collective right which may be too vague to benefit any group."[16] Magnet sums up the prospects for section 27 as follows:

> The multiple-meaning aura radiated by section 27 is important. It allows a court or other interpreting body latitude to apply the multiculturalism principle to a wide range of situations in imaginative, polymorphous and multitudinous ways. Given the embryonic development of the multiculturalism principle in current government policy, and always on the assumption that the courts will strain seriously to actualize this multicultural ideal in practice, the array of opportunities for interpretation offers hope to multiculturalism's supporters – and a challenge to authorities applying the Charter.[17]

Magnet's comments at least take section 27 seriously. Section 27 expressly states a Canadian constitutional *value*, a principle that is relevant, and certainly not neutral, to constitutional decision making. Interpretative obligations arising from the *Charter* itself are not of the same order as are principles of statutory interpretation, and, accordingly, the obligation to give effect to section 27 carries a different interpretational burden.[18] It is incumbent upon the Court to give section 27 effect. The *Charter* must form the basis of a (relatively) coherent and principled jurisprudence: section 27 suggests that judicial choice should be exercised, wherever relevant, to support the goal of preservation and enhancement of multicultural heritage. But the questions surrounding the effect of multiculturalism as a policy cannot be answered simply by translating a term used by policy makers into legal principle. The debate concerning policy and its effects is also translated into section 27: how judicial choice is exercised remains dependent on judicial understanding of the legal obligation to "preserve and enhance."

The interpretative obligations expressed in section 27 are distinct from the provisions of the Constitution of Canada, which accord certain minority groups protection through special constitutional status. For historical and political reasons, the Canadian Constitution accords to four disparate groups – Aboriginal peoples, the national minority of Quebec, denominational communities, and English and French linguistic minorities – separate institutional and legal rights in relation to the maintenance of their status. The Constitution accords each of these groups a degree of autonomy, designed to help the group to survive as a distinct community within Canada. Changes to their status require constitutional amendment: despite the Court's assertion to the contrary,[19] the special status accorded these groups therefore suggests a hierarchy in the Canadian constitutional settlement that privileges language, Aboriginal, and denominational communities.

The extent to which groups other than those accorded special constitutional status might possibly make any similar claims to rights based on group status is, as Magnet puts it, a "claim at the outer extremes (or perhaps beyond the limits) of section 15 of the Charter."[20] Section 15, the equality guarantee, states:

> Every individual is equal before and under the law and has the right to equal protection and benefit of the law without discrimination and, in particular, without discrimination based on race, national or ethnic origin, colour, sex, age or mental or physical disability.

But Magnet's comment raises the question, what is the legal effect of the multicultural principle and policies on section 15 of the *Charter*? How does, or should, the fact that Canada's is a multicultural society affect understanding of equality law? What sorts of claims, if any, can persons or groups who are not given special constitutional status make? While the Court has developed a complex equality jurisprudence, which recognizes diversity as a fundamental aspect of equality, equality and multiculturalism per se have sat uneasily together. Magnet cautions us regarding the limits of the non-discrimination principle in interpreting and giving effect to section 27:

> The antidiscrimination principle emanates from ideals of equality, not multiculturalism. To some extent, a concentrated focus on advantages one group obtains vis-à-vis other groups is counterproductive to enhancement and development of the distinctive cultural pluralism which inspires section 27. The equality perspective gives rise to unprofitable but compelling arguments that it is illegitimate to confer benefits on one group, without simultaneously making such benefits available to all others. The practical effect of this limit is to retard progress for all groups.[21]

Perhaps this sort of caution is in part responsible for the rare invocation of section 27 in the Supreme Court's equality analysis. However, in the context of elaborating the purposes of equality law, section 27 was referred to by McIntyre J. in *Andrews v. Law Society of British Columbia*:

> the promotion of equality under s. 15 has a much more specific goal than the mere elimination of distinctions. If the *Charter* was intended to eliminate all distinctions, then there would be no place for sections such as 27 (multicultural heritage); 2(*a*) (freedom of conscience and religion); 25 (aboriginal rights and freedoms); and other such provisions designed to safeguard certain distinctions.[22]

The Court clearly contemplated that section 15 must be interpreted so as to accommodate distinctions that are permitted by section 27. Nevertheless, section 27 has been virtually ignored by the Court, apart from dissenting judgments in rare cases. But before analyzing the (limited) role section 27 has had in interpreting section 15, it is useful to consider that section 27 has been influential in recognizing diversity as a protected aspect of other substantive rights and in directing a reading of the *Charter*'s limitation provision so as to protect, and promote respect for, diverse cultures within Canada.

Multiculturalism and Substantive Rights

The Court has tended to invoke section 27 in one of two ways. First, in support of a liberal interpretation of substantive rights, which favours diversity. For example, in *R. v. Big M Drug Mart Ltd.*,[23] the Court invalidated a federal statute imposing Sunday as a day of rest for religious reasons. The chief justice commented that "to accept that Parliament retains the right to compel universal observance of the day of rest preferred by one religion is not consistent with the preservation and enhancement of the multicultural heritage of Canadians."[24] The *Charter* sanctioned a secular day of rest because of the "diversity of belief and non-belief, the diverse socio-cultural backgrounds of Canadians."[25]

Similarly, in *Edwards Books and Art Ltd. v. The Queen*,[26] the Court found that the *Retail Business Holidays Act* infringed upon freedom of religion by giving an economic advantage to Sunday observers as compared to observers of other days. However, the *Act* was lawful under the *Charter*'s limitation provision, in part because there was an exemption in it for small businesses to stay open Sunday if they remained closed the previous day. The chief justice considered that freedom of religion means nothing more or less than protection from direct and indirect coercion: any more restrictive interpretation would be "inconsistent with the Court's obligations under s. 27."[27] La Forest J. agreed, but he had difficulty with the result insofar as it gave an incomplete answer to the multicultural issue: "it is not at first sight easy to see why an exemption is not constitutionally required for Moslems, if it is required for Jews and other Saturday observers ... s. 27, favouring multiculturalism would reinforce this way of looking at things."[28] Wilson J., dissenting, would have invoked section 27 to invalidate the *Retail Business Holidays Act.* The reason: some but not all of the minorities who observed a Saturday Sabbath could do business on Sundays. That, she said, creates "an invidious distinction into the group and severs the religious and cultural tie that binds them together."[29]

Section 27 has also been invoked in support of justificatory factors under section 1, the limitation provision of the *Charter.* In *R. v. Keegstra,* the Criminal Code proscription against hate propaganda was held to infringe the right to freedom of expression but was justified under section 1. The Court invoked the preservation and enhancement of Canada's multicultural heritage to support the objective of limiting activity that promotes hatred among groups in Canadian society. The chief justice approved of the approach of Cory J.A., which held that "multiculturalism cannot be preserved let alone enhanced if free rein is given to the promotion of hatred against identifiable cultural groups."[30] The Court read the *Charter* as supporting the "need to prevent attacks on the individual's connection with his or her culture, and hence upon the process of self-development."[31]

L'Heureux-Dubé has commented that the Court in *Keegstra* "accorded equality rights prominence in what could have been a 'pure' speech controversy."[32] And while the *Charter* provision relied on in *Edwards Books* was section 2(a), freedom of religion, the differences of opinion among the Court resulted from their characterization of the issue as essentially one of equality between different religious groups in Canadian society. Section 27 has therefore operated primarily in terms of protecting or accommodating diversity within the context of an analysis of substantive rights and on the basis of principles concerning equality of multicultural groups and their interests. Of course, none of these cases asked the Court to give effect to a claim to accommodate culture that made any demands on public funds. That claim was made squarely within a section 15 challenge.

In *Adler v Ontario,*[33] the appellant challenged the fact that Roman Catholic and secular public schools received funding and School Health Support Services for disabled students, while dissident religious-based schools received neither. The challenge was brought under section 2(a) (freedom of religion) and 15 (equality). The claim failed "because the funding of Roman Catholic separate schools and public schools is within the contemplation of the terms of section 93 and is, therefore, immune from *Charter* scrutiny"[34] as well as because of the plenary power granted the provinces to legislate public schools. The Court has consistently refused to interpret the Constitution in any way that judges the special status accorded the four protected constitutional groups against equality concerns under section 15.[35] In *Mahe v. Alberta*, the Court had justified this method for minority language educational rights by stating that

> equality between Canada's official language groups is obviously present in s. 23. Beyond this, however, the section is, if anything, an exception to the provisions of ss. 15 and 27 in that it accords these groups, the English and the French, special status in comparison to all other linguistic groups in Canada ... it would be totally incongruous to invoke in aid of the interpretation of a provision which grants special rights to a select group of individuals, the principle of equality intended to be universally applicable to "every individual." [36]

In her dissenting reasons in *Adler*, L'Heureux-Dubé J. relied on section 27 to effect an analysis that did undertake a balancing exercise between cultural groups, irrespective of the special constitutional status accorded Roman Catholics. She characterized the interests at stake as being the "recognition and continuation of these communities."[37] These interests, she reasoned, are relevant to the fundamental purposes of the *Charter* because of the principle of accommodation in the interpretation of ss. 2(a) and 15, which, she said, is consonant with section 27. She relied on *Big M Drug Mart Ltd.* and *Edwards Books and Art Ltd.* for authority that the obligation in section 27 – to preserve and enhance – imposed a duty to accommodate religious minorities where an adverse secular law required it. She stated:

> At issue here are the efforts of small, insular religious minority communities seeking to survive in a large, secular society. As such, the complete non-recognition of this group strikes at the very heart of the principles underlying s. 15 ... [We] cannot imagine a deeper scar being inflicted on a more insular group by the denial of a more fundamental interest; it is the very survival of these communities which is threatened.[38]

She rejected any justification based on lack of funding under section 1. The "purely financial" failure to fund was insufficient to overcome the severe breach of an insular minority group's equality rights for the purposes of furthering majoritarian interests. She conceded that partial funding might be an option but that, as the case was presented, the respondents did not discharge the section 1 burden.

In her dissenting reasons, McLachlin J. referred not to section 27 but, rather, to Canada's "multicultural society." She held that section 15 was violated because the appellants were denied equal benefit of the law by a lack of funding to schools consistent with their religious beliefs. The fact that they chose their religion and the need for religious schools did not negate that discrimination. However, she held that the infringement was justified because of its purpose, which was "to foster a strong public secular school system attended by students of all cultural and religious groups." The result:

> Children of all races and religions learn together and play together. No religion is touted over any other. The goal is to provide a forum for the development of respect for the beliefs and customs of all cultural groups and for their ethical and moral values. The strength of the public secular school system is its diversity – diversity which its supporters believe will lead to increased understanding and respect for different cultures and beliefs.[39]

In the end, the goal of encouraging a more tolerant and harmonious multicultural society was considered by McLachlin J. as a pressing and substantial objective, sufficient to justify an infringement of section 15, with respect to funding of the schools. In many respects, it is McLachlin J.'s view that accords most closely with Canadian multicultural policy as it has developed over the years. The *Strategic Evaluation of Multicultural Programs*,[40] published in the same year that *Adler* was decided, emphasized integration rather than accommodation and concluded that "greater integration efforts and the promotion of social cohesion – currently ill-defined – are deemed essential to strengthening multicultural policy."[41]

For L'Heureux-Dubé J., the preservation and enhancement of Canada's multicultural heritage gave rise to the duty to accommodate difference among religious minorities. For McLachlin J., multiculturalism offered a justification for discrimination because it supported the legislature's goal of encouraging a more tolerant and harmonious society. She emphasized that diversity within the public school system was designed to recognize difference, while at the same time promoting better social cohesion. But L'Heureux-Dubé likewise appealed to social cohesion through accommodation of difference: funding would foster "the values of a pluralist democratic society, including the values of cohesion, religious tolerance, and understanding."[42] Despite the differences between the two justices, both consider that social cohesion within a multicultural society is an aspect of equality concerns under the *Charter*. And both justices share a view of equality that necessitates the contemplation of some measure of accommodation of difference for cultural communities and requires justification for measures that support integrationist results.

Equality Law, Diversity, and Human Dignity

Apart from rare cases such as *Adler*, multiculturalism, when it is referred to at all by the Court, is not referred to in terms of the interpretative principles in respect of "preservation and enhancement" under section 27. If the reluctance on the part of the Supreme Court echoes Magnet's caution that an equality perspective for section 27 gives rise to arguments comparing the conferring of benefits on groups, then it is suggested that the Court has perhaps too cautiously avoided another aspect of section 27 in relation to equality. Drawing a sharp distinction between group rights and individual rights, and reading equality – in the context of multiculturalism – as necessarily pitting one group against another, does not always, or necessarily, flow from section 27. It has been accepted by the Court that section 27 informs the section 15 analysis. There is nothing in section 27 that precludes an interpretation that supports interests that *individuals* have – in association with group membership – that originate from their ethnocultural identity.

L'Heureux-Dubé has stated that it is the constitutionally recognized value of *diversity* that is given effect by section 27 of the *Charter*.[43] In the context of section 15, the Court has recently forged a unique equality jurisprudence that – in terms of the test set out since the leading case of *Law v. Canada (Minister of Employment and Immigration)*[44] – adopts a contextual approach that attempts to incorporate a judicial understanding of difference in order to determine whether there has been a violation of "essential human dignity." The Court has offered a "specific, albeit non-exhaustive" definition of essential human dignity:[45]

> Human dignity means that an individual *or group* feels self-respect and self-worth ... Human dignity is harmed when individuals and groups are marginalized, ignored, or devalued, and is enhanced when laws recognize the full place of all individuals and groups within Canadian society.[46]

The definition of human dignity and the elaborate test set by the Court to determine a violation of dignity have proved highly problematic in practice. Dignity concerns an individual or group feeling of self-worth and self-respect. But feelings are highly subjective, so in order to undertake the legal examination of essential human dignity, which is required in order to determine whether there is a violation of the equality guarantee, the Court assumes the perspective of "a reasonable person, dispassionate and fully apprised of the circumstances, possessed of similar attributes to, and under similar circumstances as, the claimant."[47]

It is not clear to what extent it can be said that culture, or religion, or other group characteristics legitimately shape the determination of what is reasonable. But it is clear that such characteristics are relevant to the Court's inquiry. As Iacobucci J. explained, "all of that individual's or that group's traits, history, and circumstances must be considered."[48] The subjective-objective perspective is meant to preclude a simple assertion by a claimant that the legislation makes him "feel" less worthy, while avoiding a simple reasonableness test that could easily perpetuate community prejudices. The judge overcomes each of these perspectives by adopting a "dignity in context" approach. But the contextual perspective seems to demand the virtual omniscience of the Court. In practice, the work the Court has to do to achieve an understanding of dignity in context is rarely undertaken; instead, cases have sometimes privileged "reason," ignored context, and allowed legislative purpose to carry the day. The subjective-objective perspective has resulted in crude alternatives. A claimant who takes the trouble to make a section 15 claim will almost always meet the subjective portion of the standard, so the Court is left to determine the reasonableness of that feeling. As Sheila Martin has noted: a claimant who fails is either "suffering from false consciousness (subjectively) and/or else is being unreasonable (objectively)."[49]

The notion of group dignity raises specific problems. How does a *group* feel self-respect or self-worth? Is the Court concerned with the feelings of the totality of the members or of the group as a group? If the latter, how does one determine who speaks for the group or how group feeling is to be measured? The Court has never said. And the Court has not been asked to consider the possibility of the dignity of a group pitted against that of an individual member, yet, it is in precisely these circumstances that the legal conception of dignity would be crucial. In spite of references to the dignity of the group, the definition of dignity has been elaborated by the Court solely in terms of the effect of laws or practices on individuals: "all persons" enjoy equal recognition at law as human beings. It is extremely unlikely that the dignity of a group could trump that of the individual if the "concern, respect and consideration" of the individual were found to be sufficiently compromised. The difficulty – apart from that of identifying and defining the group – is that the legal recognition and conception of a group could suffer from the same generalizations about attributes that have previously enabled stereotyping or prejudice. In the name of providing a remedial equality law, association with a disadvantaged group could, if the test is not handled with vigilance, perpetuate the very perceptions that equality law is purportedly attempting to overcome.

The section 15 test is, however, capable of supporting a concept of dignity that is relational, in which "reasonableness" is situated in the context of a (cultural) group membership. For individuals, dignity is in part defined by community or group membership; and for groups, dignity is arguably the totality of attributes that are constitutive of the group identity. That conception of human dignity – which follows from an application of the section 15 test – necessarily raises issues concerning cultural diversity and engages the interpretative obligation in section 27.

Multiculturalism, Equality, and Constitutionalism

The disagreement between McLachlin and L'Heureux-Dube J.J. in *Adler* illustrates that advocacy of multiculturalism is not determinative of outcome. One might have argued that the *Charter*'s sections 15 and 27 encourage a particular discussion, debate, and engagement with the concept of, if not multiculturalism per se, at least of diversity in Canadian society, even if the legal effects of diversity as a constitutional value remain as yet unresolved. One might have also thought that the definition of dignity and the complex test under section 15 would favour a development of such engagement. Dignity contemplates inclusion, the full place of individuals and groups in society, but the question remains: does it also give rise to the duty to accommodate such individuals and groups, where without such accommodation there would be a violation of essential human dignity? And what of challenges under section 15 with regard to differences among groups that are constitutionally protected under the *Charter* and those that are not? The current test under section 15, adopted after *Adler* was decided, at least obliges the Court to engage with the issues addressed in the alternative approaches of Justices McLachlin and L'Heureux-Dube in *Adler*.

Adler did not succeed. So Arieh Waldman took the matter to the Human Rights Committee under the *International Covenant on Civil and Political Rights* and argued a breach of articles 2(1), 26, and 27.[50] The committee formed its view on section 26, the non-discrimination provision, and, having disposed of the matter in favour of the petitioner, decided not to proceed with further elaboration:

> The Committee has noted the State party's argument that the aims of the State party's secular public education system are compatible with the principle of nondiscrimination laid down in the Covenant. The Committee does not take issue with this argument but notes, however, that the proclaimed aims of the system do not justify the exclusive funding of Roman Catholic religious schools ... [The] Committee observes that the Covenant does not oblige States parties to fund schools which are established on a religious basis. However, if a State party chooses to provide public funding to religious schools, it should make this funding available without discrimination. This means that providing funding for the schools of one religious group and not for another must be based on reasonable and objective criteria. In the instant case, the Committee concludes that the material before it does not show that the differential treatment between the Roman Catholic faith and the author's religious denomination is based on such criteria.[51]

The committee's finding, that benefits that are not required but that are nevertheless provided by a state, must be provided in a non-discriminatory manner, is consistent with the interpretation of other international human rights instruments[52] and comparative human rights methodology. No satis-factory justification was provided by the uniqueness of the Canadian con-stitutional settlement: the result flows from human rights principles, which operate irrespective of historical antecedents or political compromise. Fur-thermore, the committee's reasoning was based solely on an equality analy-sis: it did not find it necessary to express a view on article 27 of the Covenant, which is the international equivalent of section 27 of the *Charter*. But the legal effect given to article 26 was one that supported diversity and multi-culturalism nonetheless. If this effect is achieved within article 26, then the interpretative obligation to give effect to multiculturalism (which L'Heureux-Dube, at least, has interpreted as the constitutional value of "diversity") would lend support to this finding in the Canadian context. The response of international law to the claim by *Adler* is ominously reminiscent of the submission made by the Canadian Polish Congress with regard to the draft-ing of the *Charter*'s provisions for protected groups, that "a document which singles out the so-called 'founding races' for special mention and special privileges will become increasingly objectionable and irrelevant."[53]

The Supreme Court's reasoning in *Adler* was reaffirmed recently in *Gosselin (Tutor of) v. Quebec (Attorney General)*,[54] which challenged the restriction on the provision of English-language schooling to children of certain classes of persons in Quebec. The appellants, who were members of the French-language majority and who were denied English-language schooling for their children, argued that the provision violated both the *Quebec Charter of Rights and Freedoms* and the Canadian *Charter*. The Court held that the equality guarantee was not opposable to section 23 of the *Charter*, just as it was not opposable to section 93(1) in *Adler*: these provisions identify certain minor-ity groups as rights-holders that enjoy constitutional protection. Equality rights are of "immense importance," agreed the Court, but they are "just part of our constitutional fabric"; the protection of minorities is also a "key principle."[55] The Court reaffirmed the statements made in 1990 in *Mahe* that section 23 "represents a linchpin in this nation's commitment to the values of bilingualism and *biculturalism*" (emphasis added)[56] and, somewhat ironically, given the subsequent jurisprudence under the equality guaran-tee, that it would be incongruous to invoke the equality guarantee that is applicable to "every individual" in aid of interpretation of a provision re-garding select rights accorded groups.[57] The only relevance of section 27 to the decision was in reaffirming the statement made in *Mahe* that section 23 provides an exception to sections 15 and 27.

Does the unique nature of the Canadian constitutional settlement pre-clude recognition of diversity and accommodation of cultural aspects for other Canadians who are associated with groups? The reasoning of L'Heureux-Dube in *Adler* indicates that she considers that equality for some Canadians, achieved by way of accommodation, need not imply a threat to the special status of others. Of course, she accepts that any resource allocation question would need to be openly discussed and supported by the Court but insists that such issues offer an insufficient bar to the justiciability of the principle of equality among communities. In this respect, her reasoning is in confluence with international human rights law. One real test for Canadian constitutionalism, based on a careful historical compromise for interested political (or politicized) groups, will be how it can continue to withstand challenges based on principle – not compromise – that are consistent with the methodology of international and comparative human rights law.

Perhaps it is the particular nature of the constitutional settlement in Canada, which – by according certain minority groups special protection – has inhibited any real discussion of the effect of section 27 on claims of groups to other status rights, such as those arising, for example, from religious affiliation. Such claims to accommodation of difference do engage the equality guarantee; they do not impinge on the rights of minorities specially protected as such. Section 27 should seemingly provide an interpretative imperative since "multiculturalism" is also accorded constitutional status. The Court continues to rely on "Canadian values based on multiculturalism" to determine challenges based on discrete rights that require an accommodation of difference, most recently in *Multani v. Commission Scolaire Marguerite-Bourgeoys*.[58] There, the Court found that an absolute prohibition on the wearing at school of a kirpan – a religious object made of metal and worn at all times by Sikh males – violated the guarantee of freedom of religion in section 2(a) of the *Charter* as well as section 3 of the Quebec *Charter*. While there was no reference to the preservation or enhancement of the multicultural heritage of Canadians, the Court engaged in the type of analysis section 27 would support when it was stated:

> A total prohibition against wearing a kirpan to school undermines the value
> of this religious symbol and sends students the message that some religious
> practices do not merit the same protection as others. On the other hand,
> accommodating Gurbaj Singh and allowing him to wear his kirpan under
> certain conditions demonstrates the importance that our society attaches
> to protecting freedom of religion and to showing respect for its minorities.
> The deleterious effects of a total prohibition thus outweigh its salutary
> effects.[59]

Having decided the case on the basis of section 2 of the *Charter*, the Court did not find it necessary to consider the section 15 challenge. But the legal effect of "values based on multiculturalism" would be equally relevant under this provision. The failure to invoke section 27 is a missed opportunity to begin to give legal effect to "multiculturalism." There is a positive obligation to interpret constitutional guarantees so as to "preserve and enhance," which suggests that accommodation of differences is presumptively favoured. It is incumbent upon the Court to take this provision seriously and begin to unpack the legal effect of section 27 as an interpretative aid.

Conclusion

The role played in legal analysis by section 27 remains mainly to promote a liberal interpretation of substantive rights (*Big M Drug Mart*), or as a section 1 justification for government action, or as a reasonable limit on such action (*Keegstra*). Where factually relevant, a close inspection of laws measured in light of the multiculturalism principle is mandated by the interpretative obligations expressed in section 27. The current test under section 15, despite its complex and difficult application, promotes this interpretative goal: it adopts a contextual inquiry that recognizes diversity, including cultural diversity, as an inherent aspect of human dignity. What the Court has not yet done, but what it is obliged to do according to the *Charter* text, is to give effect to section 27 within the dignity-in-context approach. The Court cannot begin to give effect to such an obscure provision without looking at the policy in operation in Canada today. But that policy cannot act merely as a tool for deference to government measures: it can inform the meaning of the principle, but it cannot remove from the courts their obligation to give it legal effect. There is scope to do so under section 15, should the Court be inclined to take section 27 as seriously as it should (or must) be taken.

Notes

1 Pierre Elliott Trudeau, "Address to the House of Common on October 8, 1971."
2 *Report of the Royal Commission on Bilingualism and Biculturalism*, 6 vols. (Ottawa, Queen's Printer, 1967).
3 Ibid., book IV, 12-13. Some have assessed the policy as, in part, an effort by the Liberals to capture the increasingly large non-English-speaking and non-French-speaking vote. See Freda Hawkins, *Critical Years in Immigration: Canada and Australia Compared* (Montreal: McGill-Queen's University Press, 1989), 218. The policy has also been seen as a strategy on the part of Trudeau and the federal Liberal party to undermine French Canada's claims for equality for French with English within the Canadian confederation. See Yasmeen Abu-Laban and Daiva Stasiulis, "Ethnic Pluralism under Seige: Popular and Partisan Opposition to Multiculturalism," *Canadian Public Policy/Analyse de Politiques* 18, 2 (1992): 365-86.
4 RSC 1985, c. 24 (4th Supp.). On the evolution of policy, see Jack Jedwab, "To Preserve and Enhance: Canadian Multiculturalism before and after the Charter," *Supreme Court Law Review* 19, 2 (2003): 309.
5 See http://www.canadianheritage.gc.ca/progs/multi/what-multi_e.cfm.
6 For example, the *Citizens' Forum on Canada's Future* in 1991 reported that Canadian citizens responded positively to the growing ethnic diversity but opposed the official multiculturalism policy because it failed to ensure that citizens must learn to be Canadians *first*, while retaining ethnic and cultural identities without fear of discrimination. See Marc Leman, "Canadian Multiculturalism," Library of Parliament, Information Research Service, http://www.parl.gc.ca/information/library/PRBpubs/936-e.htm.
7 See Neil Bissoondath, *Selling Illusions: The Cult of Multiculturalism in Canada* (Toronto: Penguin Books, 1994). See also Richard Gwyn, *Nationalism without Walls: The Unbearable Lightness of Being Canadian* (Toronto: McClelland and Stewart, 1995).

8   Pat Duffy Hutcheon, "Multiculturalism in Canada," http://patduffyhutcheon.com/Papers%20and%20Presentations/Multiculturalism%20in%20Canada.htm.

9   For a survey, see Hutcheon "Multiculturalism in Canada."

10 David Hollinger, *Postethnic America: Beyond Multiculturalism* (New York: Basic Books, 1995).

11 Will Kymlicka "American Multiculturalism in the International Arena," *Dissent* (Fall 1998): 73-79.

12 See Jack Jedwab "To Preserve and Enhance," 309, 343-44.

13 Canadians overwhelmingly agree that multiculturalism and bilingualism are important to Canadian identity and that preservation and enhancement of their multicultural heritage should be supported by the federal government. See Environics Canada, Survey on Canadian Charter of Rights and Freedoms (January 2002).

14 Michael R. Hudson "Multiculturalism, Government Policy and Constitutional Enshrinement: A Comparative Study," in *Multiculturalism and the Charter: A Legal Perspective* (Toronto: Carswell, 1987), 4.

15 P.W. Hogg, *Constitutional Law of Canada and Canada Act Annotated* (Toronto: Carswell, 1982), 72.

16 Hudson, "Multiculturalism," 4, 26.

17 Joseph E. Magnet, "Multiculturalism in the Canadian Charter of Rights and Freedoms," in *The Canadian Charter of Rights and Freedoms,* ed. Gerald Beaudoin and Errol Mendes (Toronto: Carswell, 1996).

18 See s. 52, of the Constitution.

19 See *Mahe v. Alberta,* [1990] 1 S.C.R. 342.

20 Joseph. E. Magnet, "What Does 'Equality between Communities' Mean?'" (2003) 19 S.C.L.R. (2d) 277, 305.

21 Magnet, "Multiculturalism."

22 [1989] 1 S.C.R. 143, 171.

23 [1985] 1 S.C.R. 295.

24 [1985] 1 S.C.R. 295, 351.

25 [1985] 1 S.C.R. 295, 351.

26 [1986] 2 S.C.R. 713.

27 [1986] 2 S.C.R. 713.

28 [1986] 2 S.C.R. 713, 804.

29 [1986] 2 S.C.R. 713, 808.

30 [1990] 3 S.C.R. 697.

31 [1990] 3 S.C.R. 607, 757.

32 C. L'Heureux-Dubé, "Realizing Equality in the Twentieth Century: The Role of the Supreme Court of Canada in Comparative Perspective," *International Journal of Constitutional Law* 1, 1 (2003): 35, 52. See also *Canada (Human Rights Commission) v. Taylor,* [1990] 3 S.C.R. 892, 916-7.

33 [1996] 3 S.C.R. 609.

34 [1996] 3 S.C.R. 609, para. 27.

35 See, for example, *Gosselin (tutor of) v. Quebec (A.G.)* 2005 S.C.C. 15; and *Okwuoki v. Lester B Pearson School Board; Casimir v. Quebec (A.G.)* 2005 S.C.C. 14, decided together on March 31, 2005.

36 [1990] 1 S.C.R. 342, 369.

37 [1996] 3 S.C.R. 609, para. 84.

38 [1996] 3 S.C.R. 609, para. 86.

39 [1996] 3 S.C.R. 609, para. 1 p. 41 of 44.

40 Canada, Department of Canadian Heritage, Corporate Review Branch, *Strategic Evaluation of Multiculturalism Programs: Final Report* (Ottawa, March 1996).

41 J. Jedwab, "To Preserve and Enhance," 309, 339.

42 [1996] 3 S.C.R. 609, para. 97.

43 L'Heureux-Dubé, "Realizing Equality," 35, 37.

44 [1999] 1 S.C.R. 497.

45 [1999] 1 S.C.R. 497, para. 53.

46 [1999] 1 S.C.R. 497, para. 53, citing with approval the statement of Lamer C.J. in *Rodriguez v. British Columbia (Attorney General)*, [1993] S.C.R. 519 at 554.
47 [1999] 1 S.C.R. 497, para. 60.
48 Ibid.
49 See S. Martin, "Balancing Individual Rights to Equality and Social Goals," *Canadian Bar Review* 80 (2001): 299, 330.
50 Communication No. 694/1996, U.N. Doc. CCPR/C/67/D/694/1996 (November 5, 1999).
51 Para. 10.6.
52 See, for example, the Belgian Linguistics Case, European Court of Human Rights, 23/07/68.
53 Canadian Polish Conference, Brief on Constitutional Reform, 1980.
54 [2005] 1 S.C.R. 238, 2005 S.C.C. 15.
55 [2005] 1 S.C.R. 238, at para 27.
56 [2005] 1 S.C.R. 238, at para 28.
57 [2005] 1 S.C.R. 238, at para 33.
58 2006 S.C.C. 6, at para. 71.
59 2006 S.C.C. 6, at para. 79.

11
Welfare Rights as Equality Rights? Insights from the' Supreme Court of Canada
Katherine Eddy

Equality is much vaunted as a core political and moral value, but there are serious doubts as to whether a concern for equality can do all – or any – of the work when it comes to justifying our most basic rights. When we make claims about rights to food, or shelter, or basic medical care, our concern is that people not starve, or freeze, or die prematurely from a preventable disease. We are not, at least on the face of it, worried about unfair or unequal distributions; we are not asking that people have an equal share, but simply that they have enough to survive.

The peculiarly urgent nature of welfare rights claims seems,[1] therefore, to set them apart from the arguments over non-discrimination, liberal neutrality, and equal human dignity that characterize the cultural pluralism debate. My aim here is to show that this separation is merely apparent. Non-discrimination and human dignity are both promising starting points from which to begin the argument that citizens are entitled to social assistance to help them meet their basic subsistence needs. The point is not just that a concern for equality *can* justify welfare rights provision but that it *should*. When we ground welfare rights in non-discrimination and human dignity, we make clear why it would be wrong for the state not to respect them; we appeal not simply to the urgency of unmet needs but also to the wrongfulness of the state's failure to alleviate them.

There is, of course, nothing in the Canadian Constitution about the alleviation of severe poverty or the meeting of basic subsistence needs. There is a commitment expressed in section 36(1) of the Constitution to provide "essential public services of reasonable quality to all Canadians" and to promote "equal opportunities for the well-being of Canadians," but this commitment is excluded from the *Canadian Charter of Rights and Freedoms*[2] and is understood not to "alter the legislative authority of the provincial legislatures."[3] The *Charter* does, however, contain an equality guarantee, and the rights to life, liberty, and security of the person are also entrenched. In a recent case before the Supreme Court of Canada, *Gosselin v. Quebec*

(*Attorney General*),[4] the justices considered whether the right to social assistance payments at the subsistence level could be derived from either of these two existing protections.

I am not going to say much about whether I think the Supreme Court decided the case as it should have done. There is an obvious discrepancy between what counts as a good argument in the context of Canadian constitutional law and what counts as a good argument in political theory. I am interested in the case from the perspective of normative political theory: my concern is with whether Canadians *should* have constitutional welfare rights and not, at least not directly, with whether welfare rights claims can successfully be made under the *Charter*'s existing protections. I nevertheless think the *Gosselin* case, and the arguments advanced within it, offer insight into the more general debate over the merits of constitutional welfare rights. As I argue below, the Supreme Court justices' treatment of the concept of "human dignity," the arguments advanced against the thesis that the state had a responsibility to alleviate the unmet need of its citizens, and the greater favour found for the equality approach to welfare rights are important and relevant considerations for political theorists concerned to evaluate the question of whether, and on what grounds, welfare rights should be included in constitutions in the first place.

I do not hope to resolve all the questions about welfare rights as constitutional rights; instead, I weigh up the two arguments for welfare rights that appear in the *Gosselin* case: one that insists that they can be derived from considerations of *equality* and another that points to the state's responsibility to alleviate *unmet need* in order to justify the state's duty to provide for its citizens. To that end, I begin with a brief discussion of the background to the *Gosselin* case, then outline the unmet-need argument for welfare rights that appears within it. I point to the Court's reluctance to accept the unmet-need argument, and highlight the links between the reasons the Court advances and the more general worries about the unmet-need argument in the philosophical literature on welfare rights. I go on to outline the equality strategy, which, I argue, offers a way of avoiding the pitfalls of the unmet-need argument but not without leaving the case for welfare rights on precarious ground. I conclude with a sketch of two plausible ways of rescuing the equality argument for welfare rights, both of which derive welfare rights from the state's overarching duty to respect the human dignity and equal worth of its members.

The *Gosselin* Case

Let me begin with a brief summary of the facts of the case. In the 1980s, the Quebec government introduced policy setting the base amount of welfare for claimants under thirty years of age at one-third the level of that available to those over thirty. This lower-level benefit was also one-third of what the Quebec government deemed adequate for subsistence. However, if you signed up for one of the government's new work experience or education programs, you could increase your benefit to the over-thirty level, or at least come within one hundred dollars of it. This was intended as a strategy to combat the growing phenomenon of youth unemployment. The Quebec government's commitment to this goal was, however, belied by the fact that it only created 30,000 places on these programs for 85,000 welfare recipients under thirty years of age. Although the government cited lack of interest and access to other (illicit) sources of income among welfare recipients to explain why it had difficulty filling even these 30,000 places, Gosselin's lawyers pointed out that college and university graduates, as well as the illiterate, were barred from certain initiatives altogether, and they brought forward evidence of waiting lists and other difficulties associated with qualifying for the programs.[5] Though the parties disagreed about the causes of the low participation rate, they agreed on the effects: most of the welfare recipients under thirty (73 percent) were left on the lower-level benefit during the life of the Quebec government's policy.[6]

Gosselin's lawyers claimed that, given the climate of high unemployment and given the difficulties of securing a place on the work experience programs, the Quebec government left her in a position that was seriously harmful to her psychological and physical well-being and so threatened her "security of the person" as well as her life, both of which are protected under section 7 of the *Charter*. Gosselin's lawyers also argued that, by denying her the level of social assistance available to the over-thirty group, the government discriminated against her on the basis of her age, thus breaching its duties with respect to the equality guarantee in section 15(1) of the *Charter*. Her case was ultimately unsuccessful, on both counts. On December 19, 2002, the Supreme Court ruled that the Quebec government had not violated the *Charter*. The margin was slim, however: four of the nine justices dissented on the question of whether the Quebec government violated the equality guarantee, and two dissented on the question of whether it had breached its duties with respect to Gosselin's rights to "life" and "security of the person."

Unmet Need and Security of the Person: The Section 7 Claim

Consider, first, Gosselin's claim that the Quebec government, by failing to provide her with a subsistence-level benefit, breached its duties with respect to her rights to life and security of the person. Section 7 of the *Charter* reads:

> Everyone has the right to life, liberty and security of the person and the right not to be deprived thereof except in accordance with the principles of fundamental justice.

The Court found that evidence of the insecurity of Gosselin's living conditions or life-threatening need was not enough to establish a rights-violation under section 7; in order to have a valid section 7 claim, Gosselin would have to have shown that the *state* deprived of her of her life or threatened her security of the person. Delivering the opinion of the majority, Chief Justice McLachlin wrote that section 7 is best understood, given the wording of the provision and the interpretation typically adopted by the Canadian courts, as giving rise only to the right *not to be deprived* of one's life by the state: "Nothing in the jurisprudence thus far suggests that section 7 places a positive obligation on the state to ensure that each person enjoys life, liberty or security of the person."[7] Justice Bastarache concurred, pointing out that the wording of the provision made it clear that "the right is protected only insofar as the claimant is deprived of the right to security of the person by the state."[8]

In her dissenting opinion, Justice Arbour queried the claim that the language of section 7 makes it clear that the freedom protected by section 7 is only the freedom not to be deprived by the state of whatever security or liberty one happens to enjoy. Such a reading would, she argued, require us to ignore the significance of the conjunction between the two clauses of section 7. Section 7 says, she reminds us, that: "[e]veryone has the right to life, liberty and security of the person *and* the right not to be deprived thereof except in accordance with the principles of fundamental justice."[9] Thus, on her view, one can intelligibly and faithfully read section 7 as first positing a general right to life, liberty, and security, and then setting out, in the second clause, a more specific right not to be deprived of life, liberty, and security except in accordance with the principles of fundamental justice. This reading would leave open the question of the extent of the state's duties with respect to the rights set out in the first clause.[10]

Of course, even if we accept Justice Arbour's argument that the wording of the *Charter* leaves open the extent of the state's duties with respect to the rights set out in section 7, a restrictive reading of section 7 might, nonetheless, be appropriate and defensible. According to Chief Justice McLachlin, the restrictive reading is in line with the purpose of section 7 as well as the "dominant strand of jurisprudence on s. 7."[11] And yet, we should be clear that the reading favoured by the majority and by Justice Bastarache – that is, that "a s. 7 claim must arise as a result of a determinative state action that in and of itself deprives the claimant of the right to life, liberty or security of the person"[12] – implies (1) that the state can meet its duties with respect to section 7 by simple forbearance and, from this, (2) that the state has no duties to protect persons from threats to their section 7 liberties caused by non-state actors.

The difficulty is that both propositions seem at odds with the Court's earlier, and more extensive, understanding of the state's duties with respect to other fundamental *Charter* freedoms.[13] For example, when Justice Bastarache wrote the decision in an earlier civil liberties case, *Dunmore v. Ontario (Attorney General)*, he pointed out that the Court had "repeatedly held that the contribution of private actors to a violation of fundamental freedoms does not immunize the state from *Charter* review."[14] The Court found in *Dunmore* that exclusion from a legislative scheme whose purpose was to protect a particular freedom could constitute a breach of duty under the *Charter* so long as the "affected group" was rendered "substantially incapable of exercising the freedom sought without the protection of the legislation."[15] In *Dunmore*, the freedom sought was freedom of association: agricultural workers were excluded from a scheme of statutory labour rights, and their freedom to associate – protected under section 2(d) of the *Charter* – was thus rendered vulnerable to employer reprisals for organizing. Bastarache there argued that, although there was "no constitutional right to protective legislation *per se*," in some cases, "a posture of governmental restraint" would have the effect of rendering the right to freedom of association unrealizable.[16]

Why, then, was Justice Bastarache unwilling to indict the government for its posture of restraint when it came to Gosselin's rights to life and security of the person? Given his acknowledgment of the climate of mass unemployment, and the attention he drew to the fact that the government programs "were not available to all applicants at all times,"[17] one would have expected him to accept the claim that the government's failure to provide Gosselin with a subsistence-level benefit left her in a position that was life-threatening and insecure and, thus, effectively rendered her section 7 rights unrealizable.

Justice Bastarache, however, insisted that the facts of *Dunmore* and *Gosselin* were different. Unlike the agricultural workers, Gosselin had not shown a "substantial incapability of protecting her right to security. She ha[d] not demonstrated that the legislation, by excluding her, ha[d] reduced her security any more than it would have already been, given market conditions."[18] Again, this statement seems at odds with his chastisement of the Quebec government for having "created for [welfare recipients under thirty] what it defined as substandard living conditions,"[19] and it further betrays a curious unwillingness to apply the argument he advanced in *Dunmore* to the facts of *Gosselin*. Of course, a posture of governmental restraint won't reduce one's security to a level below that available "given market conditions." It nonetheless, as he earlier insisted, might leave a person "substantially incapable" of protecting a fundamental freedom and amount to a breach of duty for that very reason.

Thus, though the way was open for Justice Bastarache, and indeed for the majority, to accept that the state had a duty to assist Gosselin, they remained wedded to an understanding of section 7's purpose as limited to protecting the individual only from those threats to life, liberty, and security emanating from the state. Though Chief Justice McLachlin was willing to allow, as she put it, "the possibility that a positive obligation to sustain life, liberty or security of the person may be made out in special circumstances,"[20] as the threat to Gosselin's life could ultimately be traced to her own personal and psychological problems, there was, she thought, no reason to revisit the traditional understanding of the state's duties and to impose an undue burden on government. Justice Bastarache grounded his reading of section 7 in a similar reluctance to impute state responsibility for Gosselin's suffering: since the appellant's unfortunate situation was the result of the "vagaries of a weak economy" it would be against the aims of the *Charter* to heap blame on the Quebec government.[21] The government had not, or at least not directly, been responsible for causing her plight and so could not be taken to be morally responsible to alleviate it.

In sum, then, Gosselin's need-based section 7 claim failed not just because there was a tradition of understanding the section 7 claim as giving rise solely to negative duties but also because the justices thought that to expand the scope of the state's section 7 duty to include the duty to sustain life and security of the person would, effectively, be to impose on the state a burden of alleviating harms for which it could not be said to be morally responsible. The Court was reluctant to ground the state's duty to aid in the effects of unmet need on the individual's interests in "life" and "security of the person"; it was not convinced that the state's failure to alleviate unmet need was necessarily wrongful.

The Problem with Unmet Need: Rights without Wrongs

This is the same critique launched against welfare rights nearly thirty years ago by Charles Fried in his book *Right and Wrong*. Fried argues that "Rights are categorical moral entities such that the violation of a right is always wrong."[22] He does not mean by this that all rights are absolute; rather, he means that the violation of a right is categorically wrong in that it retains an element of wrongness about it even if it's justifiable under extraordinary circumstances. To illustrate: even if I have to push you out of the way to save a drowning child, pushing you was still wrong – not wrong "all things considered" but wrong in the sense of breaching a norm that I, under normal circumstances, would have been expected to follow.

How does this work in the context of welfare rights? The claim is that welfare rights (at least when phrased as specific rights to adequate nutrition, shelter, and basic medical care) are not real rights since it is not categorically wrong for the state to fail to provide for your basic needs.[23] From this perspective, "welfare rights" are conceptually incoherent and morally problematic: Does the state really wrong you just because it doesn't provide for your needs? Is it fair to hold the state responsible for your inability to provide for yourself or for the effects of a weak economy? And why are your needs the state's responsibility anyway?

Notice that there is no denying here that a person might really need food, shelter, and medical care, nor that it is urgent and important for her to have these things. Fried's analysis encourages us to look at fundamental rights from the potential duty-bearer's perspective: it is not categorically wrong for the state to deny a person food, but it is categorically wrong for the state to deny a person a fair trial. So a person has the right to a fair trial but no right to food. Thus, on Fried's account, individuals do not have rights to be secured access to the means to survive since rights are properly concerned with protecting individuals against categorical wrongs, and the state does not necessarily wrong the individual by doing nothing to help her meet her basic needs.

It is in light of this scepticism about the wrongfulness of state inaction in the face of unmet need that the equality argument for welfare rights starts to look promising. It begins with a seemingly less demanding premise, not:

> Individuals have rights against their states to be provided with the means to meet their basic needs.

But, rather:

> The state has a duty that its laws respect the equal worth and human dignity of its citizens.

This first premise of the equality argument does seem to pass Fried's test: if the state does not respect the dignity of its citizens, or their equal worth, then it has wronged them by denying them the protection to which their simple humanity entitles them.

Though the "duty of equal concern and respect" may seem initially more palatable (and perhaps less demanding) than the duty to provide for basic needs, part of the reason for this has no doubt to do with its vagueness. Say we are agreed that the state has a duty to treat its citizens with "equal concern and respect" and that its laws must reflect their "equal worth" and respect their "human dignity." Where do we go from here? How do we go from an abstract duty of "respect for equal worth" to welfare rights to specific levels of provision?

In what follows, I look at a version of the equality argument for welfare rights as it was put forward by Justice L'Heureux-Dubé in her dissenting opinion in the *Gosselin* case. She purports to address the concerns about the vagueness of the duty to "respect human dignity" and explains how to get from "equal worth" to welfare.

The Equality Argument

Section 15(1) of the *Charter* reads:

> Every individual is equal before and under the law and has the right to the
> equal protection and equal benefit of the law without discrimination and,
> in particular, without discrimination based on race, national or ethnic ori-
> gin, colour, religion, sex, age or mental or physical disability.

In her dissenting opinion in *Gosselin*, Justice L'Heureux-Dubé argued that
the Quebec government had discriminated against Louise Gosselin by denying her access to a subsistence level of social assistance on the basis of her
age; had she been over thirty, she would have been entitled to the full benefit without the work requirement.

Granted, the cry of age discrimination here looks a bit contrived. Chief
Justice McLachlin countered it by pointing out that those under thirty had
not been the victims of historical disadvantage, nor was it likely that the
Quebec government harboured offensive stereotypes about lazy, unemployed
youths. The reason, she insisted, that the full benefit was made conditional
on employment for under-thirties was precisely in recognition that as young
people, they had the most to lose from developing an early habit of dependence on state support.

And yet, though there may be good reasons for drawing a distinction in
law, it may nonetheless be judged discriminatory in virtue of its effects.
Justice L'Heureux-Dubé drew on a discrimination standard unanimously
agreed to in the landmark case of *Law*, known as the *Law Test*, to lend authority to her finding of age discrimination, despite the absence of stereotypes or historical disadvantage.[24]

The *Law Test*, on Justice L'Heureux-Dubé's reading, states that, if a distinction drawn in law has the effect of threatening human dignity or the
equal worth of individuals, it is discriminatory. L'Heureux-Dubé J. argued
that, if a person suffers threats to her physical empowerment and bodily
integrity, her dignity is threatened.[25] She then concluded that distinctions
drawn in law that have the effect of threatening dignity by excluding persons from the means to bodily integrity and physical empowerment are
discriminatory.[26] A distinction need not, then, be based on stereotype or be
insensitive to historical disadvantage in order to be counted discriminatory, as long as it can be shown to have the effect of threatening dignity and
the individual's sense of equal worth.[27]

But what counts as an effect? If we need to show that the threat to dignity
occurs as the effect of a law, doesn't the equality strategy leave us where we
were before: having to establish that a given law tangibly caused or exacer-
bated the agent's poverty in order to make a case for the state's duty to aid?

The greatest advantage of the equality strategy, however, is that it does not require us to establish that the state is causally responsible for the threat to the agent's physical integrity in order for the state to assume moral responsibility for the agent's plight.

Recall that section 15(1) makes explicit the duty to ensure "equal benefit" of the law. Thus, under the Canadian Constitution, a law can be said to threaten a person's dignity even if it does not make her worse off – with respect to the specific benefit conferred by the law – than she would have been in the absence of that law. To illustrate, consider the case of same-sex unions: members of same-sex couples are not made worse off (in any direct sense) by the passing of a law that confers a new spousal benefit but only on opposite-sex couples. Such a law may, nonetheless, reasonably be found to violate the equality rights of same-sex couples by omission and exclusion.[28] In the recent *Halpern* case, the Ontario Court of Appeal found that denying same-sex couples the right to legally marry "perpetuates the view that same-sex relationships are less worthy of recognition than opposite-sex relationships. In doing so, it offends the dignity of persons in same-sex relationships."[29] Thus, a law can still be deemed discriminatory in its effects even if it leaves me in no worse a position than it found me; it is discriminatory insofar as it implies, conveys, or perpetuates the view that I am less worthy of respect and concern than other members or groups in Canadian society.

It is Justice L'Heureux-Dubé's contention that a law expresses or perpetuates such a discriminatory view insofar as it effectively excludes persons or groups from the means to their physical empowerment and bodily integrity. Thus, on her account, if a law excludes me from some positive provision (1) that is necessary for my physical and psychological empowerment and (2) to which it allows others access, then it threatens my human dignity and violates my equality rights under section 15(1) of the *Charter*.

Welfare rights proponents might, nonetheless, remain dissatisfied with Justice L'Heureux-Dubé's section 15(1) argument for welfare rights. Why? Because whether or not an agent has the right to social assistance on the equality account still seems to depend on whether the state has provided it to someone else; the state could have avoided having to provide for the under-thirty group by refusing provision to the over-thirty group as well. Indeed, as Justice Bastarache noted, if the state had made the work experience programs compulsory for all age groups, there would have been no grounds for an equality-based challenge.[30] The equality strategy, then, seems to leave the argument for welfare rights on precarious ground; it fails to mirror the extent of our moral concern, leaving us with no call to object when the dignity and physical empowerment of all welfare recipients is "equally" under threat.

Rescuing the Equality Argument?

In what follows, I defend a more far-reaching version of the equality argument. It grounds welfare rights in the state's overarching duty to respect the equal worth of its citizens and their human dignity, without hinging a person's entitlement to social assistance on the contingent fact of the state's having legislated so as to provide it to others. Granted, insofar as it dispenses with the requirement that a distinction be drawn within the context of a given law in order to count as discriminatory, it may be implausible as an interpretation of the existing protections available under the Canadian Constitution. It is, however, intended to provide those who accept the concern for equal worth and human dignity at the core of the Court's section 15(1) analysis with a reason to accept the state's duty to provide for the basic needs of its citizens as consistent with that concern.

Both versions of the equality argument for welfare rights that I sketch below draw on Justice Iacobucci's memorable articulation of the concept of human dignity in the landmark *Law* case:

> Human dignity means that an individual or group feels self-respect and self-worth. It is concerned with physical and psychological integrity and empowerment. Human dignity is harmed by unfair treatment premised upon personal traits or circumstances which do not relate to individual needs, capacities, or merits. It is enhanced by laws which are sensitive to the needs, capacities, and merits of different individuals, taking into account the context underlying their differences. Human dignity is harmed when individuals and groups are marginalized, ignored, or devalued, and is enhanced when laws recognize the full place of individuals and groups within Canadian society. Human dignity within the meaning of the equality guarantee does not relate to the status or position of an individual in society per se, but rather concerns the manner in which a person legitimately feels when confronted with a particular law.[31]

The first version of the equality argument appeals directly to the link between human dignity and threats to "physical and psychological integrity and empowerment." The second "concerns the manner in which a person legitimately feels when confronted with a particular law" and is prompted by the question Justice L'Heureux-Dubé took to be central to her finding of discrimination in the *Gosselin* case: how would the reasonable person feel in the face of the government's failure to alleviate her unmet need?

The Human Dignity Argument

Consider first the human dignity argument. Recall that Justice L'Heureux-Dubé's finding of discrimination in the *Gosselin* case was grounded in the claim that "if individual interests including physical and psychological integrity are infringed, a harm to dignity results."[32] If we accept the posited relationship between human dignity and physical empowerment and bodily integrity, then the human dignity argument for welfare rights is quite simple and can be expressed as follows:

1 The state has a duty to respect the human dignity of its citizens.
2 A person's human dignity is threatened when her state avoidably excludes her from the means to physical and psychological empowerment and integrity.
   From these premises, we conclude that:
3 The state has a duty to ensure that its laws guarantee citizens access to the means to their physical empowerment and bodily integrity.

The second premise is the most controversial and in need of unpacking. On one view, the reference to avoidable exclusion is superfluous: if physical empowerment is necessary for human dignity, and a person lacks the means to physical empowerment, then we needn't establish that the state "avoidably excluded" a person from those means in order to conclude that her dignity is threatened. Her dignity is threatened simply by the fact of her unmet need.

And yet, it is not clear that human dignity is necessarily threatened by unmet need alone. Do those who willingly choose to forfeit the means to physical empowerment and bodily integrity really suffer threats to their human dignity? What about those who are members of afflicted communities all suffering together in times of unavoidable scarcity? The phrase "avoidable exclusion" is warranted if we want to account for those cases where persons have difficulty meeting their basic needs, without their dignity being threatened.[33] According to the human dignity argument being put forward here, "avoidable exclusion" is an aspect of what is dignity-threatening about the state's failure to guarantee agents secure access to the means to meet their basic needs: the state's indifference to the plight of those whose poverty it is in a position to alleviate is, at least in part, the cause of the threat to their dignity that results from its omission.

Consider another challenge to the argument: does the state's duty "not to avoidably exclude persons from the means to physical empowerment and bodily integrity" really amount to a duty "to guarantee them secure access to the means to realise their basic needs?" On one view, the two duties are not equivalent: if a subsistence farmer loses her crops in a flash flood, she may end up without secure access to food but not because the state "avoidably excluded" her from access to it.[34] (The flood, not the state, is responsible for threatening her access to food, we might say.) On the view I am putting forward here, however, a person is avoidably excluded from the means to physical empowerment insofar as there remains a possible and viable institutional arrangement under which she could be guaranteed secure access to the means to meet her basic needs. Thus, on my account, the subsistence farmer *is* "avoidably excluded" from access to food if she is denied access to food when there is a feasible institutional (re)arrangement under which she could be guaranteed secure access to it.

The Equal Worth Argument
On a second version of the equality argument for welfare rights, the starting point is, again, the state's duty to frame its laws and institutions in a way that embodies respect for citizens' equal worth and human dignity. This version of the argument is, however, broadly "contractualist" in character; that is, it considers the justice of political arrangements to be a matter of their acceptability to reasonable persons.[35]

The "equal worth" argument is more complicated than the "human dignity" argument advanced in the previous section, but the gist of it can be captured in the following sketch:

1 The state has a duty to respect the equal worth of its citizens.
2 The state fails to respect the equal worth of its citizens when it enforces a system of laws and institutions that cannot be justified to the reasonable person forced to live with the worst of its effects.
3 We could not justify to the reasonable person[36] a system of laws and institutions that (avoidably) fails to guarantee her secure access to the means to realize her basic needs.
   Therefore:
4 The state has a duty to ensure that its laws guarantee citizens access to the means to realize their basic needs.

On the contractualist account, we make sense of the state's duty to respect the equal worth and dignity of its citizens as a duty that applies to the design of the "basic structure" of the polity as a whole.[37] The claim is that, when the state enforces a system of laws and institutions that cannot be justified to those who stand to lose from them, then it has not accorded its citizens the respect for their equal worth that is their due. The state breaches its duty to respect a person's equal worth when it exercises political authority in a way that shows callous disregard for her point of view, depriving her of the respect to which she is entitled simply by virtue of being human. If we are agreed that we cannot justify to the reasonable person a system of laws the imposition of which has the effect of allowing her to starve, then we have already conceded that the enforcement of such a legal system amounts to a failure to respect her equal worth. It is as though we say to her: you are not worthy of our protection, our laws need not be tailored to your concerns.

Conclusion

Let us now take stock and see if the two versions of the equality argument have yielded the outcome hoped for. We were looking for a way of answering the objections of those who argued that state inaction in the face of unmet need was not necessarily wrongful. By appealing to a prior duty of the state to structure its laws so as to respect the human dignity and equal worth of its citizens, I have argued that we have a way of accounting for the wrongfulness of state inaction in the face of unmet need. When a person is avoidably excluded from the means to sustain her life, her human dignity is threatened, and she has been treated in a way that is inconsistent with her equal worth. If the state has a duty to respect the dignity and equal worth of its citizens, then it must at the very least take reasonable steps to protect its citizens from these threats.

Acknowledgments

I am grateful to Adam Swift, Sarah McCallum, Bruce Eddy, the members of the Oxford Graduate Workshop in Political Theory, three anonymous referees, and those who attended the University of Edinburgh's conference (Constitutionalism and Cultural Pluralism: Lessons from Canada) for very helpful comments on earlier versions of this chapter. I would also like to thank the ESRC and the British Academy for financial support.

Notes

1 Welfare rights manifest themselves in a number of rhetorical guises – the right to a "subsistence income," to the "alleviation of severe poverty," or to "social assistance at a level adequate to sustain life," to name a few. For the purposes of this chapter, I assume that we can group these different formulations under the same broad heading: welfare rights are the rights citizens hold against their states to be guaranteed secure access to the means to satisfy their basic subsistence needs. They include rights to food, shelter, and basic medical care. The term "secure access" is taken from Thomas Pogge, *World Poverty and Human Rights* (Oxford: Polity Press, 2002).
2 *Canadian Charter of Rights and Freedoms*, Part I of the *Constitution Act*, 1982, enacted as Schedule B to the *Canada Act*, 1982 (U.K.), 1982, c. 11 (hereafter *Charter*).
3 Equalisation and Regional Disparities, Part III of the *Constitution Act*, 1982, enacted as Schedule B to the *Canada Act*, 1982 (U.K.), 1982, c. 11.
4 *Gosselin v. Quebec (Attorney General)*, [2002] 4 S.C.R. 429 (hereafter *Gosselin*).
5 Per Bastarache in *Gosselin*, 534 and 587.
6 Ibid.
7 Per McLachlin in *Gosselin*, 491.
8 Per Bastarache in *Gosselin*, 209.
9 S. 7, *Charter*, emphasis added.
10 Per Arbour in *Gosselin*, 613-15.
11 Per McLachlin in *Gosselin*, 433.
12 Per Bastarache in *Gosselin*, 545.
13 On this point, see Arbour and Bastarache in *Gosselin*, 625-31 and 1045-46, respectively.

14 Per Bastarache in *Dunmore v. Ontario (Attorney General)*, [2001] 3 S.C.R. 1016 at 1049. Bastarache also cites *Lavigne v. Ontario Public Service Employees Union*, [1991] 1 S.C.R. 206 and *R. v. Edwards Books and Art Ltd.*, [1986] 2 S.C.R. 713, per Dickson, at 766.
15 Per Bastarache in *Gosselin*, 549.
16 Per Bastarache in *Dunmore*, 1046.
17 Per Bastarache in *Gosselin*, 581.
18 Ibid., 550.
19 Ibid., 564.
20 Per McLachlin in *Gosselin*, 492.
21 Per Bastarache in *Gosselin*, 548.
22 Charles Fried, *Right and Wrong* (Cambridge, MA: Harvard University Press, 1978), 108.
23 Fried does allow for the existence of a "very general right" to a "fair share of [one's] community's scarce resources," but he thinks the content of what constitutes a fair share needs to be left open as it will "vary with the circumstances and is in part a matter of what each person does." See Fried, *Right and Wrong*, 132-34.
24 Per L'Heureux-Dubé in *Gosselin*, 500. The *Law Test* is set out in *Law v. Canada (Minister of Employment and Immigration)* [1999] 1 S.C.R. 497.

> Accordingly, a court that is called upon to determine a discrimination claim under s. 15(1) should make the following three broad inquiries:
> (A) Does the impugned law (a) draw a formal distinction between the claimant and others on the basis of one or more personal characteristics, or (b) fail to take into account the claimant's already disadvantaged position within Canadian society resulting in substantively differential treatment between the claimant and others on the basis of one or more personal characteristics?
> (B) Is the claimant subject to differential treatment based on one or more enumerated and analogous grounds? and
> (C) Does the differential treatment discriminate, by imposing a burden upon or withholding a benefit from the claimant in a manner which reflects the stereotypical application of presumed group or personal characteristics, *or which otherwise has the effect of perpetuating or promoting the view that the individual is less capable or worthy of recognition or value as a human being or as a member of Canadian society, equally deserving of concern, respect, and consideration?* (emphasis added)

25 Per L'Heureux-Dubé in *Gosselin*, 508.
26 Ibid.
27 Though L'Heureux-Dubé states categorically that age is an "enumerated" ground, her discrimination argument does not rely on its status as such. She insists that "a discrimination claim should be evaluated primarily in terms of an impugned distinction's effects" and goes on to say that, "even if we accept for the moment that youth are generally an advantaged group, if a distinction were to severely harm the fundamental interests of youth and only youth, that distinction would be discriminatory."
28 See, for example, *M. v. H.*, [1999] 2 S.C.R. 3.
29 *Halpern v. Canada (Attorney General)*, [2003] 65 O.R. (3d) 161 at para. 107.
30 Per Bastarache in *Gosselin*, 591.
31 Per Iacobucci in *Law*, 530.
32 Per L'Heureux-Dubé in *Gosselin*, 508.
33 For a discussion of the effects of institutionalized exclusion on human dignity, see Avishai Margalit, *The Decent Society* (Cambridge, MA: Harvard University Press, 1996).
34 Such a view might plausibly be attributed to Thomas Pogge. Though he says in *World Poverty and Human Rights* that "avoidable insecurity of access ... constitutes official disrespect and stains the society's human rights record" (64), it is unclear whether he would count the state's failure to provide for the starving flood victim as a human rights violation since the state is not causally responsible for the flood victim's plight. See also his "Relational

Conceptions of Justice: Responsibilities for Health Outcomes," in *Public Health, Ethics and Equity*, ed. Fabienne Peter, Amartya Sen and Sudhir Anand (Oxford: Clarendon Press, 2004), 19.

35 For an account of contractualism, see T.M. Scanlon's *What We Owe to Each Other* (Cambridge, MA: Belknap Press, 1998), 201. The contractualist approach I adopt here is narrower in focus than Scanlon's: it considers the justice of legal and political institutions to be a matter of their justifiability to reasonable persons.

36 The reasonable person, insofar as the contractualist argument is concerned, is someone who has the "aim of finding principles that others, insofar as they too have this aim, could not reasonably reject" (Scanlon, *What We Owe*, 191). Reasonableness is distinct from rationality in that it has moral content, but that content is, at least in part, defined by the constraints on the contractualist exercise: the need and willingness to come to some agreement about moral principles or, in the specific case I am considering, the design of the basic legal and political institutions of a society. For an excellent discussion of the difficulties inherent in the use of the "reasonable person" standard in negligence cases, see Mayo Moran's *Rethinking the Reasonable Person: An Egalitarian Reconstruction of the Objective Standard* (Oxford: Oxford University Press, 2003). I take the reasonable person to have the normative quality Moran identifies as relevant to negligence cases: appropriate concern for the interests of others.

37 On the "basic structure," see John Rawls, *Justice as Fairness: A Restatement* (Cambridge, MA: Belknap, 2001), 10: "[T]he basic structure of society is the way in which the main political and social institutions of society fit together into one system of social cooperation, and the way they assign basic rights and duties and regulate the division of advantages that arises from social cooperation over time."

Appendix:
Canadian Charter of Rights
and Freedoms

Schedule B
Constitution Act, 1982

Enacted as Schedule B to the *Canada Act 1982* (U.K.) 1982, c. 11, which came into force on
April 17, 1982

PART I
Canadian charter of rights and freedoms

Whereas Canada is founded upon principles that recognize
the supremacy of God and the rule of law:

Guarantee of Rights and Freedoms

Rights and
freedoms in
Canada

1. The *Canadian Charter of Rights and Freedoms* guarantees
the rights and freedoms set out in it subject only to
such reasonable limits prescribed by law as can be
demonstrably justified in a free and democratic society.

Fundamental Freedoms

Fundamental
freedoms

2. Everyone has the following fundamental freedoms:
   (a) freedom of conscience and religion;
   (b) freedom of thought, belief, opinion and expression,
       including freedom of the press and other media of
       communication;
   (c) freedom of peaceful assembly; and
   (d) freedom of association.

Democratic Rights

Democratic
rights of citizens

3. Every citizen of Canada has the right to vote in an election of members of the House of Commons or of a legislative assembly and to be qualified for membership therein.

Maximum
duration of
legislative
bodies

4. (1) No House of Commons and no legislative assembly shall continue for longer than five years from the date fixed for the return of the writs of a general election of its members.

Continuation
in special
circumstances

(2) In time of real or apprehended war, invasion or insurrection, a House of Commons may be continued by Parliament and a legislative assembly may be continued by the legislature beyond five years if such continuation is not opposed by the votes of more than one-third of the members of the House of Commons or the legislative assembly, as the case may be.

Annual sitting of
legislative bodies

5. There shall be a sitting of Parliament and of each legislature at least once every twelve months.

Mobility Rights

Mobility of
citizens

6. (1) Every citizen of Canada has the right to enter, remain in and leave Canada.

Rights to move
and gain
livelihood

(2) Every citizen of Canada and every person who has the status of a permanent resident of Canada has the right
  (a) to move to and take up residence in any province; and
  (b) to pursue the gaining of a livelihood in any province.

Limitation

(3) The rights specified in subsection (2) are subject to
  (a) any laws or practices of general application in force in a province other than those that discriminate among persons primarily on the basis of province of present or previous residence; and
  (b) any laws providing for reasonable residency requirements as a qualification for the receipt of publicly provided social services.

Affirmative action programs

(4) Subsections (2) and (3) do not preclude any law, program or activity that has as its object the amelioration in a province of conditions of individuals in that province who are socially or economically disadvantaged if the rate of employment in that province is below the rate of employment in Canada.

Legal Rights

Life, liberty and security of person

7. Everyone has the right to life, liberty and security of the person and the right not to be deprived thereof except in accordance with the principles of fundamental justice.

Search or seizure

8. Everyone has the right to be secure against unreasonable search or seizure.

Detention or imprisonment

9. Everyone has the right not to be arbitrarily detained or imprisoned.

Arrest or detention

10. Everyone has the right on arrest or detention
    (a) to be informed promptly of the reasons therefor;
    (b) to retain and instruct counsel without delay and to be informed of that right; and
    (c) to have the validity of the detention determined by way of *habeas corpus* and to be released if the detention is not lawful.

Proceedings in criminal and penal matters

11. Any person charged with an offence has the right
    (a) to be informed without unreasonable delay of the specific offence;
    (b) to be tried within a reasonable time;
    (c) not to be compelled to be a witness in proceedings against that person in respect of the offence;
    (d) to be presumed innocent until proven guilty according to law in a fair and public hearing by an independent and impartial tribunal;
    (e) not to be denied reasonable bail without just cause;
    (f) except in the case of an offence under military law tried before a military tribunal, to the benefit of trial by jury where the maximum punishment for the offence is imprisonment for five years or a more severe punishment;

(g) not to be found guilty on account of any act or omission unless, at the time of the act or omission, it constituted an offence under Canadian or international law or was criminal according to the general principles of law recognized by the community of nations;

(h) if finally acquitted of the offence, not to be tried for it again and, if finally found guilty and punished for the offence, not to be tried or punished for it again; and

(i) if found guilty of the offence and if the punishment for the offence has been varied between the time of commission and the time of sentencing, to the benefit of the lesser punishment.

Treatment or punishment

12. Everyone has the right not to be subjected to any cruel and unusual treatment or punishment.

Self-crimination

13. A witness who testifies in any proceedings has the right not to have any incriminating evidence so given used to incriminate that witness in any other proceedings, except in a prosecution for perjury or for the giving of contradictory evidence.

Interpreter

14. A party or witness in any proceedings who does not understand or speak the language in which the proceedings are conducted or who is deaf has the right to the assistance of an interpreter.

Equality Rights

Equality before and under law and equal protection and benefit of law

15. (1) Every individual is equal before and under the law and has the right to the equal protection and equal benefit of the law without discrimination and, in particular, without discrimination based on race, national or ethnic origin, colour, religion, sex, age or mental or physical disability.

Affirmative action programs

(2) Subsection (1) does not preclude any law, program or activity that has as its object the amelioration of conditions of disadvantaged individuals or groups including those that are disadvantaged because of race, national or ethnic origin, colour, religion, sex, age or mental or physical disability.

Official Languages of Canada

Official languages
of Canada

16. (1) English and French are the official languages of Canada and have equality of status and equal rights and privileges as to their use in all institutions of the Parliament and government of Canada.

Official languages
of New Brunswick

(2) English and French are the official languages of New Brunswick and have equality of status and equal rights and privileges as to their use in all institutions of the legislature and government of New Brunswick.

Advancement of
status and use

(3) Nothing in this Charter limits the authority of Parliament or a legislature to advance the equality of status or use of English and French.

English and
French linguistic
communities in
New Brunswick

16.1. (1) The English linguistic community and the French linguistic community in New Brunswick have equality of status and equal rights and privileges, including the right to distinct educational institutions and such distinct cultural institutions as are necessary for the preservation and promotion of those communities.

Role of the
legislature and
government of
New Brunswick

(2) The role of the legislature and government of New Brunswick to preserve and promote the status, rights and privileges referred to in subsection (1) is affirmed.

Proceedings of
Parliament

17. (1) Everyone has the right to use English or French in any debates and other proceedings of Parliament.

Proceedings of
New Brunswick
legislature

(2) Everyone has the right to use English or French in any debates and other proceedings of the legislature of New Brunswick.

Parliamentary
statutes and
records

18. (1) The statutes, records and journals of Parliament shall be printed and published in English and French and both language versions are equally authoritative.

New Brunswick
statutes and
records

(2) The statutes, records and journals of the legislature of New Brunswick shall be printed and published in English and French and both language versions are equally authoritative.

Proceedings in courts established by Parliament

19. (1) Either English or French may be used by any person in, or in any pleading in or process issuing from, any court established by Parliament.

Proceedings in New Brunswick courts

(2) Either English or French may be used by any person in, or in any pleading in or process issuing from, any court of New Brunswick.

Communications by public with federal institutions

20. (1) Any member of the public in Canada has the right to communicate with, and to receive available services from, any head or central office of an institution of the Parliament or government of Canada in English or French, and has the same right with respect to any other office of any such institution where

(a) there is a significant demand for communications with and services from that office in such language; or

(b) due to the nature of the office, it is reasonable that communications with and services from that office be available in both English and French.

Communications by public with New Brunswick institutions

(2) Any member of the public in New Brunswick has the right to communicate with, and to receive available services from, any office of an institution of the legislature or government of New Brunswick in English or French.

Continuation of existing constitutional provisions

21. Nothing in sections 16 to 20 abrogates or derogates from any right, privilege or obligation with respect to the English and French languages, or either of them, that exists or is continued by virtue of any other provision of the Constitution of Canada.

Rights and privileges preserved

22. Nothing in sections 16 to 20 abrogates or derogates from any legal or customary right or privilege acquired or enjoyed either before or after the coming into force of this Charter with respect to any language that is not English or French.

Minority Language Educational Rights

Language of instruction

23. (1) Citizens of Canada

(a) whose first language learned and still understood is that of the English or French linguistic minority population of the province in which they reside, or

(b) who have received their primary school instruction in Canada in English or French and reside in a province where the language in which they received that instruction is the language of the English or French linguistic minority population of the province, have the right to have their children receive primary and secondary school instruction in that language in that province.

Continuity of
language instruction

(2) Citizens of Canada of whom any child has received or is receiving primary or secondary school instruction in English or French in Canada, have the right to have all their children receive primary and secondary school instruction in the same language.

Application
where numbers
warrant

(3) The right of citizens of Canada under subsections (1) and (2) to have their children receive primary and secondary school instruction in the language of the English or French linguistic minority population of a province

(a) applies wherever in the province the number of children of citizens who have such a right is sufficient to warrant the provision to them out of public funds of minority language instruction; and

(b) includes, where the number of those children so warrants, the right to have them receive that instruction in minority language educational facilities provided out of public funds.

Enforcement

Enforcement of
guaranteed rights
and freedoms

24. (1) Anyone whose rights or freedoms, as guaranteed by this Charter, have been infringed or denied may apply to a court of competent jurisdiction to obtain such remedy as the court considers appropriate and just in the circumstances.

Exclusion of evidence bringing administration of justice into disrepute

(2) Where, in proceedings under subsection (1), a court concludes that evidence was obtained in a manner that infringed or denied any rights or freedoms guaranteed by this Charter, the evidence shall be excluded if it is established that, having regard to all the circumstances, the admission of it in the proceedings would bring the administration of justice into disrepute.

General

Aboriginal rights and freedoms not affected by Charter

25. The guarantee in this Charter of certain rights and freedoms shall not be construed so as to abrogate or derogate from any aboriginal, treaty or other rights or freedoms that pertain to the aboriginal peoples of Canada including

    (a) any rights or freedoms that have been recognized by the Royal Proclamation of October 7, 1763; and

    (b) any rights or freedoms that now exist by way of land claims agreements or may be so acquired.

Other rights and freedoms not affected by Charter

26. The guarantee in this Charter of certain rights and freedoms shall not be construed as denying the existence of any other rights or freedoms that exist in Canada.

Multicultural heritage

27. This Charter shall be interpreted in a manner consistent with the preservation and enhancement of the multicultural heritage of Canadians.

Rights guaranteed equally to both sexes

28. Notwithstanding anything in this Charter, the rights and freedoms referred to in it are guaranteed equally to male and female persons.

Rights respecting certain schools preserved

29. Nothing in this Charter abrogates or derogates from any rights or privileges guaranteed by or under the Constitution of Canada in respect of denominational, separate or dissentient schools.(93)

Application to territories and territorial authorities

30. A reference in this Charter to a Province or to the legislative assembly or legislature of a province shall be deemed to include a reference to the Yukon Territory and the Northwest Territories, or to the

appropriate legislative authority thereof, as the case may be.

Legislative powers not extended

31. Nothing in this Charter extends the legislative powers of any body or authority.

Application of Charter

Application of Charter

32. (1) This Charter applies

    (a) to the Parliament and government of Canada in respect of all matters within the authority of Parliament including all matters relating to the Yukon Territory and Northwest Territories; and

    (b) to the legislature and government of each province in respect of all matters within the authority of the legislature of each province.

Exception

(2) Notwithstanding subsection (1), section 15 shall not have effect until three years after this section comes into force.

Exception where express declaration

33. (1) Parliament or the legislature of a province may expressly declare in an Act of Parliament or of the legislature, as the case may be, that the Act or a provision thereof shall operate notwithstanding a provision included in section 2 or sections 7 to 15 of this Charter.

Operation of exception

(2) An Act or a provision of an Act in respect of which a declaration made under this section is in effect shall have such operation as it would have but for the provision of this Charter referred to in the declaration.

Five year limitation

(3) A declaration made under subsection (1) shall cease to have effect five years after it comes into force or on such earlier date as may be specified in the declaration.

Re-enactment

(4) Parliament or the legislature of a province may re-enact a declaration made under subsection (1).

Five year limitation

(5) Subsection (3) applies in respect of a re-enactment made under subsection (4).

Citation

Citation

34. This Part may be cited as the *Canadian Charter of Rights and Freedoms*.

Contributors

Daniel Bourgeois is executive director of the Canadian Institute for Research on Public Policy and Public Administration. His research focuses on administrative decentralization and the allocation of public services to minority groups. He has published *The Canadian Bilingual Districts* at McGill-Queen's University Press and a dozen articles on the subject.

Marc Chevrier is a professor of political science at the Université du Québec à Montréal. He has published a collection of philosophical essays (*Le temps de l'homme fini*, 2005) and many articles on federalism, law and politics, and the political life of Quebec and of Canada.

Robert J. Currie is an assistant professor at Dalhousie Law School, Halifax, Nova Scotia, where he teaches international criminal law, evidence, civil procedure, and advocacy. He has published on a wide variety of legal topics and specializes in international and transnational criminal law.

Jameson W. Doig is senior scholar and professor emeritus in the Woodrow Wilson School and Politics Department, Princeton University. His publications include three books and a number of articles in the fields of metropolitan politics, public administration, and public law.

Katherine Eddy is British Academy Postdoctoral Fellow at the Centre for the Study of Social Justice and Anna Biegun Warburg Research Fellow in Political Theory at St. Anne's College, Oxford. She works on rights and social justice, with a focus on constitutional welfare rights.

Hugh Donald Forbes is professor in the Department of Political Science at the University of Toronto. He specializes in Canadian politics and political thought; nationalism and ethnic conflict; and the philosophy and politics of the social sciences. His books include: *Nationalism, Ethnocentrism, and Personality: Social Science and Critical Theory* (1985); *Canadian Political Thought* (editor, 1985); and *Ethnic Conflict: Commerce, Culture, and the Contract Hypothesis* (1997). A new book, *George Grant: A Guide to His Thought,* will be published in July 2007. He is currently writing a book about multiculturalism in Canada.

Andrew F. Johnson is a professor of political studies and dean of social sciences at Bishop's University, Quebec. His publications have largely focused on Canadian social policy and on public administration, but he is currently collaborating with other scholars on research related to gaps in the delivery of public policies to the anglophone minority in Quebec.

Hugh Kindred is professor of law at Dalhousie University, Halifax, where he teaches international law, commercial law, and maritime transportation. His many publications in these fields include *Maritime Law* (2003), written with Edgar Gold and Aldo Chircop, which was co-winner of the Walter Owen Book Prize in 2005. He is also co-general editor, with Phillip Saunders, of *International Law Chiefly as Interpreted and Applied in Canada,* now in its seventh edition (2006). In 2003, Professor Kindred was honoured by the Canadian Association of Law Teachers with its Award for Academic Excellence.

Will Kymlicka is the Canada Research Chair in Political Philosophy at Queen's University and a visiting professor in the nationalism studies program at the Central European University in Budapest. His books include *Liberalism, Community, and Culture* (1989), *Contemporary Political Philosophy* (1990; 2nd ed. 2002), *Multicultural Citizenship* (1995), *Finding Our Way: Rethinking Ethnocultural Relations in Canada* (1998), *Politics in the Vernacular: Nationalism, Multiculturalism, Citizenship* (2001), and *Multicultural Odysseys: Navigating the New International Politics of Diversity* (2007).

Ian Peach is the director of the Saskatchewan Institute of Public Policy. Prior to coming to the institute in 2003, he had worked for the Government of Saskatchewan for eight years, in positions in the Executive Council and the Department of Intergovernmental Affairs. During the period of the Meech Lake and Charlottetown accords, Mr. Peach worked for the Ontario Ministry of the Attorney General, two parliamentary committees on constitutional reform, and the Government of the Yukon.

Joan Small is senior lecturer in Law at City University, London. Her primary interests and expertise are constitutional law, human rights, legal theory, and public international law. She has published articles on family law, public international law, and constitutional law and human rights.

Michael Temelini is an assistant professor in the department of political science and lectures in the Humanities M.Phil program at Memorial University of Newfoundland in St. John's. He teaches social and political theory and Canadian politics, and his research focuses on multiculturalism, federalism, and Canadian social movements. He is also a frequent guest commentator for CBC radio news.

Stephen Tierney is a reader in law at the University of Edinburgh, where he specializes in comparative constitutional law and international law. His teaching and research interests in particular focus on the legal accommodation of national identity and comparative constitutional law and theory. His books include: *Accommodating National Identity: New Approaches in International and Domestic Law* (2000); *Constitutional Law and National Pluralism* (2004); *Towards an International Legal Community? The Sovereignty of States and the Sovereignty of International Law* (2006), and *Accommodating Cultural Diversity: Contemporary Issues in Theory and Practice* (2007).

Index

Florian Sauvageau, David Schneiderman, and David Taras, with Ruth Klinkhammer and Pierre Trudel
The Last Word: Media Coverage of the Supreme Court of Canada (2005)

Gerald Kernerman
Multicultural Nationalism: Civilizing Difference, Constituting Community (2005)

Pamela A. Jordan
Defending Rights in Russia: Lawyers, the State, and Legal Reform in the Post-Soviet Era (2005)

Anna Pratt
Securing Borders: Detention and Deportation in Canada (2005)

Kirsten Johnson Kramar
Unwilling Mothers, Unwanted Babies: Infanticide in Canada (2005)

W.A. Bogart
Good Government? Good Citizens? Courts, Politics, and Markets in a Changing Canada (2005)

Catherine Dauvergne
Humanitarianism, Identity, and Nation: Migration Laws in Canada and Australia (2005)

Michael Lee Ross
First Nations Sacred Sites in Canada's Courts (2005)

Andrew Woolford
Between Justice and Certainty: Treaty Making in British Columbia (2005)

John McLaren, Andrew Buck, and Nancy Wright (eds.)
Despotic Dominion: Property Rights in British Settler Societies (2004)

Georges Campeau
From UI to EI: Waging War on the Welfare State (2004)

Alvin J. Esau
The Courts and the Colonies: The Litigation of Hutterite Church Disputes (2004)

Christopher N. Kendall
Gay Male Pornography: An Issue of Sex Discrimination (2004)

Roy B. Flemming
Tournament of Appeals: Granting Judicial Review in Canada (2004)

Constance Backhouse and Nancy L. Backhouse
The Heiress vs the Establishment: Mrs. Campbell's Campaign for Legal Justice (2004)

Christopher P. Manfredi
Feminist Activism in the Supreme Court: Legal Mobilization and the Women's Legal Education and Action Fund (2004)

Annalise Acorn
Compulsory Compassion: A Critique of Restorative Justice (2004)

Jonathan Swainger and Constance Backhouse (eds.)
People and Place: Historical Influences on Legal Culture (2003)

Jim Phillips and Rosemary Gartner
Murdering Holiness: The Trials of Franz Creffield and George Mitchell (2003)

David R. Boyd
Unnatural Law: Rethinking Canadian Environmental Law and Policy (2003)

Ikechi Mgbeoji
Collective Insecurity: The Liberian Crisis, Unilateralism, and Global Order (2003)

Rebecca Johnson
Taxing Choices: The Intersection of Class, Gender, Parenthood, and the Law (2002)

John McLaren, Robert Menzies, and Dorothy E. Chunn (eds.)
Regulating Lives: Historical Essays on the State, Society, the Individual, and the Law (2002)

Joan Brockman
Gender in the Legal Profession: Fitting or Breaking the Mould (2001)